MORRIS MARINA 1972-73 AUTOBOOK

Workshop Manual for
Morris Marina Australian version 1500 cc 1972-73
Morris Marina Australian version 1750 cc 1972-73

by

Kenneth Ball
Graduate, Institution of Mechanical Engineers
Associate Member, Guild of Motoring Writers

and the

Autopress team of Technical Writers

AUTOPRESS LTD   GOLDEN LANE   BRIGHTON   BN1 2QJ   ENGLAND

The AUTOBOOK series of Workshop Manuals is the largest in the world and covers the majority of British and Continental motor cars, as well as all major Japanese and Australian models. For a full list see the back of this manual.

CONTENTS

ISBN 0 85147 343 1

First Edition   1973

© Autopress Ltd 1973

Printed and bound in Brighton England for Autopress Ltd by G Beard & Son Ltd

ACKNOWLEDGEMENT

My thanks are due to British Leyland Motor Corporation Ltd. for their unstinted co-operation and also for supplying data and illustrations.

I am also grateful to a considerable number of owners who have discussed their cars at length and many of whose suggestions have been included in this manual.

Kenneth Ball
Graduate, Institution of Mechanical Engineers
Associate Member, Guild of Motoring Writers
Ditchling Sussex England.

INTRODUCTION

This do-it-yourself Workshop Manual has been specially written for the owner who wishes to maintain his car in first class condition and to carry out his own servicing and repairs. Considerable savings on garage charges can be made, and one can drive in safety and confidence knowing the work has been done properly.

Comprehensive step-by-step instructions and illustrations are given on all dismantling, overhauling and assembling operations. Certain assemblies require the use of expensive special tools, the purchase of which would be unjustified. In these cases information is included but the reader is recommended to hand the unit to the agent for attention.

Throughout the Manual hints and tips are included which will be found invaluable, and there is an easy to follow fault diagnosis at the end of each chapter.

Whilst every care has been taken to ensure correctness of information it is obviously not possible to guarantee complete freedom from errors or to accept liability arising from such errors or omissions.

Instructions may refer to the righthand or lefthand sides of the vehicle or the components. These are the same as the righthand or lefthand of an observer standing behind the car and looking forward.

CHAPTER 1

THE ENGINE

1:1 Description

The four cylinder in-line single overhead camshaft engine of the Australian Marina is basically that of the Morris 1500 or English Austin Maxi. In the Marina, however, it is mounted in the conventional fore-and-aft position. A four-speed synchromesh gearbox, or the alternative automatic transmission, is attached to the rear of the engine and drive is taken to the rear wheels through a propeller shaft and live axle.

Two engines sizes are available and are known as the 1500 and 1750. The former is of 1485 cc with a bore and stroke of 76.2 x 81.28 mm. The latter is of 1748 cc having dimensions of 76.2 x 95.75 mm. The TC model is a twin-carburetter version of the 1750 with a slightly higher compression ratio. The 1500 model is available with the manual gearbox only, but on 1750 and TC models either manual or automatic transmission is available.

FIG 1:1 is an exploded view of the engine components. The front of the cylinder block 1 encloses the lower part of the camshaft drive chain 47. The bottom flange of the block is on the centre line of the crankshaft and is bolted to the oil reservoir (sump) casting 87 thus forming an extremely rigid crankcase assembly.

The forged steel counterbalanced crankshaft 7 is carried in five main bearings. At the front of the crankshaft is the pulley 19 for the water pump, fan and alternator drive belt. Behind the pulley is an oil seal 18, the camshaft chain sprocket 16 and a skew gear 15 which drives an almost vertical shaft 23. This shaft at its top end drives the distributor while at the lower end it drives the rotor type oil pump 24 through a quill shaft 28. The lower end of shaft 23 also incorporates a cam which operates the fuel pump 94 through a push rod 95.

The main bearings 5 are of the renewable steel backed type with reticular tin-aluminium running surfaces. The connecting rods 8 have horizontally split big ends which will pass upwards through the cylinder bores for removal of piston and rod assemblies. The big end bearings 11 are of the same material as the mains. The gudgeon pins 12 float in the piston bosses but are a tight press fit in the connecting rods. The solid skirt pistons 13 carry two compression rings and an oil control ring each.

The cast iron cylinder head 29 is provided with valves set at small angle from the vertical. There are eight separate ports, the inlet ports being round and the exhaust rectangular. Inlet and exhaust manifolds for single carburetter 77 and for twin carburetter 84 are cast in one piece.

Bolted to the top face of the cylinder head is an aluminium camshaft carrier 32 which carries the overhead

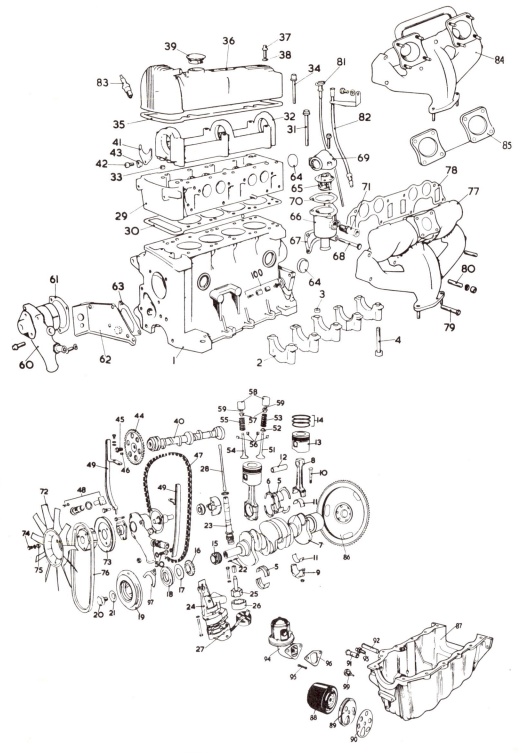

FIG 1:1   The engine components

camshaft 40 in three bearings machined directly in the casting. The valves 51, 54 are operated through inverted bucket type tappets 58 and clearance is adjusted by fitting shims 59 between tappet and valve. As there is no side thrust on the valve stems wear is negligible and therefore the valves operate directly in the head without guides.

The oil pump takes oil from the reservoir and passes it to a renewable external filter of the full flow type 88 which conceals a non-adjustable oil relief valve 92 fitted in the reservoir. From the filter, oil under pressure passes to drillings feeding the various bearings in the usual way. A crankcase ventilation air filter 100 is situated at the rear of the lefthand side of the engine (See **Section 1:14**). Cooling is by means of the impeller assisted thermo syphon system with thermostat and a crossflow radiator (see **Chapter 4**).

1:2 Overhauling methods

Before giving detailed instruction on engine overhaul we draw the reader's attention to the general 'Hints on Maintenance and Overhaul' at the end of this manual. As many operations involve raising and supporting the car, particular attention is drawn to the paragraph on 'Safe Working Conditions'. Where a single post contact hoist is available, the front adjustable lifting pads should contact the front chassis member at a point in line with the front edge of the front door (see **Fig 1:2**). The rear pads should contact the short crossmember between the rear spring support and the outside edge of the body. Where this type of equipment is not available, access to the underside of the car can be obtained by working over a pit or by supporting the front wheels on a sound pair of ramps. Where it becomes necessary to support one end of the car on stands, use two of the support points shown in **FIG 1:2**, using suitably large hardwood pads between stands and chassis to avoid damage.

References to right and left are to those sides of the car as seen from the driver's seat looking forward. No. 1 cylinder is at the front of the engine and the firing order is 1-3-4-2.

Operations with the engine in the car:

The conventional front engine/rear wheel drive layout of the Marina means that most operations on the engine can be carried out without its removal from the car. These include all work on the head, attention to valves, camshaft

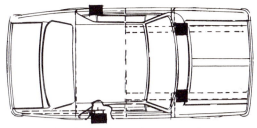

FIG 1:2   Jacking and support points

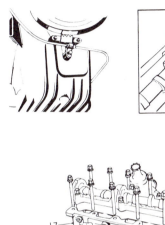

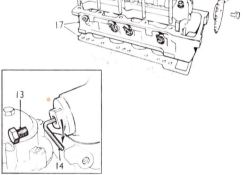

FIG 1:3   Removal of cylinder head

Key to Fig 1:1   1 Cylinder block   2 Main bearing cap   3 Main bearing cap dowel   4 Main bearing cap bolt   5 Main bearing shells   6 Crankshaft thrust washers   7 Crankshaft   8 Connecting rod   9 Connecting rod cap   10 Connecting rod cap bolt   11 Big-end bearing sheels   12 Gudgeon pin   13 Piston   14 Piston rings   15 Distributor shaft drive gear   16 Crankshaft sprocket   17 Oil thrower   18 Crankshaft pulley oil seal   19 Crankshaft pulley   20 Crankshaft pulley bolt   21 Crankshaft pulley lock washer   22 Key for distributor drive gear and sprocket   23 Distributor and fuel pump drive shaft   24 Oil pump body   25 Oil pump shaft assembly   26 Oil pump rotor   27 Oil pump base   28 Oil pump drive shaft   29 Cylinder head   30 Cylinder head gasket   31 Cylinder head bolt   32 Camshaft carrier   33 Camshaft carrier dowel   34 Camshaft carrier bolt   35 Camshaft cover gasket   36 Camshaft cover   37 Camshaft cover screw   38 Camshaft cover screw 'O' ring   39 Oil filler cap   40 Camshaft   41 Camshaft locating plate   42 Camshaft locating plate screw   43 Lockwasher   44 Camshaft sprocket   45 Camshaft sprocket bolt   46 Camshaft sprocket dowel   47 Timing chain   48 Timing chain tensioner assembly   49 Timing chain guides   50 Guide adjuster   51 Inlet valve   52 Inlet valve spring seat and seal   53 Inlet valve spring   54 Exhaust valve   55 Exhaust valve spring   56 Valve cotters   57 Valve spring cups   58 Tappets   59 Tappet adjusting shims   60 Water pump   61 Water pump gasket   62 Engine plate   63 Engine plate gasket   64 Welch plugs   65 Thermostat   66 Thermostat housing   67 Thermostat housing gasket   68 Thermostat housing bolt   69 Water outlet elbow   70 Water outlet elbow gasket   71 Heater hose connection   72 Fan   73 Fan pulley   74 Fan screw   75 Fan insert   76 Fan belt   77 Inlet and exhaust manifold   78 Manifold gasket   79 Manifold bolt   80 Manifold stud   81 Oil dipstick   82 Oil dipstick tube   83 Spark plug   84 Inlet and exhaust manifold (twin carburetters)   85 Carburetter gaskets   86 Flywheel   87 Oil reservoir   88 Engine oil filter   89 Adaptor plate   90 Gasket   91 Oil pump connector   92 Pressure relief valve   93 Bolt—retaining   94 Fuel pump   95 Fuel pump push rod   96 Spacer   97 Oil seal retainer   98 Fan spacer   99 Oil reservoir drain plug   100 Crankcase air filter

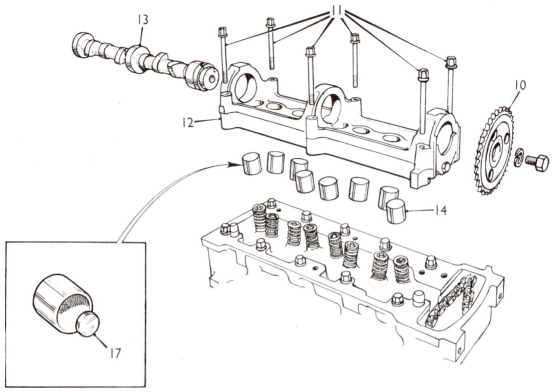

FIG 1:4   Camshaft and tappet removal

Key to Fig 1:4   10 Camshaft sprocket   11 Camshaft housing bolts   12 Camshaft housing   13 Camshaft   14 Tappets
17 Tappet adjusting shims

and camshaft drive, removal of water pump, removal of sump and oil pump and the renewal of big-end bearing shells. As the big-ends will pass upwards through the cylinder bores, removal of the head and sump permits removal of connecting rods, pistons and rings. On manual transmission models access to the clutch and flywheel ring gear is possible by removing the gearbox only.

Operations involving engine removal:

For removal of the crankshaft and attention to main bearings it is essential to remove the engine. Moreover, if a large number of operations are to be carried out on the engine, it may be more convenient to work on the engine out of the car, even if individual jobs are possible without its removal.

Engine emission control:

This car has been designed with engine emission control in accordance with legislation requirements. It should be noted that after attention to valves, tappet clearances, valve timing, ventilation filter, carburation or manifolds and exhaust system, emission checks must be carried out. These checks involve the use of specialized equipment and should be entrusted to an Austin-Morris dealer.

1:3 Removing the engine

On cars with manual (synchromesh) transmission the engine can be lifted upwards and removed separately leaving the gearbox in the car. Alternatively, if suitable equipment is available, engine and gearbox can be lowered as a unit and withdrawn from underneath the car. On cars with automatic transmission, the engine and transmission are removed as a unit. Note however that in either case it is possible to remove the gearbox or transmission separately leaving the engine in the car (see **Chapters 6** and **7**).

Engine removal (cars with manual gearbox only):

1 Remove the bonnet (see **Chapter 13**).
2 Drain the cooling system (see **Chapter 4**). It is also advisable to drain the sump by removing the drain plug (99 in **FIG 1:1**).
3 Disconnect both battery terminals.
4 Disconnect all electrical leads and all controls from the engine. It is advisable to label the leads to ensure they can be correctly reconnected.
5 Disconnect the exhaust pipe from the manifold and remove the bolt from the clip securing the pipe to the engine backplate (**FIG 1:26**).

6 Disconnect radiator hoses, heater hoses and servo vacuum hose where applicable. Remove the radiator (see **Chapter 4**) and cooling fan.

7 Disconnect the fuel feed pipe from the tank at the pump end, plugging it to prevent loss of fuel.

8 Bolt the lifting brackets (Part No. 18GA.041) to the front and rear of the cylinder head and attach suitable lifting equipment.

9 Remove all bolts securing the engine backplate to the clutch housing. Support the gearbox with an adjustable axle stand or a jack. Replace sump drain plug to prevent spillage of oil dregs when tilting engine.

10 Take the weight of the engine on the crane or hoist and disconnect the front engine mounts from the brackets on the chassis. Ensure that the weight of the gearbox is still taken by the jack, as the front of the car will rise as the engine weight is taken off the suspension.

11 Move the engine forward to disengage the first motion shaft from the crankshaft and clutch, taking care that the weight of the engine or gearbox does not hang on the gearbox shaft during the operation or damage to the clutch may result.

12 Make a final check to ensure that no leads or hoses connecting the engine to the car have been overlooked.

13 Lift the engine clear of the car.

Removing engine and gearbox as a unit (manual or automatic models) :

Before undertaking this operation, note that it involves raising and supporting the front of the car while the power unit is lowered and withdrawn from underneath. If professional garage equipment is not available, ensure that equipment used is adequate for safe handling of the weights involved.

1 Remove the bonnet (see **Chapter 13**).

2 Disconnect both battery terminals. Disconnect all electrical leads from the engine and gearbox.

3 Drain the cooling system (see **Chapter 4**). Disconnect radiator hoses, also heater and vacuum hoses where applicable. Remove the radiator.

4 Engine and gearbox oil may be drained at this stage. The engine drain plug is shown at 99 **FIG 1 : 1**. When draining automatic transmission note that after a run the oil may be hot enough to cause severe burns.

5 Remove the carburetter assembly and lay to one side. Disconnect the exhaust system (**FIG 1 : 26**) sufficiently to enable it to be moved clear of the engine. Replace engine and gearbox drain plugs.

6 (Manual models only). Disconnect the clutch slave cylinder.

7 Fit engine lifting brackets part No. 18GA.041 to the cylinder head.

8 Raise and support the front of the car. Attach lifting equipment to the engine and just take the weight of the power unit, taking care not to lift the car off its supports.

9 Disconnect the propeller shaft from the gearbox by removing the four flange bolts, having marked the flange relationship with paint. Tie the propeller shaft up to a suitable point on the chassis.

10 Disconnect the speedometer cable from the gearbox. On manual models, disconnect the gearlever. On automatic models, disconnect the selector rod and the inhibitor and reverse switch wiring.

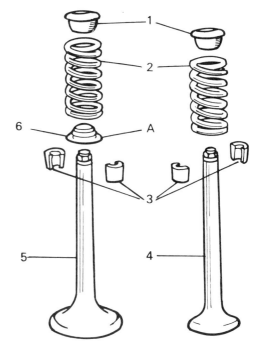

FIG 1 : 5 Valves and components

Key to Fig 1 : 5   1 Spring cup   2 Valve springs   3 Valve cotters   4 Exhaust valve   5 Inlet valve   6 Spring seat and seal assembly

The combined spring seat and seal assembly is only fitted to the inlet valves and the rear exhaust valve

11 Remove the crossmember from under the gearbox.

12 Remove the righthand front engine mounting from the chassis bracket.

13 Remove the lefthand mounting complete.

14 Make a final check to ensure that no leads or controls between the power unit and the car have been overlooked.

15 Place a suitable trolley jack under the power unit. Lower the unit on to it, taking care not to damage the alternator. After ensuring that the power unit cannot shift on the trolley, remove the lifting chain.

16 Place a lift bar through the towing eyes at the front of the car, attach lifting equipment and raise the front of the car sufficiently to allow the power unit to be pulled clear.

1 : 4 Lifting the head

It is possible to remove and refit the camshaft without lifting the cylinder head, but if head and valves are to be serviced with the engine in the car it is best to remove the head complete with camshaft. All work on head and valves including adjustment of valve clearances can then be carried out on the bench. The head complete with camshaft is then ready for refitting to the car as a unit. To remove the head complete proceed as follows:

1 Disconnect the battery. Remove the air cleaner. Disconnect vacuum, breather and fuel pipes. Disconnect the carburetter.

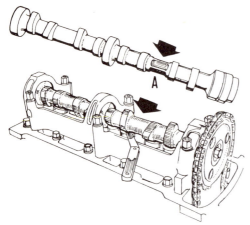

FIG 1:6 Camshaft spanner flats and method of checking valve clearances

2 Disconnect servo and exhaust pipes. Drain the cooling system and disconnect all hoses from the thermostat housing.

3 Disconnect leads from sparking plugs and thermal transmitter.

4 Referring to **FIG 1:1** remove the six screws 37 and lift off the camshaft cover 36. Referring to **FIG 1:3** turn the engine until the crankshaft pulley marks are in line with No. 1 cylinder at TDC on firing stroke. The marks on camshaft and housing 12A should then also be in line.

5 From low down near the fuel pump remove bolt 13 from the chain tensioner adaptor. Insert a 1/8 Allen key in the socket and turn the tensioner clockwise.

6 Remove the camshaft sprocket 15 and rest the timing chain on the guides. Do not turn the engine after this. Using a diagonal sequence slacken the cylinder head bolts 16 part of a turn at a time until they can be removed. Lift off the head and gasket 17. Note that the head is located by two dowels in the righthand side of the cylinder block near cylinders 1 and 4.

1:5 Servicing the head

Removing camshaft:

Assuming the head has been removed complete with camshaft as described in the previous Section proceed as follows with reference to **FIG 1:4**:

Slacken bolts 11 a little at a time in a diagonal sequence until all pressure from the valve springs is released. When the camshaft housing 12 is lifted still more the tappets 14 will fall clear to enable the camshaft 13 to be withdrawn to the rear. Now remove the tappets and store them in the correct order for replacement. Some numbered nails in a strip of wood could be used, or simply an indication to show which nail and tappet is located at the front end of the engine.

Examine the camshaft and housing bearing surfaces for signs of scoring and excessive wear. The journal diameters are given in Technical Data at the end of this manual. See that the cam surfaces are not worn or pitted and that the sprocket driving dowel is a perfect fit. Check the fit of the tappets in the housing and renew worn parts.

End float and location of the camshaft is controlled by plate 41 in **FIG 1:1**. This will be found bolted to the camshaft housing behind the sprocket. If end float of the camshaft exceeds .002 to .007 inch it must be cured by fitting a new plate.

Removing valves:

Before removing the valves scrape as much of the carbon as possible from the combustion chambers. This will minimize risk of damaging valve seats in the process. Using a suitable spring compressor the valve springs 2 in **FIG 1:5** and remove the cotters 3, the spring cups 1 and the springs 2. Remove the oil seals and spring seats from the inlet valves. Remove the valves and store them in the correct order so that they can be replaced in their respective guides during reassembly.

If the valves and seats have seen considerable service it will be necessary to have them reconditioned by an agent with the proper tools. Valve seats can be reground to the correct angle of $45\frac{1}{4}$ deg., but if the seatings in the head need reconditioning, the following operations are required:

1 The glazing of the seats must be removed.
2 The seats must be recut to an angle of 45 deg., removing the minimum of metal.
3 The seats must be narrowed to the correct width.

The valves can then be lapped in with fine grinding paste. Note that seats in the head which have gone too far can be restored by having inserts fitted. This is done by accurate machining with special equipment. After fitting, the insert seats are cut to the correct dimensions.

To grind in the valves, put a light spring under the head and smear the valve seat with a little fine grinding paste. Use a reciprocating movement of a suction tool stuck to the head of the valve. Let the valve rise occasionally under the influence of the spring so that the paste becomes evenly distributed and concentric scoring of the seats is avoided. Grind no more than is necessary to produce an even matt grey finish.

Refitting the valves:

Ensure that all traces of carbon dust and grinding paste have been removed from the head and valve guides. Lubricate the valve stems with EP 140 oil before inserting in the guides. The fitting of a new set of valve springs is to be recommended. Also examine the valve cotters and renew any showing signs of wear. Fit new spring seat and seal assemblies to inlet valves and rear exhaust valve only. Ensure that the cotters are fully home in their recesses and are not displaced when releasing the spring compressor.

Refitting camshaft:

Refit the camshaft housing, turning bolts 11 (**FIG 1:4**) to engage two or three threads only. Fit the tappets in the correct order, holding the shims in place inside the tappets with a spot of petroleum jelly. Refit the camshaft and tighten the camshaft housing bolts a little at a time against the pressure of the valve springs in the sequence shown in **FIG 1:7**. Next check the valve clearances and adjust if necessary. These operations are more easily carried out on the bench.

Valve clearances:

Valve clearances are checked by means of a feeler gauge between the back of each cam and the tappet as shown in **FIG 1:6**. The camshaft has spanner flats as shown at A to enable it to be turned. Use the following sequence when checking:

Check No. 1 tappet with No. 8 valve fully open
Check No. 3 tappet with No. 6 valve fully open
Check No. 5 tappet with No. 4 valve fully open
Check No. 2 tappet with No. 7 valve fully open
Check No. 8 tappet with No. 1 valve fully open
Check No. 6 tappet with No. 3 valve fully open
Check No. 4 tappet with No. 5 valve fully open
Check No. 7 tappet with No. 2 valve fully open

Write down the clearances in the correct order. Notice that each line of numbers adds up to nine. This enables checking to proceed without constant reference to the table.

1 The standard setting of the tappet clearance is .018 inch for inlet valves and .022 inch for exhaust valves. Adjustment is only necessary if the clearance for either valve is reduced to less than .012 inch, if new parts have been fitted or if valve grinding has been carried out.

2 From the list of recorded clearances take the first tappet to need clearance adjustment and measure the thicknesses of the shim removed from it. Let 'A' be the clearance as measured, 'B' the thickness of the shim removed and 'C' the correct clearance specified in Operation 4. The thickness of shim required can then be calculated from the formula $A + B - C$. Shims are available in the following thicknesses:

.097 inch .105 inch .113 inch
.099 inch .107 inch .115 inch
.101 inch .109 inch .117 inch
.103 inch .111 inch .119 inch

Check the shimming of all the other tappets with incorrect clearances.

3 Stick the shims inside the tappets with a little petroleum jelly and refit all the dismantled parts in the reverse order of dismantling. Check the tappet clearance again when the camshaft is in place.

1:6 Refitting head. Valve timing

Refitting the cylinder head is a reversal of the removal procedure but the following points should be noted:

1 Ensure that the cylinder head bolt holes on the cylinder block are free of foreign matter. Check the cylinder block face for damage especially around the bolt holes.

2 Place a new cylinder head gasket over the two dowels in the cylinder block. The gasket should be installed dry.

3 Tighten the cylinder head bolts gradually in the sequence shown in **FIG 1:7**.

4 If the camshaft carrier assembly has not already been fitted as described in the previous Section it should now be installed and valve clearances checked.

Valve timing:

1 Align the crankshaft timing marks (**FIG 1:3**) with No. 1 cylinder on TDC of compression stroke. The distributor rotor will be pointing towards No. 1 HT lead.

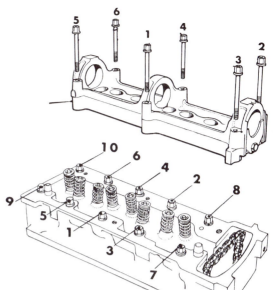

FIG 1:7 Bolt tightening sequences camshaft carrier and cylinder head

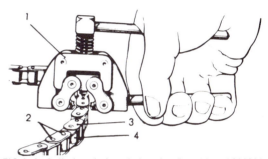

FIG 1:8 Splitting timing chain using Renold tool 311006
Key to Fig 1:8 1 Tool 2 Bearing pin 3 Sideplate 4 Roller

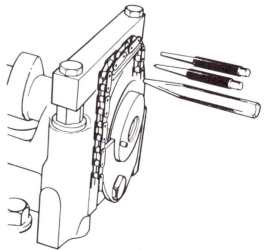

FIG 1:9 Riveting timing chain using tool No. 18GA.017

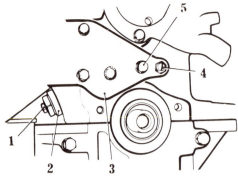

FIG 1:10   Timing chain adjustment

Key to Fig 1:10   1 Set screw   2 Tensioner body   3 Front engine plate   4 Cam adjuster   5 Dowel bolt

(If the camshaft marks were aligned before removing sprocket and cylinder head as instructed in **Section 1:4** and the engine has not been turned, operation 1 can be omitted).

2 Align the camshaft timing marks as shown in **FIG 1:3**.

3 Fit the sprocket in the timing chain with the chain tight on the guides so that the dowel hole in the sprocket lines up with the camshaft dowel. During this operation the camshaft and crankshaft must not be rotated.

4 Fit the sprocket to the camshaft with the chain engaged keeping the chain taut on the fixed guide side.

5 Release the chain tensioner. Check and if necessary adjust chain tension (see **Section 1:7**).

6 Recheck timing by turning engine in direction of rotation until crankshaft timing marks are again aligned at TDC compression stroke on No. 1 cylinder.

7 Tighten the camshaft sprocket nut to 35 lb ft. Refit the camshaft cover and tighten the screws evenly to 6 lb ft. Refit the other components in reverse order of removal.

1:7 Camshaft drive gear. Front oil seal

Removing camshaft chain:

If the chain only is to be renewed proceed as follows:

1 Remove camshaft cover and align camshaft timing marks. Retract and lock chain tensioner. (See **Section 1:4**, operation 4).

2 Remove the camshaft sprocket taking care not to move the crankshaft or the camshaft. Leaving a section of the timing chain accessible, block the timing chain aperture with a piece of lint free cloth to keep out dirt or parts which may be dropped.

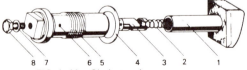

FIG 1:11   Chain tensioner components

Key to Fig 1:11   1 Slipper assembly   2 Spring   3 Plunger   4 Washer   5 Tensioner body   6 Oil hole   7 Copper washer   8 Set screw

3 Split the chain using the chain link remover or rivet extractor Renold part No. 311006. To use the tool first turn the centre screw anti-clockwise to retract. Open the jaws by squeezing the two handles together as shown in **FIG 1:8**. Place the tool over the chain at one bearing pin and close the jaws against the roller by releasing the handles. Turn the screw clockwise until the tip contacts one bearing pin and continue turning until the pin end is just released from the side plate. Unscrew the tool and repeat operation on the other pin of the same side plate.

4 Ensure that both ends of the chain are secured so that they will not drop into the aperture. Remove the loose link noting that this must not be reused as unrivetting destroys the fit of the part.

Refitting camshaft chain:

1 Remove the cloth from the aperture. Attach the new chain to the old with a piece of wire so that the new chain can be pulled through by means of the old one. When the new chain is located round the guides, tensioner and crankshaft sprocket replace the cloth in the aperture to ensure that links or tools cannot drop into the sump.

2 Secure the anvil of the timing chain link replacer 18GA 017 to the camshaft carrier bolts using the bolts supplied with the tool (see **FIG 1:9**). Connect the two ends of the chain with a new rivetting link and position the chain on the anvil as shown.

3 Fit the chain side plate over the pins and tap into position using the hollow punch. Ensure that both ends of the side plate are fully home but keep the plate parallel during the operation to avoid risk of bending it.

4 Spread the ends of the pins with the centre punch and finally peen over with the concave punch.

5 Ensure that the link just rivetted has sufficient side clearance to prevent binding. If it cannot be freely moved by hand gently tap the link side plates to produce face movement. Remove the anvil of the link replacer. Remove the cloth from the aperture.

6 Adjust the valve timing as described in **Section 1:** and refit other parts in reverse order of dismantling.

Removing timing chain tensioner:

1 Drain the cooling system, disconnect radiator hoses. Remove radiator, fan pulley and belt (see **Chapter 4**).

2 Remove crankshaft pulley. Referring to **FIG 1:10** remove front engine plate 3. Remove fuel pump and pushrod (**Chapter 2**).

3 Retract and lock chain tensioner as described in **Section 1:4**, operation 4. Remove the tensioner body 5 in **FIG 1:11** (also 2 in **FIG 1:10**).

4 Referring to **FIG 1:10** turn the cam adjuster 4 to give maximum chain slack. Lever the chain away from the tensioner and turn tensioner through 180 deg. Finally push the chain inwards and remove the tensioner through the front plate aperture.

5 In some cases it may be necessary to remove the camshaft sprocket to allow sufficient chain movement. For instructions refer to **Section 1:4**.

Refitting chain tensioner:

1 Referring to **FIG 1:11** push the chain inwards and place slipper assembly 1 in position. Adjust the chain by means of screw 4 **(FIG 1:10)**.
2 Referring to **FIG 1:11** fit spring 2 and plunger 3 in tensioner and lock by turning a 1/8 Allen key clockwise.
3 Screw in the tensioner body 5 while holding the tensioner against the chain. Remove the access screw 8 insert Allen key and release plunger by turning key anticlockwise.
4 Reverse the remainder of the removal operations.

Timing chain guides:

1 Drain the cooling system and disconnect radiator hoses. Remove the fan, pulley and belt.
2 Remove cam cover. Slacken the crankshaft pulley and camshaft sprocket bolts.
3 Align the valve timing marks **(Section 1:4)**. Remove crankshaft pulley and camshaft sprocket taking care not to turn crankshaft or camshaft.
4 Remove dowel bolt 10 (see **FIG 1:12**) and retaining bolts 11, taking care not to drop bolts, washers or tools into the sump. Lift and withdraw the fixed guide 12. Disengage lower end of guide 13 from adjuster.
5 Refitting is in the reverse order of dismantling. Tighten retaining bolts 11 to 20 lb ft. Check valve timing.

Front oil seal:

To remove:
1 Slacken the fan belt and remove (see **Chapter 4**).
2 Referring to **FIG 1:1** tap back the bolt lockwasher 21, and remove crankshaft pulley bolt 20. Remove pulley 21 and remove crankshaft pulley bolt 20. Remove pulley 19.
3 Remove the seal retainer plate 97. Remove the seal by levering its outer edge from the cylinder block.
To fit new seal reverse the removal procedure noting the following points:
1 Lightly coat the outside diameter of the seal with jointing compound.
2 Ensure that the seal is squarely pressed into position. Refit the seal retainer.
3 Lubricate the seal and crankshaft pulley running surface before fitting pulley.
4 Tighten the pulley nut to 60 to 70 lb ft.

1:8 Removing sump and oil pump

The sump or oil reservoir contains the oil pump and also carries the fuel pump. To ensure alignment of the drive for these components the sump flange has two stepped dowels with their larger ends in the crankcase. The sump needs only be removed for access to oil pump and pickup strainer or to big end bearings. To remove the sump:

1 Disconnect the battery. Drain the engine oil and raise the vehicle to a suitable working height or work over a pit.
2 Remove the distributor (see **Chapter 3**). Withdraw the square-ended quill shaft **(FIG 1:1** item 28) from the distributor drive shaft. A tool similar to 18GA 1147 can be made up for this purpose **(FIG 1:13)**.

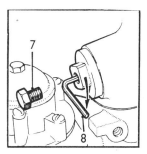

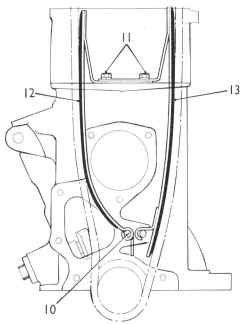

FIG 1:12   Removing and refitting timing chain guides

Key to Fig 1:1   7 Bolt for tensioner adapter   8 Allen key
9 Camshaft sprocket   10 Dowel bolt for lefthand guide
11 Guide retaining bolts   12 Lefthand guide
13 Righthand guide

3 Remove the fuel pump and pushrod **(Chapter 2)**.
4 Remove the oil filter. Remove the dipstick tube **(FIG 1:1** item 82) and brackets.
5 Carefully drift the two dowels out of the sump flange.
6 Remove the bolts securing the sump to the crankcase and engine back plate. Remove the sump complete taking care not to damage the backing plate gasket.

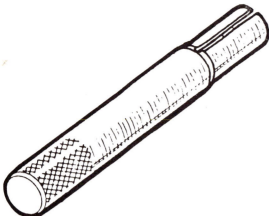

FIG 1:13 Tool No. 18GA.1147 Quill shaft remover/replacer

Removal of oil pump:

Having removed the sump as already described:

1 Remove the oil filter adaptor plate. Remove the oil pump connector 1 in **FIG 1:14**.
2 Referring to **FIG 1:15** remove the two retaining bolts 3 with their copper sealing washers. Remove the bolt 8 in **FIG 1:16** securing the strainer to the sump. The pump and strainer assembly can now be removed as a unit.
3 The strainer can be removed from the pump by undoing the two bolts 9. Wash the strainer gauze with a brush and clean fuel. On no account use fluffy rags for any lubrication parts.

Refitting:

Refitting of oil pump and sump are a reversal of removal procedure but the following points should be noted:

1 Renew gasket 6 (**FIG 1:16**) if this has been disturbed. Renew the two copper sealing washers on bolts 3 (**FIG 1:15**).
2 If the gasket between the engine backplate and sump has been damaged cut a new gasket through the centre in such a manner that the bolt holes will line up and the ends mate with the ends of the existing gasket. Coat liberally with sealing compound.

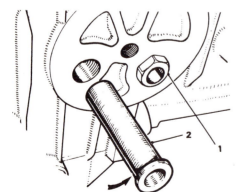

FIG 1:14 Oil pump connector and oil pressure relief valve

3 Loosely fit all bolts to the sump. Run up the backplate bolts and the bolts adjacent to and opposite the dowels, Align the dowel holes and refit the dowels using a suitable G-cramp. Tighten all bolts to the recommended torque.

1:9 Dismantling oil pump

FIG 1:16 shows the components of the oil pump. Dismantling is straightforward but the efficiency of the pump depends on a minimum variation from original dimensions and working clearance between the parts. Dimensions are given in Technical Data but in the event of serious oil pump trouble the owner is recommended to fit a replacement pump complete.

1:10 Removing clutch and flywheel. Starter ring gear

This section only deals with the removal and refitting of the clutch and all other matters relating to the clutch will be found in **Chapter 5**.

The parts are only accessible after the engine has been separated from the gearbox. Depending on what further work is to be carried out remove the engine from the car (see **Section 1:3**) or remove the gearbox from the car (see **Chapter 6**). If the complete power unit has been taken out separate the gearbox from the engine.

The attachments of the clutch are shown in **FIG 1:17**. Make alignment marks 2 and 8 on the clutch cover and flywheel so that the parts will be reassembled in their original alignment. Progressively and diagonally slacken the attachment bolts 3. **The bolts must be progressively slackened otherwise the pressure of the spring will distort the clutch cover.** When all the bolts are free lift off the clutch assembly and remove the driven plate 6.

Mark the flywheel to crankshaft relationship with paint.

Spigot bush:

Whenever the clutch is removed, the spigot bush in the end of the crankshaft should be checked for wear or chatter marks. Renew the bush if it is damaged.

The bush can possibly be removed by tapping a thread in it and using a bolt screwed in to pull it out. If this does not succeed find a suitable tube as a spacer and in combination with a flat washer make an extractor so that the bush is pulled out as the bolt is tightened. If a tap is not available, or a suitable internal extractor, find or turn a piece of rod that is a snug fit in the bush. Fill the bush and recess in the crankshaft with grease, avoiding air pockets. Press the rod into the bush and with light hammer blows on the end of the rod the hydraulic pressure of the grease will force the bush out.

Press a new bush into place and lubricate it lightly with high melting-point grease.

Reassembly:

The parts are refitted in the reverse order of removal. Renew any parts, gaskets or seals that are damaged.

Refit the flywheel, making sure that the contact faces are perfectly clean and aligning any previously made marks. Use a new lockplate if the old one is damaged and tighten the bolts to a torque of 40 lb ft (5.5 kg m) before locking them.

Fit the driven plate to the flywheel with the spring housing facing outwards and hold it in place with the centralizing mandrel 18GA 032 as shown. **The mandrel is essential as it centralizes the driven plate so that the gearbox input shaft can be passed through it into the spigot bearing when refitting the gearbox.** Refit the clutch cover assembly, aligning the marks and secure it in place by evenly and progressively tightening the attachment bolts. Tighten the bolts to a torque of 60 lb ft.

Starter ring gear (Manual models):

If the teeth on the ring are badly worn or damaged a new ring can be fitted to the flywheel. Remove the flywheel. Carefully drill through partially at the root of a tooth and use a cold chisel to split the ring at this weak point. **Take great care not to damage or mark the flywheel itself.**

Thoroughly clean the periphery of the flywheel by scrubbing it with a wire brush and removing high spots with emerycloth.

Polish the new ring at a few points around it, using emerycloth, as the colour of these points will give an indication of the temperature of the ring. Heat the ring to a temperature of 300 to 400°C (572 to 752°F) indicated by the polished patches being from grey/brown to light blue in colour. The best method is to use a stove to heat the ring but it can be heated using two or more blow lamps while laid on a sheet of asbestos. If blow lamps are used keep the flames moving so that local overheated spots do not develop. **Overheating will ruin the temper of the metal.** When the ring is hot, lay it into

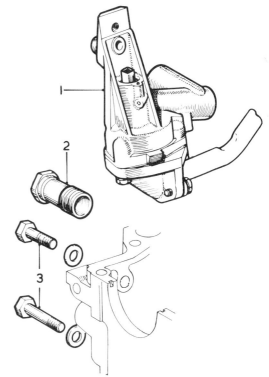

FIG 1 :15   Oil pump attachments

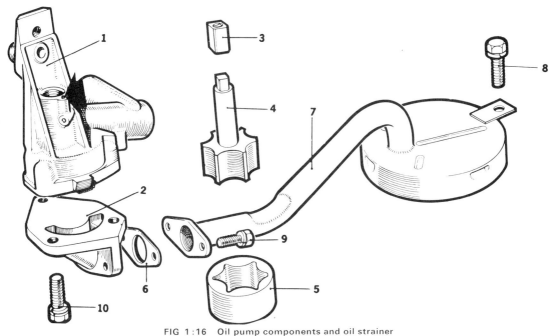

FIG 1 :16   Oil pump components and oil strainer

Key to Fig 1 :16   1 Pump body   2 Base   3 Square drive   4 Rotor shaft   5 Outer ring   6 Gasket   7 Pick-up and strainer assembly   8 Strainer securing bolt   9 Flange bolt (2 off)   10 Base securing bolt (3 off)

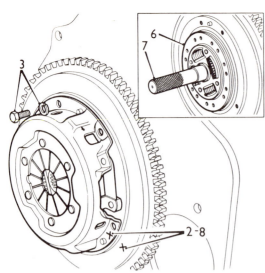

FIG 1:17   Clutch and flywheel attachments

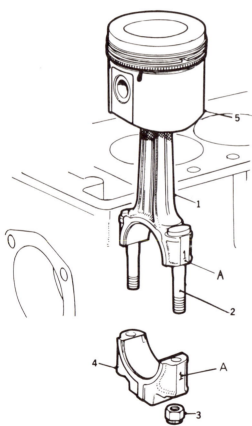

FIG 1:18   Piston and connecting rod

Key to Fig 1:18   1 Connecting rod   2 Connecting rod cap bolt   3 Cap nut   4 Cap   5 Piston   A Bore number

place on the flywheel and tap it fully into place with soft-metal drifts. The lead-in on the teeth should face towards the clutch side of the flywheel. Leave the ring to cool fully before moving the flywheel.

Automatic models:

With automatic models the starter ring gear forms part of the converter drive plate and it is serviced as a complete assembly only.

Removing:

1 Drain the gearbox oil. **(Note precautions given in Chapter 7).**
2 Remove the gearbox.
3 Remove the starter motor.
4 Remove the converter housing.
5 Remove the 4 bolts securing the converter to the drive plate.
6 Remove the bolts securing the drive plate to the crankshaft noting the position of the spacer plates.

Refitting:

1 Loosely mount the new drive plate on the crankshaft with the spacers and lockwashers assembled in the correct order.
2 Check that the lead on the ring gear teeth face the engine backplate.
3 Secure the plate to the crankshaft.
4 Refit the converter to the drive plate diagonally tightening the securing bolts to the figure given in Technical Data.
5 Align the drive slots in the gearbox oil pump drive gear with the driving tangs on the converter.
6 Refit the gearbox and replace the remaining components in the reverse order to which they were removed.

1:11 Splitting big-ends, removing rods and pistons

1 Remove the cylinder head (see **Section 1:4).** Remove sump (see **Section 1:8).** Refer to **FIG 1:18** and check the markings on rod and cap A. These should coincide with the cylinder bore numbers starting with No. 1 at the front end of the engine.
2 When the big-end nuts 3 are removed they must be scrapped, so be prepared to fit new nuts on reassembly. When the nuts are off, tap the connecting rod bolts upwards until a downward pull on the caps 4 will release them. Remove the bearing shells 11 in **FIG 1:1** keeping them in the order of removal.
3 If the engine is due for decarbonizing there will be a ring of carbon round the top of each cylinder bore. Remove this with a scraper and then push the connecting rod and piston upwards and out. If the bearing shells and caps are restored to their respective rods there will be no confusion when it comes to reassembly.

A design feature of the piston and connecting rod assembly is that the gudgeon pin is a tight press fit in the small-end of the rod. Removing and refitting the pin involves the use of the tool 18G A 06 **(FIG 1:19)** or a carefully chosen substitute. The drawbolt 1 has its larger diameter A just small enough to pass through the hole in the piston while its smaller diameter B passes through the gudgeon pin and is threaded to take nut C. The part 2 has its internal diameter large enough to accommodate the gudgeon pin while its outer diameter presses against the piston boss without risk of damage to the piston. Before removing gudgeon pins mark to ensure that piston pin and connecting rod can be reassembled in their original positions.

Check all parts for wear, renewing the assembly if the gudgeon pin is slack in the piston bosses. The correct diameter of the pin is .8123 to .8125 inch.

Refitting gudgeon pin:

1 Lubricate the gudgeon pin with thin oil and fit it into the bore on one side of the piston.
2 Clamp the gudgeon pin remover/replacer tool 18GA 06 in a vice with the small length boss uppermost.
3 Position the tool screw through the gudgeon pin, connecting rod and tool and fit the nut and thrust bearing assembly to the screw.
4 Screw the nut up by hand and ensure that all parts are squarely aligned. Tighten the nut preferably using a torque wrench which should read at least 10 lb ft if the pin is a sufficiently tight fit in the rod.
5 Referring to **FIG 1:20** tighten until the pin is $\frac{1}{16}$ below the piston face as shown at A. This ensures that when the rod is midway between the bosses the ends of the pin will be flush. Check that the piston moves freely on the pin.

1:12 Refitting rings, pistons and con-rods

Renew the piston rings if they have seen much service and check the ring gap before fitting them (see 17 in **FIG 1:21**). Press each ring about 1 inch down the bore with a piston and measure the gap with feeler gauges. It should be .008 to .016 for 1500 and .008 to .017 for 1750 and TC. Judicious filing of the ring ends will enable gaps which are too small to be increased. Check the fit of the rings in the piston grooves, but first clean the grooves free from carbon without scraping the metal. The ring to groove clearance 18 of the top two rings must lie between .002 to .0035 for 1500 and .0015 to .0035 for 1750 TC models. Dimensions for widths of rings and ring grooves are given in Technical Data at the end of this manual.

Refitting rings:

FIG 1:22 shows details of the piston rings.
1 Fit the bottom rail 1 of the oil control ring to the piston and position it below the bottom groove.
2 Fit the oil control expander 3 into the bottom groove.
3 Move the bottom oil control ring rail 2 into the bottom groove.
4 Fit the top oil control rail into the bottom groove.
5 Check that the ends of the expander are butting but not overlapping. (See lower inset).
6 Set the gaps of the rails and the expander at 90 degrees to each other.
7 Fit the second compression ring 5 with the scalloped face of the ring towards the bottom of the piston.
8 Fit the top compression ring 6 to the groove with the inner shouldered face towards the top of the piston.

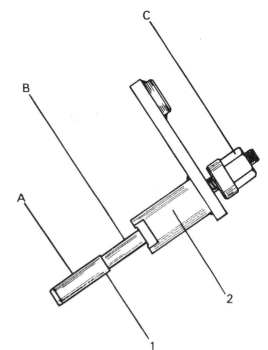

FIG 1:19   Gudgeon pin tool No. 18GA 06

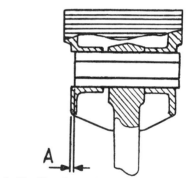

FIG 1:20   Showing position of gudgeon pin after fitting

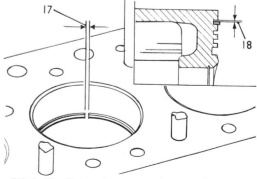

FIG 1:21   Piston ring gaps and groove clearances

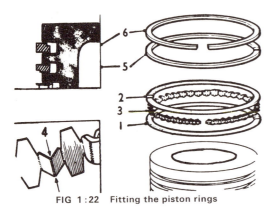

FIG 1:22 Fitting the piston rings

Key to Fig 1:22 1 Oil ring bottom rail 2 Oil ring top rail 3 Oil ring expander 4 Expander ends butted 5 Second compression ring 6 Top compression ring

Refitting pistons and connecting rods:

Reverse the dismantling sequence but be careful to ensure that each assembly is fitted into its correct bore. The piston crown is marked 'FRONT' and the connecting rod oil hole must be on the distributor side. Use a piston ring compressor to introduce the piston into the oiled bore and then pull the assembly down until the upper bearing shell can be fitted to the rod. Be careful to fit the tag on the shell into the notch in the rod and oil the big-end journal. Fit the cap and lower shell with the marks aligned and screw **new** nuts on the bolts. Tighten to a torque of 31 to 35 lb ft.

1:13 Servicing crankshaft and main bearings

Removing crankshaft:

1 Remove the engine or power unit (see **Section 1:3**). Remove the gearbox, clutch, and flywheel or automatic components where applicable.
2 Remove engine backplate and seal assembly.

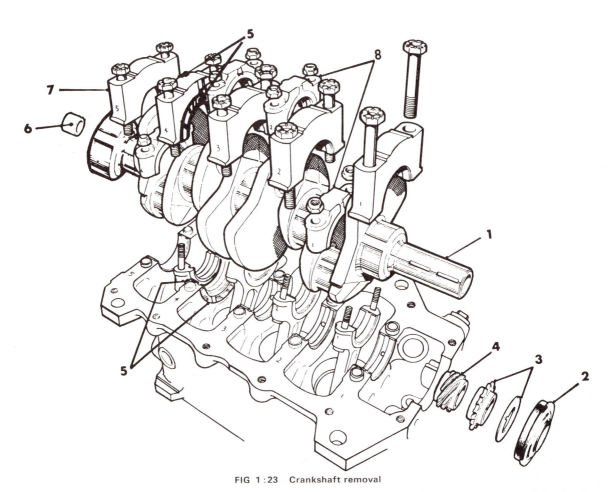

FIG 1:23 Crankshaft removal

Key to Fig 1:23 1 Crankshaft 2 Crankshaft pulley oil seal 3 Crankshaft sprocket 4 Distributor drive gear 5 Crankshaft thrust washers 6 Input shaft spigot bush 7 Main bearing cap 8 Connecting rod cap

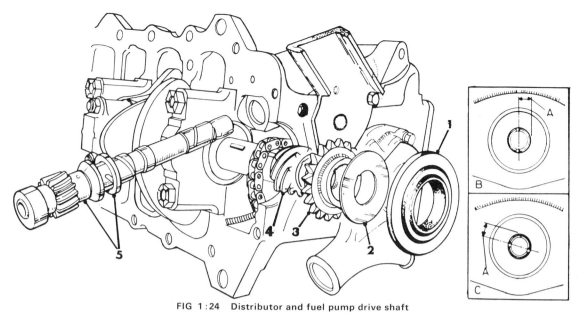

FIG 1:24 Distributor and fuel pump drive shaft

Key to Fig 1:24 1 Pulley oil seal 2 Oil thrower 3 Sprocket 4 Drive gear and thrust washer 5 Drive shaft and thrust washer

3 Remove the dipstick and tube, distributor and quill shaft, and the petrol pipe, pump to carburetter.

4 Retract and lock the chain tensioner, as described in **Section 1:4.**

5 Remove the camshaft cover, camshaft sprocket and fuel pump.

6 Remove the oil reservoir complete (see **Section 1:8**). Remove distributor drive shaft. Remove the crankshaft front seal retainer, seal, oil slinger, crankshaft sprocket and distributor drive gear.

7 Before dismantling further, check the crankshaft end float. Use a dial gauge on one end of the crankshaft and lever the shaft backwards and forwards to check.

8 Check the big-end markings A in **FIG 1:18** and the main bearing marks in **FIG 1:23**. In each case No. 1 should start at the front end of the engine. Remove big-end caps 8 and main bearing caps 7.

9 Lift away the crankshaft 1. On each side of No. 4 main bearing there are thrust washers to control end float. They are shown as items 6 in **FIG 1:1**. Keep the bearing shells with their caps so that they can be fitted in their original positions if they are not to be renewed.

Refitting the crankshaft:

Check the main and big-end bearings for wear. Diametrical clearance and end float figures will be found in Technical Data at the end of this manual. If necessary, the main and big-end journals can be reground to undersizes of .010, .020, .030 and .040 inch and undersize bearings fitted. Excessive end float is cured by selecting suitable thrust washers 5 **(FIG 1:23)**. Renew all bearing shells which are scored or show signs of breaking up.

Adjustment of main and big-end clearances by filing the caps and shells is not permissible. It immediately renders the parts unacceptable on an exchange basis. The shells are ready to fit and the running clearances will be correct without any need for adjustment. If a bearing has run flush out all oil passages under high pressure and inject fresh engine oil.

If the crankshaft is a new or reconditioned one it will be necessary to line-ream the three small dowel holes at the flywheel end with those in the flywheel. Oversize dowels can then be fitted. Proceed to refit the crankshaft as follows:

1 Oil the journals and lower the crankshaft into place after positioning the timing chain correctly. Make sure the thrust washer halves are correctly fitted and have their oilways facing outwards.

2 Check that the bearing shell tags are seated in their notches and fit the main bearing caps. Tighten the bolts to a torque of 70 lb ft.

3 Fit the big-end caps, tightening the nuts to a torque of 31 to 35 lb ft.

Refitting distributor drive shaft:

Next refit the distributor drive shaft (see **FIG 1:24**).

Some care is needed in this operation because the shaft turns as the gear teeth are meshed. **It is essential, for the accuracy of ignition timing, to ensure that the drive slot at the top end finishes up in the right position.** Proceed as follows:

1 Fit the thrust washer to the drive shaft.

2 Ensure the timing marks are set at TDC with No. 1 on compression stroke.

3 Fit the drive shaft with the drive slot at 12 o'clock with the large offset segment A as shown in inset B.

4 Fit the driving gear noting the distributor shaft will turn through 70 deg. anticlockwise to bring the drive

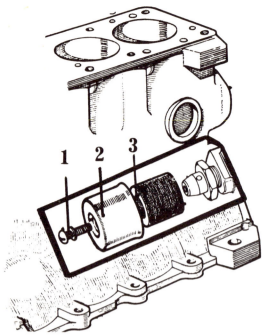

FIG 1:25 Engine breathing system

slot to 10 o'clock with the large offset segment A uppermost giving the correct positioning for No. 1 cylinder firing. Refer inset C.

5 At this point check that with the distributor fitted the rotor arm is set to fire on No. 1 cylinder and the contact points are just beginning to open.

Reassembly:

Replace in the remaining parts in the reverse order to which they were removed, checking the valve timing and ignition timing. The distributor may be temporarily installed for this purpose.

Note that after installation of engine in car the oil pump must be primed (see **Section 1:16**).

1:14 External oil filter and relief valve. Ventilation filter

The external oil filter is of the fullflow throwaway canister type. To remove unscrew the canister from the base using a universal canister removing/replacing tool. Turn anticlockwise to unscrew. Screw on the new filter assembly which includes new sealing rings and tighten first by hand only. Mark the filter position and then tighten a further half turn using the tool. Start the engine and check for oil leaks.

The oil pressure relief valve (**FIG 1:14**) is a sealed unit and if defective it must be renewed. To remove, remove the oil filter assembly including the adaptor plate and gasket. Withdraw or lever out the relief valve 2. When refitting ensure that the discharge hole in the valve is facing downwards into the sump as shown by arrow in **FIG 1:14**. Fit a new oil filter adaptor plate gasket using jointing compound and ensuring that the word 'TOP' stamped on the gasket is facing outwards.

Ventilation filter:

Fresh air is filtered into the crankcase through a filter mounted on the lefthand rear of the crankcase as shown in **FIG 1:25** and item 100 in **FIG 1:1**. Crankcase fumes are drawn upwards through the timing chain compartment into the camshaft cover, oil being filtered out by a separator at the front of the camshaft cover. A hose connects the camshaft cover with the carburetter intake so that fumes are drawn into the combusion chambers and eliminated.

To test the functioning of the air filter, remove the sealed oil filler cap while the engine is running. Engine speed should drop noticeably. If it remains constant the filter element must be renewed. It should in any case be replaced every 12,000 miles or at shorter intervals in very dusty conditions.

Referring to **FIG 1:25**, remove the screw 1 and cover 2. Remove and discard the element 3. Clean the cover and element container. Fit new element, replace cover and screw.

1:15 Reassembling stripped engine

All the operations concerned with dismantling and refitting the various components of the engine have been covered in **Sections 1:3** to **1:14**. The task of reassembling the transmission to the engine is covered early in **Chapter 6**. It is essential to be clean and methodical when performing the operations and to lubricate all bearing surfaces liberally with clean engine oil. Always renew all joint gaskets as these are available in complete sets.

Start off by fitting the crankshaft. As each bearing cap is tightened check the freedom of the shaft. If it suddenly becomes tight, dismantle the last cap to be tightened and check the bearing shells for dirt and burrs. This method must also be adopted when refitting the big-ends. Make quite sure that the shaft has been correctly assembled with all gears and the timing chain in position. Continue to refit the components in the reverse order to dismantling, being careful to use the torque wrench figures given in the text and also in Technical Data at the end of this manual. Always check that the crankshaft and camshaft are correctly positioned so that the ignition and valve timings are not wrongly set.

Fit a new gasket before attaching the inlet and exhaust manifold. There are four short bolts in the top row, two long bolts in the outer holes in the bottom row and two nuts and spring washers for studs in the third and fourth bottom holes.

The servicing of associated components such as the carburetter fuel pump, generator and water pump are covered in the various Chapters devoted to those subjects.

1:16 Refitting engine in car

Refitting engine or complete power unit is a reversal of the removal procedure, but the following points should be noted:

1 On manual models where engine only has been removed it will be lowered from above, while the gearbox is supported on a jack or small hoist.

2 Lightly lubricate the spigot bearing in the crankshaft end, into which the gearbox input shaft fits, with a little high-melting point grease.

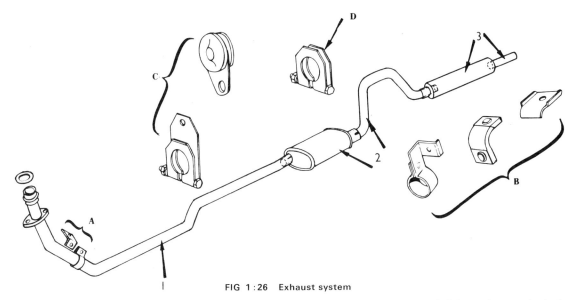

FIG 1 : 26   Exhaust system

Key to Fig 1 : 26   1 Front pipe   2 Muffler and intermediate pipe   3 Resonator and tail pipe.   **A** Exhaust pipe to engine back plate bracket   **B** Tail pipe to body mounting   **C** Muffler to body mounting   **D** Muffler to exhaust pipe clamp

3 Lower the engine back into place and make fine adjustments on the hoist and jack so that the gearbox input shaft is accurately aligned with the clutch. Slide the engine rearwards, without using force, so that the input shaft slides through the clutch. Turn the input shaft slightly if the splines do not line up. With the engine still on the hoist, align the engine mouting bolt holes and then fit and tighten the bolts.

On automatic or manual models where the complete unit has been removed it must be refitted from beneath the car.

On all models refit all ancillary parts and remake all connections removed before engine removal. On manual models where gearbox has also been removed do not forget to refill and bleed clutch hydraulic system. Where servo is fitted do not forget servo vacuum hose connection.

Refill the cooling system and check for possible leaks. If the bottom half of the engine has been dismantled, sump removed and crankshaft removed, the oil pump should be primed before starting the engine as follows:

1 Fill sump to indicated level on dipstick.
2 Remove sparking plugs and disconnect main coil lead.
3 Crank engine until oil gauge records normal pressure or oil warning light goes out.
4 Check oil level, refit plugs and lead.

1 : 17 Exhaust pipe

FIG 1 : 26 shows the components of the exhaust system which is rigidly attached to the backplate at A but flexibly mounted at B and C.

Removal of the complete exhaust system as an assembly presents a certain amount of difficulty. It is however available for service purposes in three parts,

numbered 1, 2 and 3 in the diagram, thus facilitating replacement. Replacement muffler and resonator are supplied with longer and larger diameter inlet pipes which fit over the original pipes using clamps thus making welding unnecessary.

When assembling, note that the system must be unstressed and correctly aligned, therefore proceed as follows:

1 Loosely fit the manifold clamp and rear strap assembly.
2 Align the pipe immediately in front of the muffler so that the two parts of mounting C are in line and vertical.
3 Tighten the manifold clamp and engine backplate bracket.
4 Align the exhaust pipe between the muffler and the resonator to run parallel to the body sidemember.
5 Tighten all clamps and mountings.

1 : 18 Fault diagnosis

(a) Engine will not start

1 Defective coil
2 Faulty distributor capacitor (condenser)
3 Dirty, pitted or incorrectly set contact breaker points
4 Ignition wiring loose or insulation faulty
5 Water on plug leads, damp distributor
6 Battery discharged, terminals corroded
7 Faulty or jammed starter. Switch defective
8 Plug leads wrongly connected
9 Vapour lock in fuel pipes due to heat
10 Defective fuel pump or float mechanism
11 Overchoking or underchoking sticking carburetter piston
12 Blocked petrol filter or carburetter jet
13 Leaking valves, broken springs
14 Sticking valves
15 Valve timing incorrect
16 Ignition timing incorrect

(b) Engine stalls

1 Check 1, 2, 3, 4, 5, 10, 11, 12, 13 and 14 in (a)
2 Sparking plugs defective or gaps incorrect
3 Retarded ignition
4 Mixture too weak
5 Water in fuel system
6 Petrol tank vent blocked
7 Incorrect valve clearances

(c) Engine idles badly

1 Check 2, 4 and 7 in (b)
2 Air leak at manifold joints
3 Carburetter jet wrongly positioned
4 Air leak in carburetter
5 Over-rich mixture
6 Worn piston rings
7 Worn valve stems or guides
8 Weak exhaust valve springs

(d) Engine misfires

1 Check 1, 2, 3, 4, 5, 8, 10, 12, 13, 14, 15 and 16 in (a); 2, 3, 4 and 7 in (b).
2 Weak or broken valve springs

(e) Engine overheats (see **Chapter 4**)

(f) Compression low

1 Check 13 and 14 in (a), 6 and 7 in (c) and 2 in (d)
2 Worn piston ring grooves
3 Scored or worn cylinder bores
4 Breakdown of head gasket

(g) Engine lacks power

1 Check 3, 10, 11, 12, 13, 14, 15 and 16 in (a); 2, 3, 4 and 7 in (b); 6 and 7 in (c) and 2 in (d)
2 Leaking joint washers
3 Fouled sparking plugs
4 Automatic ignition advance not operating

(h) Burnt valves or head seats

1 Check 13 and 14 in (a); 7 in (b); 2 in (d) and also check (e)
2 Excessive carbon build-up round valve seats and head

(j) Sticking valves

1 Check 2 in (d)
2 Bent valve stem
3 Scored valve stem or guide
4 Incorrect valve clearance

(k) Excessive cylinder wear

1 Check 11 in (a) and see **Chapter 4**
2 Lack of oil
3 Dirty oil
4 Piston rings gummed up or broken
5 Badly fitting piston rings, gaps too small
6 Bent connecting rod

(l) Excessive oil consumption

1 Check 6 and 7 in (c) and check (k)
2 Ring gaps too wide
3 Oil control rings defective
4 Scored cylinders
5 Oil level too high
6 Leaking oil seals, filter, joints
7 Ineffective inlet valve stem oil seals

(m) Crankshaft or connecting rod bearing failure

1 Check 2 in (k)
2 Restricted oilways
3 Worn journals or crankpins
4 Loose bearing caps
5 Very low oil pressure
6 Bent connecting rod

(n) Internal water leakage (see **Chapter 4**)

(o) Poor water circulation (see **Chapter 4**)

(p) Corrosion (see **Chapter 4**)

(q) High fuel consumption (see **Chapter 2**)

(r) Engine vibration

1 Loose generator bolts
2 Mounting rubbers loose or ineffective
3 Exhaust pipe mountings defective
4 Engine steady loose or faulty
5 Misfiring due to mixture, ignition or mechanical faults

CHAPTER 2

THE FUEL SYSTEM

2:1 The fuel tank

The attachments of the fuel tank are shown in **FIG 2:1**.

Tank removal:

Disconnect both battery leads. Raise the rear of the car and place it securely on axle stands. Remove the drain plug 2 and drain the fuel into a suitable container. If the fuel is contaminated or dirty it can be used for cleaning operations. Disconnect the lead 3 from the tank unit. Disconnect the vent and fuel pipes 4, using pliers to squeeze the legs of the clips open. Release the vent pipe 5 by the filler cap. Support the tank and remove the securing bolts and plates. Lower the tank down and out of the car.

If the tank unit is removed from the tank, **take great care not to damage or bend the float arm.**

The fuel tank is refitted in the reverse order of removal.

2:2 Fuel pump operating principles

The Goss mechanical fuel pump, item 94 in **FIG 1:1** is mounted on the righthand side of the sump and operated by an eccentric on the distributor drive shaft 23 through the pushrod 92.

The pump is shown in exploded form in **FIG 2:2**. The pushrod moves the rocker arm 18 which in turn operates the link 16 pivoting on the same spindle 20 but not attached to the rocker arm. The link pulls the diaphragm 10 down against its spring 11 drawing fuel in through the inlet valve 9. The spring then pushes the diaphragm upwards, closing the inlet valve and forcing fuel through the outlet valve 9A into the feed pipe and carburetter.

As soon as the carburetter float chamber is full its needle valve closes and the back pressure on the pump holds the diaphragm down. A small spring 15 keeps the rocker arm in contact with the pushrod and they continue to reciprocate but without operating the link.

2:3 Fuel pump testing

As a quick roadside test, disconnect the fuel line from the carburetter float chamber and point it well away from the engine. Crank the engine on the starter motor and if the pump is supplying fuel there should be a good spurt from the pipe at every other revolution of the engine.

A more sophisticated version of this test is shown in **FIG 2:3**. Disconnect the fuel line 1 from the carburetter float chamber and insert the end into a suitable glass

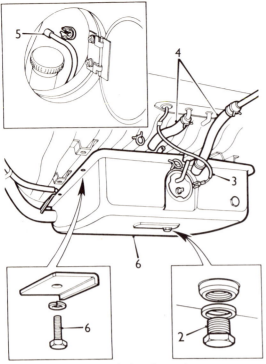

FIG 2:1 The fuel tank attachments

tightened to a torque of 15 to 18 lb ft. Note also that when installing the flexible pipe to the short inlet pipe on the pump both pipes should be set upwards at an angle of 30 deg. as shown in **FIG 2:5.** ·

Overhauling:

Clean the outside of the pump before starting to dismantle. Referring to **FIG 2:2** mark the relative positions of upper body 7 and lower body 14 before removing the screws 5 to separate the two parts. To remove the diaphragm and pullrod assembly 10 press down against the spring and turn through 90 deg. right or left to release the pullrod from the link 16. The rocker pin 20 is secured by the two clips 19.

Thoroughly clean all parts for examination and renew any that are worn or corroded. Renew the diaphragm assembly if the diaphragm shows any signs of cracking or hardening. Check the upper and lower castings for cracks and the flanges for truth. Not more than .010 wear is permissible on the working face of the rocker arm. The valve assemblies are staked into the underside of the upper body. Note the relative positions of inlet and outlet before removal. Major and minor repair kits are available.

2:5 Carburetter operating princiles

The 1500 model is fitted with an SU.HS4 carburetter, while the 1750 has the slightly larger HS6. The TC model is fitted with two HS6 carburetters. All are semi-downdraught units inclined at 20 deg. from the horizontal. The twin carburetters are fitted with a different type of air filter, see **Section 2:11**.

FIG 2:6 is a sectioned view of an HS4 carburetter, the HS6 being of basically similar construction. Its components are also shown in the exploded view **FIG 2:7**.

The throttle butterfly valve on the right is connected to the accelerator pedal by a mechanical linkage and cable. The feed tube 4 is connected to a conventional type float chamber, where the action of the float on the needle valve keeps the fuel level within limits.

When the engine is running, all the air for combustion is drawn through the carburetter. As airflow speeds up there is a reduction in pressure and the bridge below the air valve forms a reduction in the throat area, causing the flow to speed up and the static pressure to drop. This reduction in pressure draws fuel from the jet so that the fuel is mixed with the air. The pressure reduction is also transferred (by ports in the air valve piston) to the suction chamber above the air valve. The air valve will then rise to a position where the suction is balanced by the weight of the piston and the pressure of the return spring. If the throttle is opened, allowing more air to pass to the engine and speed it up, the increased airflow will first cause a further reduction in static pressure by the bridge and this will raise the air valve to a new point of balance. Conversely if the throttle is closed and the airflow reduced the static pressure will rise allowing the air valve to drop until normal suction is again restored.

As the weight of the piston and pressure of the return spring are virtually constant, the vacuum across the bridge will also be kept constant under all running conditions of the engine, with the air valve rising as the airflow increases. The jet area is fixed but the needle attached to the air valve slides up and down in the

container. Disconnect the white lead 2 from the ignition coil, **keeping the free end well away from any metal parts to prevent shortcircuits,** so that the engine will not start on the fuel in the float chamber.

Crank the engine over on the starter and check the flow. If there are good spurts of fuel and the container fills up rapidly then the pump is operating satisfactorily. If the flow starts off well but then dies away, check the vent system of the fuel tank as it may be blocked, causing a vacuum to form in the tank. If it is suspected that the vent is blocked, remove the filler cap. The pump flow should speed up immediately and the inrush of air into the tank can be heard. Other causes of the flow dying are blocked filters (note that some models are fitted with a filter on the inlet in the tank unit) or a partially blocked fuel line. If air bubbles keep emerging with the fuel then there is a leak on the suction side. If there is no flow, remove the pump from the engine and dry test. If the pump is satisfactory then the fuel lines are completely blocked, but do remember to check that there is fuel in the tank as fuel gauges can go wrong.

2:4 Removing and servicing fuel pump

Removal:

Referring to **FIG 2:4,** disconnect the fuel pipes 1, remove nuts 2 and lift away the pump with insulator block and two gaskets. Withdraw the pushrod 3.

Refitting:

Refitting is a reversal of the removal procedure, but new gaskets should be used and the securing nuts

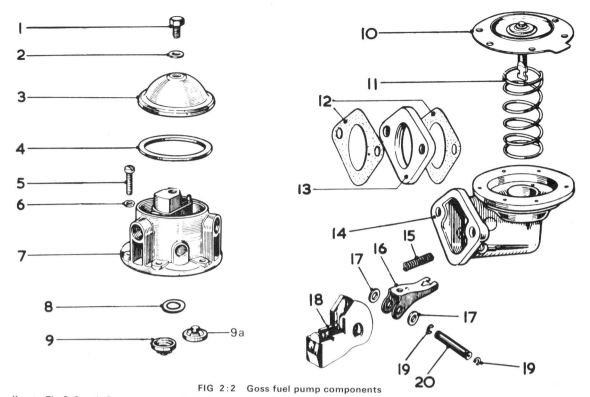

FIG 2:2 Goss fuel pump components

Key to Fig 2:2 1 Screw—cover   2 Gasket—screw   3 Cover   4 Gasket—cover   5 Screw—body   6 Washer—screw
7 Upper body (sediment chamber)   8 Gasket—valve   9 Inlet valve   9A Outlet valve   10 Diaphragm and pull rod assembly
11 Spring—diaphragm   12 Gasket   13 Block—insulator   14 Lower body   15 Spring—rocker arm   16 Link   17 Washer
18 Rocker arm   19 Clip—rocker arm pin   20 Pin—rocker arm

jet. The needle is tapered so that as it is withdrawn the effective area of the jet is increased. The vacuum being kept constant, the fuel flow through the jet will be proportional to the effective area. The jet effective area is governed by the position of the needle and therefore the height of the air valve and, as the height of the air valve is in turn proportional to the airflow, then the fuel flow will be proportional to the air flow. When the airflow is

small, the air valve will be low down and only small amounts of fuel will be drawn through the jet. The mixture strength is therefore kept within limits for all running conditions of the engine.

For cold starts, the jet head 3 can be drawn downwards so that the jet operates on a thinner portion of the needle and the effective area of the jet will be increased, allowing more fuel to be drawn through to make the

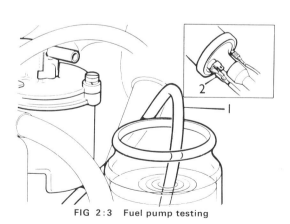

FIG 2:3 Fuel pump testing

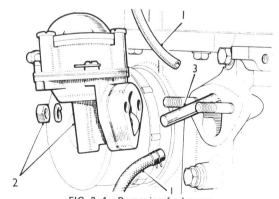

FIG 2:4 Removing fuel pump

Key to Fig 2:4 1 Fuel pipes   2 Pump and retaining nuts
3 Pushrod

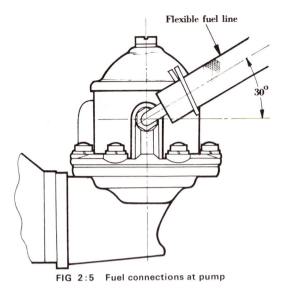

FIG 2 : 5   Fuel connections at pump

mixture richer. The mixture strength throughout the range can be altered by limiting the maximum height of the jet using the adjusting screw 2.

An oil filled damper assembly 7 is fitted to the air valve piston. The damper serves the dual function of an accelerator pump and preventing rapid fluctuations of the air valve. When the throttle valve is opened for acceleration, the damper causes the air valve to lag. The suction increases temporarily beyond its normal value and excess fuel for acceleration is then drawn through the jet.

A piston lifting pin 5 is usually fitted to allow the piston to be raised slightly, when adjusting the carburetter without having to remove the air cleaner.

The components of a carburetter are shown in **FIG 2 : 9**.

2 : 6 Routine maintenance

1 At intervals of 6000 miles (10,000 kilometres) or 6 months, whichever occurs the sooner, unscrew and remove the plug and damper 7 from the top of the carburetter 8, shown in **FIG 2 : 8**. Add a little engine oil, if necessary, to bring the level approximately $\frac{1}{2}$ inch (13 mm) above the top of the hollow piston rod, as shown by the arrows. Push the damper back into position and tighten the plug firmly.

2 At the same time as topping up the carburetter damper, check the carburetter linkages for full and free movement, cleaning and lightly lubricating the pivot points. Adjust the carburetters and their linkage if performance or economy have dropped or the operation seems poor.

2 : 7 Jet centring. Float level

Two types of metering needle and jet assembly may be found in HS carburetters: **Type 1** fixed needle assembly (see **FIG 2 : 9A**). **Type 2** spring-loaded needle assembly (see **FIG 2 : 9B**).

The needle and jet assemblies, and other associated parts are not interchangeable.

Jet centring (Fixed needle only):

This operation is necessary if it is suspected that the piston sticks and that this sticking is not due to grit in the top chamber. Refer to **FIG 2 : 10** and carry out the following procedure:

1 Remove screw 1 to disconnect the link from jet 3. Disconnect fuel feed pipe 2 from the float chamber. Pull out the jet.

2 Remove the jet adjusting nut 5 and spring 4. Refit the nut without the spring and screw it on as far as possible. Refit the jet.

3 Slacken the jet locking nut 7. When the locking nut is loose it allows jet bearing to move about freely in its enlarged bore.

4 Remove the piston damper 8. Press down on piston 9 by introducing a pencil or piece of rod into the bore vacated by the damper. While the piston is firmly pressed down, tighten locknut 7.

5 Lift the piston with pin 11 and check that it falls freely. Lower the adjusting nut and check again. If there is any difference in the sound of piston impact, repeat the jet centring operation.

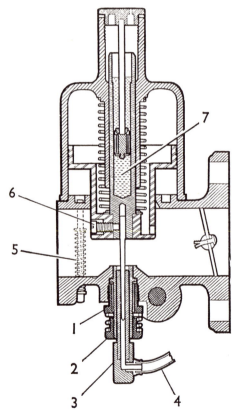

FIG 2 : 6   Sectioned view of SU Carburetter

Key to Fig 2 : 6   1 Jet locking nut   2 Jet adjusting nut 3 Jet head   4 Feed tube from float chamber   5 Piston lifting pin   6 Needle securing screw   7 Oil damper reservoir

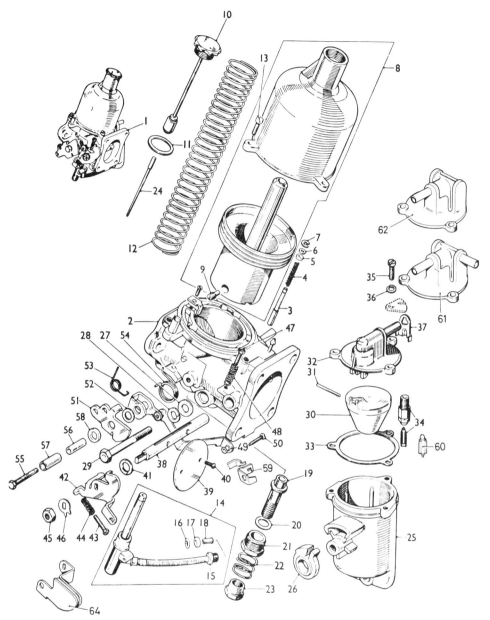

FIG 2:7 Carburetter components

Key to Fig 2:7   1 Carburetter assembly   2 Carburetter body   3 Piston lifting pin   4 Spring and pin   5 Neoprene washer
6 Brass washer   7 Circlip—pin   8 Chamber and piston assembly   9 Needle locating screw   10 Piston damper   11 Fibre washer
12 Piston spring   13 Screw—chamber to body   14 Jet assembly   15 Nut   16 Washer   17 Gland   18 Ferrule   19 Jet bearing
20 Brass washer   21 Jet locking nut   22 Jet locking spring   23 Jet adjusting screw   24 Needle   25 Float chamber   26 Adapter
27 Plain washer   28 Spring washer   29 Bolt—float chamber to body   30 Float   31 Hinge pin—float to lid   32 Float chamber
lid   33 Float chamber lid gasket   34 Needle and seat assembly (2nd type)   35 Screw   36 Spring washer   37 Baffle plate lid
38 Throttle spindle   39 Throttle disc   40 Screw-disc to spindle   41 Brass washer—spindle   42 Throttle return lever   43 Cam
stop screw   44 Spring—screw   45 Throttle spindle nut   46 Tab washer—nut   47 Throttle adjusting screw   48 Spring—screw
49 Pick-up lever and links   50 Screw-link to jet   51 Cam lever   52 Washer—cam lever   53 Cam lever spring   54 Pick-up
lever spring   55 Pivot bolt   56 Pivot bolt tube   57 Outer tube   58 Distance washer   59 Pick-up lever and link   60 Needle
(1st type)   61 Float chamber lid   62 Float chamber lid   64 Throttle linkage

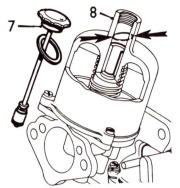

FIG 2:8 Topping up carburetter damper

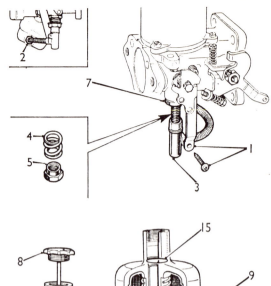

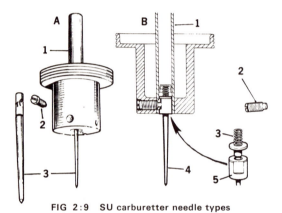

FIG 2:9 SU carburetter needle types

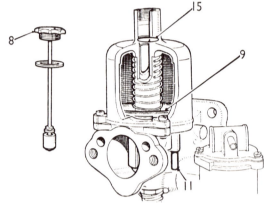

FIG 2:10 Centring carburetter needle and jet

Key to Fig 2:9 **A** Fixed needle **1** Piston rod **2** Needle securing screw **3** Metering needle **B** Spring loaded needle **1** Piston rod **2** Guide locking screw **3** Spring **4** Needle **5** Needle support guide

Key to Fig 2:10 **1** Jet link and fixing **2** Fixing for fuel pipe to float chamber **3** Jet **4** Spring **5** Jet adjusting nut **7** Jet bearing locknut **8** Damper **9** Piston **11** Piston lifting pin **15** Damper oil well

6 Remove the jet. Remove the adjusting nut, refit the spring and restore the nut. Connect up the fuel pipe and the jet link. Finally top up the damper oil well with 20W engine oil until it is $\frac{1}{2}$ inch above the hollow piston rod and refit the damper. Check the idling speed and mixture strength as described in **Section 2:6**.

Float level check:

The parts of the float chamber are shown in **FIG 2:11**. The float chamber can be removed from the carburetter by disconnecting the jet feed tube (undo nut 15 in **FIG 2:7**) and taking out the bolt 30, though this is not necessary other than for full dismantling of the carburetter.

Disconnect the fuel line from the float chamber cover 25. Take out the three screws 28, lightly scribe across the cover 25 and body 21 to assist in reassembly, and remove the cover 25 complete with the float and needle valve. Collect the gasket 22. Remove the pin 24 so that the float 23 can be taken off, taking care not to lose the needle of the valve 26. Discard the float and fit a new one in its place if it is damaged, leaks or contains fuel.

Unscrew the seat of the valve 26 from the cover. Blow through the inlet tube of the cover to clear out any dirt and wash the valve assembly 26 in clean fuel. Check the tapered end of the needle for signs of wear and renew the complete valve 26 if the needle is worn or the valve leaks when blown through with the needle held closed on its seat.

Refit the parts to the cover in the reverse order of removal. Do not overtighten the seat of the valve 26. The fuel level on SU carburetters is not particularly critical but it should be checked as shown in **FIG 2:12**.

The all nylon float used in this carburetter does not permit the raising or lowering the fuel level by the usual method of bending the metal crank attached to the float, as used in other models. To raise the fuel level, add an extra gasket under the float chamber lid after ensuring that only one gasket exists between the float needle seat and the float chamber lid. To lower the fuel level insert an additional washer between the float needle seat and the float chamber lid, after making sure that there is only one gasket between the float chamber and the lid.

Blow and brush out any sediment from inside the float chamber. Refit the cover assembly in the reverse order of removal and reconnect the fuel line.

2:8 Carburetter tuning

Carburetters on new cars have been factory tuned to meet the exhaust emission regulations of the Transport Authorities to give less than 4.5% carbon monoxide content to the exhaust gas. Where overhauls adjustments or tuning become necessary the owner is strongly advised to entrust such work to a service agent having the necessary exhaust gas analyser equipment to ensure that emission is kept within the required limit. It is realized however that occasions will arise when specialized equipment is not available and the owner mechanic has to carry out immediate repairs. A brief description of tuning methods is therefore given.

Single carburetter tuning:

Before attempting to tune the carburetter, make sure that the ignition system is in good working order and correctly set. Leaking manifold gaskets or an engine that is in poor condition will also make it difficult or impossible to tune the carburetter satisfactorily.

The idling speeds can be set roughly by ear but for the best results use a tachometer. Electronic test tachometers which can be clipped into the ignition system are available.

The adjustment points on the carburetter are shown in **FIG 2:13**.

1 Start the engine and run it until it has reached its normal operating temperature, with the choke fully returned. When the engine is hot give it a short burst at 2500 rev/min to clear the plugs. The engine should be run up to 2500 rev/min after every three minute period at idling to keep the plugs clear.

2 Check that the throttle cable operates smoothly and make sure that the choke 8 has $\frac{1}{16}$ inch (1.6 mm) of free movement when the control is fully returned. Make sure that the oil in the damper 1 is at the correct level of $\frac{1}{2}$ inch (13 mm) above the hollow piston rod. Make sure that the fast-idle screw on the interconnecting linkage is set so that it is clear of its stop and not affecting the slow-running speed.

3 With the engine running, check the slow-running speed. The idle speed should be 550 rev/min. If the slow-running speed is incorrect adjust it using the screw 5, clockwise to increase and anticlockwise to decrease. If a smooth idle cannot be obtained check the mixture strength.

4 Stop the engine and use the pin 5 (**FIG 2:6**) to raise the air valve piston, after having unscrewed the damper plunger. Release the pin and check that the air valve falls freely under its own weight and hits the bridge in the intake with a distinct clock. If the valve does not appear to fall freely, remove the air cleaner and raise the piston with a small tool through the air intake. Release the piston and check that it falls freely. If the piston does not fall freely there is an internal defect.

5 If the piston falls satisfactorily, refit the damper plunger (and air cleaner if it has been removed) and start the engine. Turn the jet adjusting nut 1 up or

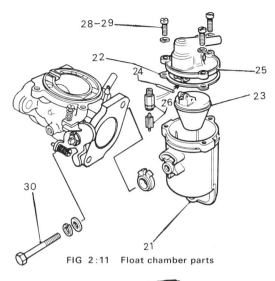

FIG 2:11 Float chamber parts

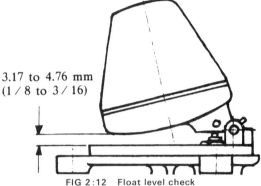

3.17 to 4.76 mm
(1 / 8 to 3 / 16)

FIG 2:12 Float level check

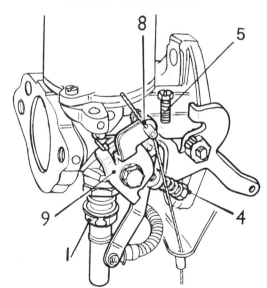

FIG 2:13 Adjustment points, single carburetter
Key to Fig 2:13   1 Adjusting nut   4 Fast idle screw
5 Throttle adjusting screw   8 Choke cable   9 Jet lever

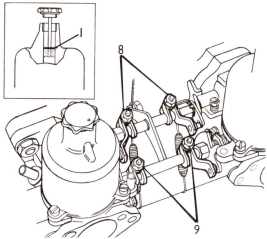

FIG 2:14 Interconnecting clamps twin carburetters

down, one flat at a time, until the fastest idling speed is obtained, consistent with smooth running. Screwing the nut up weakens the mixture and down enriches it. When the fastest idling speed has been obtained. making sure that the jet head is pressed firmly up against the adjusting nut, slowly turn the nut 1 upwards until the idling speed just begins to fall. Readjust the idling speed to the correct value.

6 When the mixture is correct, the exhaust beat should be regular and even. If the exhaust is irregular with a splashy type of misfire and colourless then the mixture is too weak. A rich mixture will cause a regular misfire with a blackish exhaust smoke. Check the adjustment by lifting the piston with the pin 5 by $\frac{1}{32}$ inch (.75 mm). If the engine speed increases and stays faster then the mixture is too rich. If the speed immediately decreases or the engine stops, the mixture is too weak. If the engine momentarily increases speed slightly then the mixture is correct.

7 Switch off the engine and operate the choke several times, making sure that the jet head returns fully against the adjusting nut every time. If the jet head sticks, the parts will have to be dismantled and cleaned.

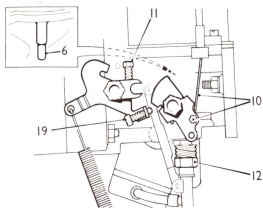

FIG 2:15 Adjusting points twin carburetters

Note that if the carburetter mixture adjustment has been completely lost a rough setting for starting the engine can still be made. Remove the air cleaner and use the adjusting nut 1 to set the jet so that its top end is flush with the bridge in the air intake—or as far as it will go. Turn the adjusting nut 1 down from this position by 12 flats (two complete turns) and this will give a mixture setting enabling the engine to be run.

The slow-running adjustment screw 5 can also be roughly set to give sufficient idling speed for the engine to run and warm up. Turn the screw in until it just contacts its stop, with the throttle valve fully closed, and then screw it in a further $1\frac{1}{2}$ turns to open the throttle valve.

When all adjustment and tuning have been completed, adjust the fast-idle screw on the interconnecting linkage until the engine is running at 1000 to 1100 rev/min when the choke is operated but without sufficient choke to move the jet head.

Twin carburetter tuning:

As the carburetter is of the same manufacture, many of the instructions for single carburetter installations are relevant (see previous Section). The engine, ignition system and manifolds must all be in good order otherwise the carburetters cannot be synchronized accurately. The rough starting settings for each of the twin carburetters are the same as for a single carburetter.

An electronic tachometer will be more accurate than the one fitted to the car, provided a special test one is used, and it will also be easier to see. Some form of balance meter will make the adjustments more accurate and easier to carry out, though it is not essential.

1 Remove the air cleaner so that the carburetter intakes are accessible. Take out the damper plungers, shown in FIG 2:14, and check that the air valve pistons fall freely and fully under their own weight after they have been lifted and released. Make sure that the oil level is approximately $\frac{1}{2}$ inch (13 mm) above the top of the hollow piston rod and refit the damper plungers. Check that the accelerator and choke linkages move freely, that there is $\frac{1}{16}$ inch of free movement when the choke control is fully returned and that both jet heads return fully against the adjusting nuts when the choke is released.

2 Start the engine and run it until it has reached its normal operating temperature. Run the engine up to 2500 rev/min to clear the plugs and after every three minutes at idling during the adjustments run it up to this speed again to keep the plugs clear. Slacken the clamp nuts 8 and 9, shown in FIG 2:14, to make the carburetters independent of each other.

3 Refer to FIG 2:15. Slacken the nut that secures the inner cable 10 of the choke control. Adjust the slow-running stop screws 11 on both carburetters until the correct idling speed of 550 rev/min is attained and the airflow is the same through both carburetters. A balance meter will make this task easier. If a meter is not available use a short piece of hose to listen to the 'hiss' at each intake and adjust the screws 11 until the hiss is the same in each carburetter intake.

4 Check the mixture strength at each carburetter and if necessary adjust it as described for single carburetters. Note that the references to the damper plunger and air

cleaner must be ignored and the adjusting nut given as 1 is the same as the adjusting nut 12 shown in **FIG 2:15**. If the original static setting of 12 flats down is used as a starting point, the two carburetters may well have a different number of flats alteration from this point after they have been adjusted and on worn carburetters there may be as much as two complete turns of the nut variation between the two. Once the mixture has been correctly set, readjust the idling speed using the two screws 11 and keeping the carburetter air flows in balance.

5 Set the throttle interconnecting clamping levers, (see items 8 in **FIG 2:14**), until the lever pins rest on the lower arm of the forks. Insert a .020 inch (.5 mm) feeler gauge 16 between the throttle shaft operating lever and the choke control interconnecting rod at A. Tighten the nuts and bolts 8, making sure that the interconnecting rod has an end float of approximately $\frac{1}{32}$ inch (.8 mm). Remove the feeler gauge. The clearance B should now be equal on both sides between each lever pin and the bottom of the fork on both carburetters, and the clearance should be .12 inch (.3 mm).

6 Position the choke control interconnecting rod so that it has an end float of approximately $\frac{1}{32}$ inch (.8 mm) and tighten the clamp nuts 9, after making sure that both jet heads are fully up against their adjusting nuts. Set the choke control cable 10 to a free movement of $\frac{1}{16}$ inch (1.6 mm) and make sure that the cable operates freely with the jets returning fully. Start the engine and pull out the choke control for approximately $\frac{1}{2}$ inch (13 mm) until the linkage is just about to move the jets. Adjust the fast-idle speed to 1000 to 1100 rev/min with the engine hot by turning both screw 19 on the carburetters.

7 Disconnect and remove the tachometer and refit the air cleaner assembly.

2:9 Removing and refitting carburetters

Single carburetters:

1 Disconnect battery earth lead.
2 Remove the air filter complete with intake pipe by removing the two 5/16 UNF nuts.
3 Release choke and accelerator cables.
4 Release petrol feed pipe and crankcase emission control pipe.
5 On automatic transmission models disconnect the throttle downshift cable.
6 Remove carburetter mounting nuts and washers. Lift away the carburetter.

Refitting is a reversal of removal procedure but the following points should be noted: Make sure all faces are clean. Renew the three gaskets (between carburetter and heat shield, heat shield and spacer, spacer and manifold). Check and adjust choke and accelerator cables and on automatic transmission models the throttle down-shift cable.

Twin carburetters:

1 Disconnect the battery earth lead.
2 Dismantle and remove the air filters (see **Section 2:11**).
3 Release the choke and accelerator cables and the three throttle return springs.

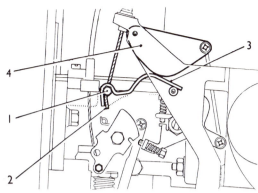

FIG 2:16 Adjusting throttle cable

Key to Fig 2:16 1 Cable fixing   2 Inner cable   3 Lever
4 Cam

4 Disconnect the petrol pipes at the carburetters.
5 Disconnect the crankcase emission control pipe.
6 On automatic transmission models release the throttle downshift cable.
7 Remove the nuts and washers holding each carburetter and remove both carburetters from the manifold studs complete with heat shields and carefully separate from the linkage.

Refitting is a reversal of the removal procedure. Ensure all contact faces are clean. Fit three new gaskets to each carburetter and connect the three throttle return springs. Check and adjust choke and accelerator cables and on automatic transmission models check throttle down-shift cable.

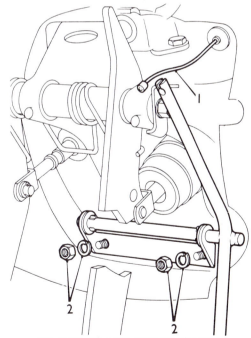

FIG 2:17 Throttle pedal attachments

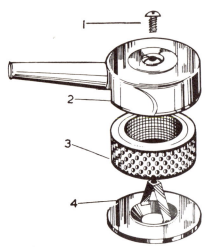

FIG 2:18 Single carburetter air filter

Key to Fig 2:18 1 Retaining screw 2 Cover 3 Element 4 Base

2:10 Throttle cable and pedal

To adjust the cable, refer to **FIG 2:16** and do the following:

1 Slacken the cable trunnion bolt 1. Pull down on inner cable 2 until all free play of the accelerator pedal is eliminated.

2 With the cable held taut, raise lever 3 until it just contacts cam 4. With the parts held in this position, slide the trunnion up the cable and tighten the bolt.

3 The final check is to press down on the accelerator pedal to see whether there is about $\frac{1}{16}$ inch of free movement in the cable before the cam operating lever starts to move.

The accelerator pedal and its attachments are shown in **FIG 2:17** which is self-explanatory.

2:11 Air filters

1500 and 1750 models:

FIG 2:18 shows the paper element type of air cleaner fitted to all single carburetter models. The element is of the throwaway type and should be renewed at intervals of 12,000 miles, or more frequently in very dusty conditions. Proceed as follows:

1 Remove the centre screw 1.

2 Withdraw the cover 2 and discard the element 3.

3 Thoroughly clean the container and install the new element.

4 Refit the cover and tighten centre screw. Do not disturb the element or cover at any other time.

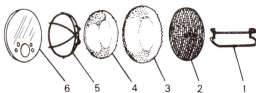

FIG 2:19 Lynx Ramflo air filter (twin carburetter models)

Key to Fig 2:19 1 Wire clip 2 Wire grille 3 Outer element 4 Inner element 5 Wire former 6 Back plate

TC model:

Twin carburetter models are fitted with two Lynx Ramflo air cleaners of the type shown in **FIG 2:19**. Each filter contains two elements. These are of different porosity, the outer element 3 being coarse and the inner one 4 fine. The two combined are capable of preventing the entry of dust particles as small as 1 to 5 microns.

Every 3000 miles, or more frequently in very dusty conditions, the cleaners should be serviced as follows:

1 Remove the wire clip 1.

2 Remove the wire grille 2 complete with filter elements 3 and 4.

3 Remove the inner wire former 5.

4 Separate the two filter elements and wash them in warm soapy water or a suitable solvent and allow them to dry.

5 Reassembly is a reversal of the dismantling procedure, but when refitting the grille to the backplate ensure that the edges of the grille are inside the upturned edges of the backplate. When refitting the wire clip attach one end first and then stretch lengthwise and snap into position.

2:12 Fault diagnosis

(a) Leakage or insufficient fuel delivered

1 Fuel tank vent restricted
2 Fuel pipes obstructed
3 Air leaks at pipe connections
4 Filters obstructed
5 Pump gaskets faulty
6 Pump diaphragm defective
7 Pump valves sticking or damaged
8 Fuel vaporizing in lines due to heat

(b) Excessive fuel consumption

1 Carburetter(s) require adjusting
2 Fuel leakage
3 Sticking controls or choke linkage
4 Dirty air cleaner
5 Excessive engine temperature
6 Brakes binding
7 Tyres under-inflated
8 Car overloaded

(c) Idling speed too high

1 Rich fuel mixture
2 Carburetter controls sticking
3 Slow-running incorrectly adjusted
4 Worn carburetter butterfly valve

(d) Noisy fuel pump

1 Loose mountings
2 Air leaks on suction side and at diaphragm
3 Clogged pump filter

(e) No fuel delivery

1 Float needle stuck
2 Fuel tank vent blocked
3 Pipe line blocked
4 Fuel pump defective
5 Bad air leak on suction side of pump
6 Fuel tank empty

CHAPTER 3

THE IGNITION SYSTEM

3:1 Distributor. Automatic timing controls

The distributor is of Lucas make, type 29.D4. It incorporates two automatic timing controls, the first being a centrifugal mechanism and the second a vacuum unit. These can be seen in **FIG 3:1**.

In the centrifugal device, weights fly outwards against the tension of small springs as engine speed rises. This movement advances the contact breaker cams relative to the distributor driving shaft, so that the points open earlier to give advanced ignition timing.

The vacuum unit is connected to the carburetter by a small-bore pipe. Depression in the carburetter intake system operates the vacuum unit, the suction varying according to engine load. At small throttle openings, with no load on the engine, there is a high degree of vacuum which causes the unit to advance the ignition timing. Large throttle openings with low speeds and a heavily-loaded engine—conditions which are met when hill-climbing, result in a much-reduced degree of vacuum. The unit will then retard the ignition.

Note that the distributor shaft is driven in an anticlockwise direction.

3:2 Distributor maintenance

The following operations should be carried out every 6,000 miles:

Distributor lubrication:

1 Refer to **FIG 3:2** which shows the lubrication points. Free the two side clips and remove the cap.
  Use an oilcan filled with 20W engine oil. Remove the rotor arm 20 in **FIG 3:1**.
2 Apply a thin smear of grease to the cam 13 in **FIG 3:2**.
3 Apply one drop of oil to the contact breaker pivot 14.
4 Apply two or three drops of oil into the recess marked 16. **Do not remove the central screw.** There is clearance provided for oil to pass.
  When lubricating, make quite sure that no oil reaches the contact breaker points. Wipe off all surplus oil and grease.

Distributor checking:

With the cap removed, turn the rotor arm in the direction of the arrow and then release it. It should return freely to its original position.

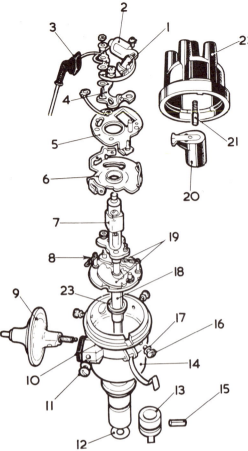

FIG 3:1 Lucas 29 D4 Distributor. Exploded view

Key to Fig 3:1 1 Movable contact 2 Condenser 3 Low tension lead 4 Fixed contact 5 Moving contact breaker plate 6 Contact breaker base plate 7 Cam 8 Automatic advance springs 9 Vacuum unit 10 Sealing grommet 11 Vacuum unit securing screw 12 Thrust washer 13 Driving dog 14 Body 15 Parallel pin 16 Base plate mounting screw 17 Spring washer 18 Shaft and action plate 19 Weight 20 Rotor arm 21 Brush and spring 22 Cap 23 Distance spacer

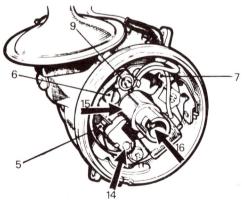

FIG 3:2 Contact breaker and lubrication points

The contact breaker plate 5 in **FIG 3:1** should be free to move. Push on the plate at the point indicated by the upper arrow.

Adjusting and cleaning the contact breaker:

To adjust the contact points refer to **FIG 3:2** and do the following:

1 Turn the crankshaft until the points 5 are fully open. This can be done by removing the sparking plugs, engaging top gear and moving the car gently in the required direction.

2 Check the gap between the points with feeler gauges. It should be .014 to .016 inch. If adjustment is necessary, slacken screw 6 and insert a screwdriver in the notches indicated at 7. Turning the screwdriver clockwise will decrease the gap and turning it anticlockwise will increase it. Retighten the securing screw when satisfied.

To clean the contact breaker points unscrew nut 9. Lift off the washers, insulator and terminals. The spring and moving contact can then be lifted off. Remove screw 6 to release the fixed contact. The contact points should be a clean matt grey. It is normal, after much service, for one of them to have a central pip and the other a small depression. Using a fine carborundum stone or emery cloth, dress the points to remove any pip or rim. The points must finish up quite flat, so that when they are installed they meet squarely. It is not necessary to remove all the depression just mentioned, only the pip. Clean off all emery dust and refit the points, taking care to fit the insulator, the terminals and the washers in the correct order when reassembling the fixed end of the spring (see **FIG 3:1**). Adjust the contact gap when the assembly is complete.

The rotor arm:

Slight erosion of the outer edge of the brass plate is normal and is not detrimental to performance. When refitting the arm, ensure that it is clean and free from oil and that the key correctly engages the slot in the shaft.

The distributor cap:

Clean the cap inside and out and look for signs of 'tracking' round the brass segments. This shows as a black line on the inner surface of the cap and is evidence of arcing. The only cure is to fit a new cap. Slight signs of erosion of the segments is not harmful.

Check the carbon brush 21 in the central boss inside the cap (see **FIG 3:1**). It must be free to move when pressed in, and should spring out when released.

3:3 Testing ignition system

If the ignition system is suspected as the cause of engine failure, the first step is to test the spark in the following way:

1 Remove the centre lead from the distributor cap. It is a simple push fit. Switch on the ignition and turn the engine by means of the starter. At the same time get an assistant to hold the detached cable **by the insulation** with the metal end about $\frac{3}{16}$ inch away from a good earth such as the cylinder block. As the engine rotates there should be regular sparking across the gap.

2 If there is no spark, remove distributor cap. Examine the plug leads 2 in **FIG 3:3** and renew them if the insulation is cracked or perished. Make sure the conductor makes good contact at the ends. The carbon brush 4 is housed in the central moulding inside the cap. It should protrude, and when pressed in, should spring out again quite freely. The end will be polished where it contacts the rotor arm (see 20 in **FIG 3:1**). The rotor arm should have a bright spot where the brush has been rubbing. If all is well, test the rotor arm by substitution to ensure that it is not at fault.

3 If none of these tests and possible rectification leads to successful sparking, carry out more intensive testing with a voltmeter as follows:

Testing the low-tension circuit in the event of ignition failure:

1 Remove the distributor cap and rotor arm. Locate the LT terminal on the coil. There will be a white cable with a black tracer in it attached to the terminal. Do not disturb the wiring but connect a 0-20-volt moving coil meter between the terminal and a good earth.

2 Look at the contact breaker points 5 in **FIG 3:3** and if they are closed, separate them with a piece of clean card.

3 Switch on the ignition and watch the voltmeter. It should read 12-volts. If there is no reading with the contacts separated, transfer the voltmeter lead from the LT terminal to the other terminal on the coil which has a white lead attached to it. If there is now a reading, disconnect the white/black cable from the coil terminal and reconnect the voltmeter to the disconnected terminal. No reading will indicate a faulty coil. A reading of battery voltage indicates faulty contact breaker insulation or a faulty capacitor (condenser). Check the capacitor by substitution. The correct capacity is .18 to .24 mF.

4 If the voltmeter reads 12-volts with the contact points separated, remove the card. The reading should drop to zero as the points meet. If it does, the LT ignition circuit is in order. If there is still no spark it will probably be due to a break in the secondary winding of the coil. The easiest way to check this is to substitute the suspected coil with one of known performance. If the battery voltage reading persists with the points in contact, or the reading does not drop right back to zero, transfer the voltmeter lead to the LT terminal on the distributor.

5 If the reading now drops back to zero then the cable between the coil and the distributor is at fault. If the reading is still at battery voltage it means that the contact points are not making electrical contact. If a low reading on the voltmeter persists it indicates a high resistance across the points. Clean or renew the contact points.

Testing the high-tension circuit:

Having tested the low-tension circuit as just described, and having rectified any faults, proceed to recheck for sparking as outlined at the beginning of this Section.

3:4 Servicing the distributor
Removal:

The attachments of the distributor are shown in **FIG 3:1** and the ignition timing marks in **FIG 3:4**.

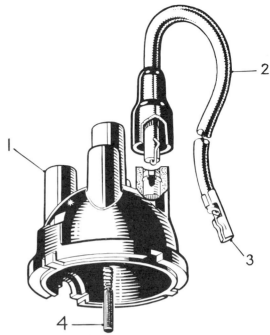

FIG 3:3 Distributor cap

Key to Fig 3:3   1 Cap   2 Sparking plug lead (HT)
3 Plug connector   4 Carbon brush and spring

Disconnect the battery. Remove the distributor cap 22 and turn the engine until the timing marks align and the brass end of the rotor arm 20 is pointing towards the position of the electrode in the cap connected to the sparking plug of No. 1 (front cylinder).

Provided that the bolt and nut that secure the clamp to the base of the distributor are not slackened or the clamp rotated about the distributor, the distributor can be removed and refitted without losing the ignition timing. Before removing the distributor, make aligning marks across the clamp and crankcase and refit the distributor so that these marks again align accurately. If there is any doubt, correctly set the ignition timing as described in the next section.

Disconnect the LT lead 3 from the distributor. Disconnect the vacuum pipe to the vacuum unit 9.

Remove the two bolts that secure the clamp and withdraw the distributor from the engine.

Refit the distributor in the reverse order of removal, turning the shaft until the rotor arm is approximately in the right position and then making slight adjustments to its position so that the offset on the driving dog slips into the slot in the drive shaft. Align the marks and tighten the bolts to a torque of 8 to 10 lb ft (1.1 to 1.4 kg m).

Dismantling (see FIG 3:1):

1 Remove the rotor arm 20. To ensure correct reassembly, check the relationship between the rotor slot and the offset driving dog 13.

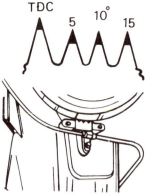

FIG 3:4 Ignition timing marks

2 Check distributor shaft end float with a feeler gauge inserted between the driving dog and thrust washer 12 End float should be .004 to .008.

3 Remove screw 11, disconnect the vacuum actuating link and withdraw the vacuum unit 9.

4 Remove the three screws 16 with spring washers 17 securing the baseplate 6. Push the LT lead grommet into the distributor body and withdraw baseplate assembly with lead. Remove the nut retaining the lead. Remove the flat washer, leads and insulator.

5 Remove the screw flat washer and spring washer and lift off the movable contact from the baseplate. Release the advance springs 8 and remove cam spindle securing screw. Mark the cam base to ensure it is returned to the same driving post.

6 To remove the driving dog 13, mark the dog and shaft to ensure correct reassembly and drive out the parallel pin 15.

Examine all parts for wear and renew as necessary. Reassembly is a reversal of the dismantling process. Lubricate the distributor shaft with engine oil and put a spot of oil on each of the weight pivot pins. Check that the rotor slot/driving dog relationship has not been altered or the timing will be 180 deg. out.

3:5 Setting the ignition timing

1 Remove the sparking plugs and turn the engine over by hand until No. 1 (front) piston is at the timing point on the compression stroke. The timing marks are shown in **FIG 3:4**. The correct timing is 10 deg. BTDC.

As the engine is being turned over, place a thumb over the hole for No. 1 sparking plug and the pressure inside the cylinder will be felt to rise as the piston comes up on the compression stroke. Turn the engine until the correct timing point is reached. If the mark is overshot, turn the engine well back and then turn it forwards to the point, otherwise the backlash in the system will not be taken up. The position can also be found if the rocker cover is off, as the valves on No. 4 (rear) cylinder will be at the point of balance when the No. 1 piston is near the correct point.

2 Remove the distributor cap and disconnect the low-tension lead from the terminal on the distributor. Reconnect the lead with a low-wattage test lamp fitted in series and switch on the ignition.

3 Slacken the pinch bolt that secures the clamp to the distributor body. Press the rotor arm lightly in a clockwise direction to take up any backlash and turn the distributor body slightly either side of its position until the point is found where the light has just gone out, indicating that the points have just opened. Tighten the pinch bolt on the clamp.

4 Rotate the engine in a forward direction for two full turns. Towards the end of the second revolution slow down the rate of turning and stop immediately after the test lamp goes out. If the timing is correct the timing marks will again be in exact alignment.

5 Remove the test lamp, after switching off the ignition, and correctly reconnect the distributor lead. Refit the distributor cap and sparking plugs. Reconnect the HT leads. If the leads were not marked on removal, No. 1 lead is connected to the electrode in the cap opposite to the rotor arm and the remainder of the leads are connected anticlockwise around the cap in the firing order (1-3-4-2).

Stroboscopic timing:

This method may be used as an accurate setting and checking, but the static setting must be made with reasonable accuracy to allow the engine to run safely. Connect the light as instructed by the makers of the instrument. **Take great care to keep tools, hands or clothes out of the moving fan belt and cooling fan.** The range of advance is given in Technical Data. Disconnect the vacuum advance pipe and adjust the idling speed to 500 rev/min.

3:6 Sparking plugs and leads

The correct sparking plugs are Champion, type N9Y. It is good practice to renew the complete set every 12,000 miles or every 12 months depending on the condition of the engine. Faulty carburation or excessive oil consumption may cause sparking plug troubles due to overheating or fouling, so that more frequent renewal may be necessary until the troubles are cured.

The sparking plugs should be cleaned and adjusted every 6,000 miles. Remove them with a box spanner, taking great care to keep the spanner square. If it is allowed to tilt it may contact the plug insulator and crack it. Examine the deposits round the electrodes for the evidence which gives a clue to firing conditions.

A normal deposit should be brown to greyish tan in colour, this being the result of correct carburation and a mixture of high-speed and low-speed driving. If the deposits are white or yellowish they indicate greater heat due to long periods of constant-speed driving, probably rather fast. Black, wet deposits are caused by oil entering the combustion chamber past worn pistons and bores or down valve stems. If the black deposits are dry and fluffy they usually indicate running with a rich mixture, but they may also be due to incomplete combustion through defective ignition or excessive idling.

Overheated sparking plugs have a white, blistered look about the centre electrode and the side electrode may be badly eroded. The cause may be poor cooling, wrong ignition timing or sustained high speeds with heavy loads.

Although some cleaning can be done by hand it is difficult to reach the inner surfaces and the best plan is to have the plugs cleaned on a shot-blasting machine. They can be tested under pressure at the same time. A sparking plug which shows a good spark in the open air may not spark at all under pressure. The garage will also set the gaps correctly. If the owner does this setting himself, it is most important to make sure the electrodes are bright and clean and the gap adjusted by bending the side electrode. **Never try to bend the central electrode.** The correct gap is .024 to .026 inch.

The plugs should screw in easily by hand. Any difficulty will be due to deposits on the threads. Clean those on the plugs with a wire brush. The holes in the head can be cleaned out with a tap or by using an old plug with crossed saw cuts down the threads. Always fit new gaskets and do not overtighten. The correct torque wrench figure is 30 lb ft. Wipe over the insulators after fitting to remove any smears from oily fingers. Oil on the insulators makes dirt adhere more readily.

Sparking plug leads and cap:

Renew the plug leads if there is any suspicion that they have deteriorated in any way. Make sure the end connections make good metallic contact with the core of the cable.

3:7 Fault diagnosis

(a) Engine will not fire

1 Battery discharged or terminals dirty
2 Distributor points dirty or incorrectly adjusted
3 Distributor cap dirty, cracked or tracking
4 Carbon brush inside distributor cap defective
5 Faulty or loose connections in low-tension circuit
6 Distributor rotor arm cracked, or omitted on reassembly
7 Faulty coil
8 HT coil lead defective
9 Broken contact spring
10 Contacts stuck open
11 Internal shortcircuit in distributor
12 Damp or dirt on HT leads, distributor cap and ignition coil

(b) Engine misfires

1 Check 2, 3, 5 and 7 in (a)
2 Weak contact breaker spring
3 Defective HT lead
4 Sparking plug(s) loose
5 Sparking plug insulation cracked
6 Sparking plug gap incorrectly set
7 Ignition timing too far advanced

NOTES

CHAPTER 4

THE COOLING SYSTEM

4:1 Description

Coolant passes through the internal passages in the crankcase and cylinder head, collecting excess heat from the engine. The coolant then passes through the radiator where it is cooled by the passage of air over the fins before returning to the engine. A natural thermo-syphon action is set up and the coolant would circulate unassisted. To ensure that there is a positive flow at all times and that the coolant circulates rapidly a centrifugal pump is fitted into the system. The pump is driven by a belt from the crankshaft pulley. To assist the airflow through the radiator, particularly when the car is stationary or travelling slowly, a cooling fan is fitted to the water pump.

A thermostat valve is fitted into the outlet from the cylinder head to ensure that the engine temperature stays reasonably constant and to give a shorter warming-up period from cold. When the coolant is cold the valve stays closed, preventing the coolant from passing through into the radiator. The coolant recirculates directly back to the engine through a bypass hose and the warming-up period is considerably reduced because the amount of coolant to be heated is reduced and there are no heat losses through the radiator. When the coolant reaches its normal temperature, the valve opens and allows the coolant to pass through the radiator.

The radiator is fitted with a plug that can be removed for filling the system and it is connected by a hose to an expansion tank. The expansion tank is fitted with a pressure cap which allows the pressure in the cooling system to rise to 13 lb/sq inch (.91 kg/sq cm) before it opens and allows surplus air to escape. The cap is also fitted with a vacuum relief valve to ensure that air can return into the expansion tank when the system cools. **Never remove the radiator filler cap when the system is hot.** If the system is overheated or boiling, allow it to cool before taking off the filler cap on the expansion chamber. If the cap is removed the sudden reduction in pressure will cause the coolant to boil and force out scalding water over the operator's hand, while air in the expansion tank will force out coolant if the radiator filler cap is removed. The system is pressurized as this raises the boiling point of the coolant and allows the engine to be run hotter without danger of boiling at localized hot spots.

4:2 Routine maintenance

There are no lubrication points in the system. Periodically check the level of the coolant in the expansion tank. The correct level is marked on the outside of the tank and it should be topped up to this mark. If water only is used for topping up, have the specific gravity of the coolant

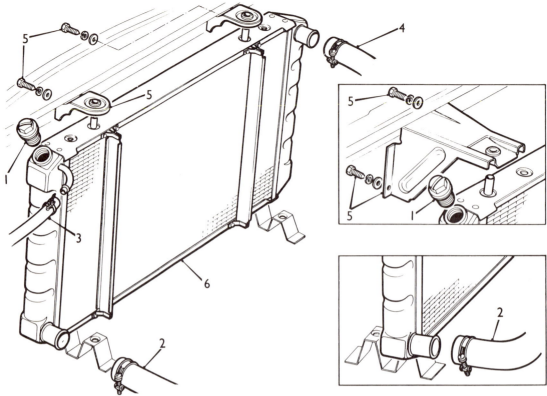

FIG 4:1 The radiator and its attachments

checked before winter to ensure that it still contains sufficient antifreeze to protect the system down to the lowest temperatures expected.

Regularly check the fan belt tension and adjust if it is slack (see **Section 4:4**).

Antifreeze has a life of approximately two years, after which the corrosion inhibitors lose their effect, so the system should be drained, flushed and refilled with fresh coolant every two years.

4:3 The radiator and expansion tank

Draining:

The radiator and its attachments are shown in **FIG 4:1**. If the system is being drained for any reason other than renewing the coolant, the coolant in the system should be drained into clean containers so that it can be used again.

If the system is hot, the filler cap on the expansion tank should be carefully undone to its first unlock position so that the pressure in the system can escape. Do not attempt that if the engine is very hot, but allow it to cool and as a safety precaution swathe the hand in rags.

Remove the radiator filler cap 1 and the filler cap from the expansion tank. Remove the cylinder block drain plug and then disconnect the bottom radiator hose 2 from the radiator 6. To drain the coolant from the expansion tank, disconnect the hose 3 from the radiator and allow the coolant to run out.

Flushing:

Proprietary compounds may be used, in which case the instructions on the tin should be followed accurately.

Water alone can be used for flushing. Reconnect the bottom hose 2 to the radiator. Remove the thermostat valve and refit the water outlet to the cylinder head, after disconnecting the top radiator hose 4 from it. Refit the radiator filler plug 1. Insert a hosepipe into the water outlet on the cylinder head and use rags to make the joint reasonably tight. Turn on the hose and let water run through until it comes out clean through the radiator top hose 4 and engine drain hole. In extreme cases it may be necessary to remove the radiator, invert it and flush through so that the water carries out any scale or dirt from the water passages. Refit the thermostat valve and water outlet to the cylinder head and reconnect the top hose.

Filling:

Make sure that all the hoses are correctly connected and that the cylinder block drain plug is fitted. Fill the system through the filler 1 on the radiator and top up the expansion tank to the level marked on its side. Refit the radiator filler cap and the expansion tank cap. Start the engine and run it at a fast-idle for 30 seconds. Stop the engine and remove the radiator filler cap 1 again. Fill the radiator right up and refit the filler plug. Start the engine and run it until it has reached its normal operating

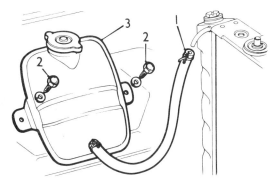

FIG 4:2 The expansion tank

temperature. Stop the engine and allow it to cool before finally topping up the expansion tank to the correct level.

Clean soft water should be used in the system as this helps to prevent corrosion and the formation of scale. It is advisable to use a mixture of antifreeze and water as the antifreeze contains corrosion inhibitors and will raise the boiling point as well as lowering the freezing point.

Radiator removal:

The attachments of the radiator are shown in **FIG 4:1**. Drain the cooling system by removing the filler 1, and disconnecting the bottom radiator hose 2. Full draining will not be required and the cylinder block drain plug can be left in place. Disconnect the hose 3 to the expansion tank and the top radiator hose 4. Remove the screws 5 that secure the brackets to the body and lift out the radiator 6.

Refit the radiator in the reverse order of removal and fill the cooling system.

It should be noted that dust and insects will gradually block the air passages through the radiator. Occasionally blow through the radiator fins from the rear, using an airline or hosepipe to remove the accumulation. In extreme cases remove the radiator so that it can be soaked and scrubbed in a hot weak detergent solution.

The expansion tank:

The attachments of the tank are shown in **FIG 4:2** and the figure is self-explanatory.

4:4 The fan belt

Every 6,000 miles, check the fan belt and its adjustment. If there are cracks or frayed edges, renew the belt by slackening off the tension. Lift the belt off the pulleys and manoeuvre it over the fan blades.

To adjust the tension of the belt, refer to **FIG 4:3**. First check the tension by applying moderate finger pressure to the longest run of the belt. The amount of deflection should not exceed $\frac{1}{2}$ inch. Do not run the engine with a tight belt as it causes rapid belt deterioration and possible damage to alternator and pump bearings. A slack belt might result in overheating and lack of charging current from the alternator.

The correct tension can be obtained by slackening the two alternator fixing bolts 1 in the illustration. Also slacken

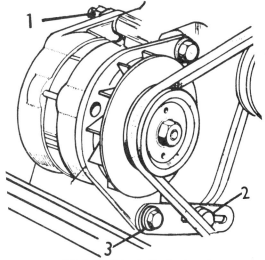

FIG 4:3 Drive belt adjustment

Key to Fig 4:3 1 Alternator top mounting bolt 2 Adjusting link bolt 3 Adjusting link anchor bolt

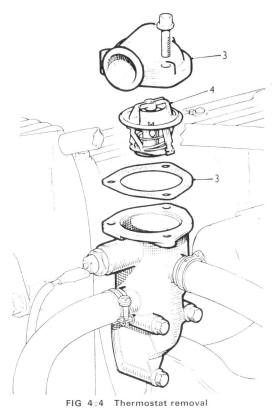

FIG 4:4 Thermostat removal

Key to Fig 4:4 3 Cover and gasket 4 Thermostat

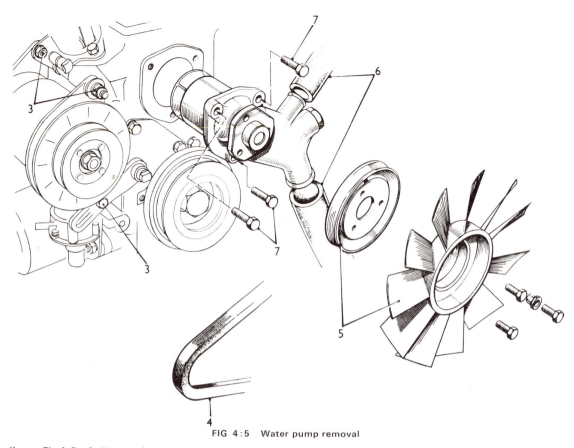

FIG 4:5   Water pump removal

Key to Fig 4:5   3 Alternator fixings   4 Drive belt   5 Fan and pulley   6 Hoses   7 Pump fixing bolts

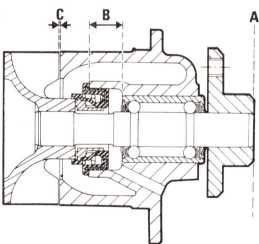

FIG 4:6   Sectioned view of water pump

Key to Fig 4:6   **A** Hub flush with spindle   **B** Edge of bearing to face of seal   **C** Clearance between impeller and housing

the adjusting link bolt 2. Lift the alternator by hand pressure, tighten the bolts and check the tension. **If it is necessary to lift the alternator with a lever, apply it at the driven end bracket only.** Tighten the bolts to a torque of 18 to 20 lb ft.

4:5 The thermostat and housing

Removing thermostat:

Refer to **FIG 4:4**. Drain the cooling system and disconnect the top hose from the thermostat cover 3. Remove the three bolts and lift off the cover and gasket. Lift out the thermostat 4.

Checking thermostat:

There are two possible causes of trouble with a thermostat. If it sticks open it leads to overcooling and a slow warming-up period. If it remains persistently closed it will cause overheating. In case of overheating it is possible to run without the thermostat until it can be renewed.

To check the action of thermostat, suspend it in a container of water so that it is fully immersed but not touching the bottom or sides. Using a thermometer, heat the water and watch the valve. It should start to open at the temperature stamped on the base. The correct thermostat settings are:

Standard	82°C or 180°F
Hot countries	74°C or 165°F
Cold countries	88°C or 190°F

If the thermostat is found to be faulty do not try to repair it or to modify its performance.

Refitting:

This is a reversal of the removal sequence.

Removing thermostat housing:

Disconnect the cable from the thermal transmitter, and all three hoses, after draining the cooling system. Remove the three long bolts securing the housing to the cylinder block and lift it away. Take care of the gasket.

Refitting:

Reverse the dismantling sequence, but use a new gasket between the housing and the block. Refill the cooling system as described in **Section 4:3**.

4:6 Servicing the water pump

Removal:

Refer to **FIG 4:5** and follow these instructions:
1 Drain the cooling system. Remove the radiator as in **Section 4:3**.
2 Slacken the three generator fixings 3 and remove the fan belt 4.
3 Remove three bolts to detach the fan pulley 5. Disconnect the hoses 6 from the pump.
4 Remove bolts 7 and withdraw the pump from the block. Note that there is a gasket under the mounting flange, which is not shown.

Dismantling:

The pulley hub and impeller are press fits on the shaft. Be prepared to renew the parts if this fit is impaired during dismantling.
1 Remove the pulley hub from the shaft.
2 Press the spindle and bearing assembly rearwards from the body.
3 Withdraw the impeller from the shaft.
4 Remove the seal assembly.

Reassembling:

1 Referring to **FIG 4:6,** press the pulley hub on to the spindle checking that the face of the hub is flush with the end of the spindle as at A.
2 Press the spindle and bearing assembly into the housing until the distance B between the edge of the bearing and the face of the seal seating is 0.596 to 0.606.
3 Fit the seal to the pump body, checking that the seal is seated correctly.

4 Press the impeller on to the spindle until the clearance C between the impeller and housing is between 0.020 and 0.030. Ensure that the impeller is pressed on squarely as cracking can easily occur.

Refitting:

Refitting is a reversal of the removal procedure. Use a new gasket between the pump and the cylinder block and tighten the securing bolts to a torque of 18 to 20 lb ft.

4:7 Frost precautions

When a vehicle is operating in conditions where the temperature is likely to drop below freezing, an antifreeze solution should be added to the coolant. Ethylene glycol antifreeze to Specification BS 3151 or BS 3152 is recommended. Except for severe climates a 25 per cent solution is used. After draining and flushing the radiator (see **Section 4:3**) two pints (Imp) of antifreeze should be added to the radiator and topped up with water. An additional $\frac{1}{2}$ pint of antifreeze should be added to the pint of water in the expansion tank.

For severe winter conditions a larger proportion of antifreeze is used. In these circumstances follow the directions given by the manufacturers of the antifreeze.

4:8 Fault diagnosis

(a) Internal water leakage

1 Cracked cylinder wall
2 Cracked cylinder head
3 Loose cylinder head nuts
4 Defective cylinder head gasket

(b) Poor circulation

1 Radiator core blocked
2 Engine water passages restricted
3 Low coolant level
4 Loose fan belt
5 Defective thermostat
6 Perished or collapsed hoses

(c) Corrosion

1 Impurities in the water
2 Neglected draining and flushing

(d) Overheating

1 Check (b)
2 Sludge in crankcase
3 Incorrect ignition timing
4 Low oil level in sump
5 Tight engine
6 Choked exhaust
7 Binding brakes
8 Slipping clutch
9 Incorrect valve timing
10 Mixture too weak

NOTES

CHAPTER 5

THE CLUTCH

5:1 Description

A Repco diaphragm spring clutch of $7\frac{1}{2}$ inch diameter is fitted. Driven plate linings on 1500 and 1750 single carburetter models are AMCO 3271. The TC model has MINTEX BM-79 linings.

Two types of driven plate are used depending on the model of gearbox fitted. The 12V gearbox has a clutch driven plate with 23 splines, while the 18V gearbox has a clutch driven plate with 20 splines.

The clutch hub incorporates four coil springs to act as a shock absorber. The clutch release bearing is a radial ballbearing prepacked with lubricant during manufacture.

5:2 Maintenance

At regular intervals check the fluid level in the master cylinder reservoir. The brake and clutch master cylinders are shown in **FIG 5:1**. **Wipe the top and filler cap clean before removing the cap,** to prevent dirt from falling into the reservoir. If the fluid is low, top up to the correct level shown on the side of the reservoir. **Use only approved fluids as the incorrect type can be dangerous.**

5:3 The clutch master cylinder
Removal:

From inside the car, extract the splitpin and remove the clevis pin (item 11 in **FIG 5:2**) to free the master cylinder pushrod from the pedal.

Syphon out or drain the fluid from the reservoir and disconnect the pipe 18, **using rags to catch any spillage as hydraulic fluid quickly removes paint.** Remove screw 16 and nut 17 and withdraw master cylinder.

Refit the master cylinder in the reverse order of removal Fill and bleed the hydraulic system as described in **Section 5:5**.

Dismantling:

The components of the master cylinder are shown in **FIG 5:2**.
1 Detach the dust cover 13. Depress the piston to take the load off the circlip 10 and remove the circlip and pushrod assembly 9. Withdraw the piston assembly.
2 Referring to **FIG 5:3**, bend the thimble leaf 2 outwards just enough to free the plunger 4 and separate it from the thimble 3 (item 6 in **FIG 5:2**).

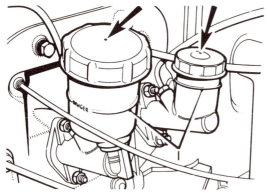

FIG 5:1 Checking fluid level in master cylinder reservoirs. The master cylinder with the smaller reservoir is for the clutch

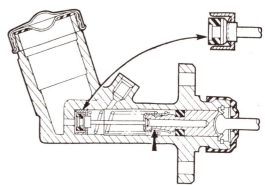

FIG 5:4 Clutch master cylinder sectional view. Heavy arrow indicates thimble leaf. Detail shows correct assembly of centre valve

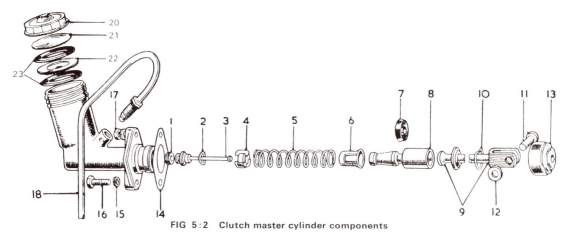

FIG 5:2 Clutch master cylinder components

Key to Fig 5:2   1 Valve seal   2 Curved washer—valve stem   3 Valve stem   4 Valve spacer   5 Spring   6 Spring retainer (thimble)   7 Plunger seal   8 Plunger   9 Push-rod   10 Circlip—push-rod   11 Clevis pin—pedal to master cylinder   12 Plain washer   13 Dust cover   14 Packing   15 Spring washer   16 Screw   17 Nut—stud   18 Master to slave cylinder pipe   20 Filler cap   21 Flat plate   22 Baffle plate   23 Rubber seals

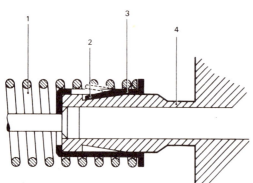

FIG 5:3 Clutch master cylinder thimble and plunger assembly

Key to Fig 5:3   1 Spring   2 Thimble leaf   3 Thimble   4 Plunger

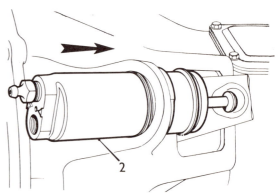

FIG 5:5 Clutch slave cylinder removal

3 Remove the plunger seal 7. Compress the spring 5 and allow the valve stem 3 to pass through the keyhole in the thimble. Separate the thimble, spring, valve stem, valve spacer 4 and curved washer 2. Remove the seal 1 from the valve stem.

Examination:

Wash all the parts in methylated spirits or hydraulic fluid. **No other solvent may be allowed to come into contact with the seals otherwise they will swell and perish.**

It is most advisable to renew the seals, available in service kits, and only if the old seals are in perfect condition should they be used again. Do not turn the seals inside out as this will damage them.

Examine the bore of the cylinder and renew the complete unit if the bore is at all pitted, scored or worn.

Check that all the ports are clear.

Reassembly (FIG 5:2):

1 Dip all parts in brake fluid and assemble while wet.
2 Replace the valve seal 1 so that the flat side is correctly seated on the valve head.
3 Fit the curved washer 2 with the domed side against the underside of the valve head and hold it in position with the valve spacer 4 the legs of which should face the valve stem.
4 Refit the spacer to the return spring 5 and insert the thimble 6 into the opposite end. Compress the spring until the valve stem engages in the keyhole in the thimble.
5 Fit a new plunger seal 7 with the flat of the seal against the plunger. Insert the small end of the plunger into the thimble as far as it will go and lock the plunger in the thimble by depressing the leaf (2 in **FIG 5:3**) so that it engages in the thimble shoulder, then centralise the spring on its seating.
6 Insert the plunger assembly into the cylinder bore, easing the lip of the plunger in carefully. On no account must the lip be bent back in this process. Position with the pushrod 9 and retaining washer and secure with the circlip 10.
7 Smear the sealing areas of the dust cover 13 with rubber grease and fit the pushrod. Pack the dust cover with rubber grease and fit to the cylinder body.

When refitting the master cylinder ensure that the pushrod is in line with the clutch pedal. Fit the clevis pin and washer and secure with a new splitpin. Refill the reservoir and bleed the system as described in **Section 5:5.**

5:4 The slave cylinder

To remove the slave cylinder, remove the retaining circlip shown in **FIG 5:5**. Remove the screw securing the flexible pipe to the bulkhead and withdraw the cylinder with the flexible pipe attached. Unscrew the pipe from the slave cylinder and secure the end at a point higher than the master cylinder to avoid loss of fluid.

When refitting the slave cylinder, make sure that the bleed screw is uppermost. Reconnect the hydraulic pipe then fill and bleed the hydraulic system as instructed in **Section 5:5**.

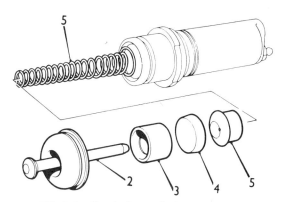

FIG 5:6 Clutch slave cylinder components

The components of the slave cylinder are shown in **FIG 5:6**. To dismantle the unit, pull back the dust cover and remove the pushrod 2. The internal parts (piston 3, seal 4 and cup filler 5) can be removed by tapping the open end of the cylinder onto the palm of the hand or by gently blowing down the inlet port.

Wash the parts in methylated spirits and renew the cup seal 4. Renew the complete unit if the bore of the cylinder is scored, worn or damaged.

Wet the internal parts with hydraulic fluid before refitting them. Fit the spring 5 with its larger diameter end leading, followed by the cup seal spreader 5. Carefully insert the seal 4, lips leading, taking great care not to damage or bend back the lips. Slide in the piston, flat face leading. Smear both ends of the pushrod 2 with Girling rubber grease and refit it, holding it in place with the dust cover.

5:5 Bleeding the hydraulic system

The method is shown in **FIG 5:7**. Bleeding is only required when air has entered the system after dismantling and reassembly or by allowing the fluid level in the reservoir to fall so low that air is drawn into the master cylinder.

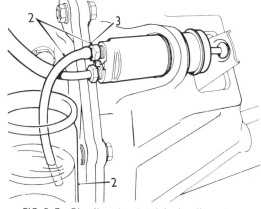

FIG 5:7 Bleeding the clutch hydraulic system

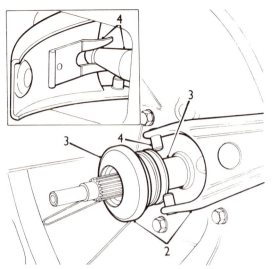

FIG 5:8 Clutch release bearing and lever

5:7 Servicing the clutch

The removal of the clutch from the flywheel, after the gearbox has been removed, is dealt with in **Chapter 1, Section 1:10,** and the instructions for refitting it are also given in this section.

If either the cover assembly or the driven plate is defective, the parts cannot be repaired and new items must be fitted in their place.

Cover assembly:

The unit must not be washed in any solvent, as this will remove the lubricant from the pivot points in the cover. Loose dust and dirt should be removed using an airline, or tyre pump, and brush. If there is oil on the pressure plate face or cover, wipe it off with a cloth moistened in fuel or suitable solvent that will evaporate completely.

Check the pressure plate face for burn or score marks as well as hairline cracks. Check the cover for cracks or distortion, paying particular attention to the areas around the attachment holes and any rivets.

Driven plate:

The driven plate must be renewed if the linings are worn down nearly to the rivet heads, the linings are contaminated with oil or grease or the assembly is mechanically defective.

Do not attempt to rivet new linings into place. Check the driven plate for loose or pulled rivets as well as for loose or broken damper springs. Slide it back onto the gearbox input shaft and check that it slides freely without excessive rotational play.

The linings are at their maximum efficiency when they have an even, polished finish through which the grain of the friction material is clearly visible. Small amounts of oil will leave dark coloured smears on the linings, while larger amounts will leave a dark glaze which hides the grain of the friction material. Large amounts of oil will be obvious from the oil-soaked appearance of the linings and the free oil in the housing. Provided that the grain of the friction material can be seen, and the unit is mechanically satisfactory, it can be used again. Do not forget to find and cure the source of the oil leak before reassembling the parts.

Before starting the operation, fill the master cylinder up as far as it will go without spilling and then keep a constant check on the level as bleeding progresses, topping up as required.

Discard fluid that has been bled through the system unless it is perfectly clean. If the fluid is clean, **do not return it directly to the reservoir** but allow it to stand in a sealed clean container for at least 24 hours to allow all the air to disperse. Use only a recommended fluid.

Attach a length of small-bore plastic or rubber tube 2 to the bleed screw 3 on the slave cylinder and dip the free end of the tube into a little clean fluid in a clean glass container.

Open the bleed screw approximately $\frac{3}{4}$ turn and have an assistant press the clutch pedal down. Close the bleed screw when the pedal reaches the end of its travel and allow the pedal to return. Again open the bleed screw and repeat the cycle of operations until the fluid coming out of the bleed tube is completely clear and free from air bubbles.

Top up the master cylinder reservoir to the correct level and remove the bleed tube from the slave cylinder, making sure that the bleed screw is closed.

5:6 The release bearing assembly

The parts are shown in **FIG 5:8.** Before they can be removed, the gearbox must be taken out of the car (see **Chapter 6, Section 6:2**).

Release the operating lever from its ballpin 4 and the lugs from the release bearing 3. Slide off the release bearing and remove the operating lever.

Renew the release bearing 3 if it is worn or operates noisily. The parts are refitted in the reverse order of removal.

5:8 Fault diagnosis

(a) Drag or spin

1 Oil or grease on the driven plate linings
2 Air leak in the hydraulic system
3 Leaking master cylinder, pipe or slave cylinder
4 Driven plate hub binding on input shaft splines
5 Distorted driven plate
6 Warped or damaged pressure plate
7 Broken driven plate linings

(b) Fierceness or snatch

1 Check 1 in (a)
2 Worn driven plate linings

(c) Slip

1 Check 1 in (a) and 2 in (b)
2 Weak diaphragm spring
3 Seized piston in slave cylinder

(d) Judder

1 Check 1, 5, 6 and 7 in (a)
2 Pressure plate not parallel with flywheel
3 Contact area on friction linings not evenly distributed
4 Bent input shaft in gearbox
5 Faulty engine or gearbox mountings
6 Worn suspension shackles
7 Weak rear springs
8 Loose propeller shaft bolts

(e) Rattle

1 Broken springs in driven plate
2 Worn release mechanism
3 Excessive backlash in transmission
4 Wear in transmission bearings
5 Release bearing loose on lever

(f) Tick or knock

1 Worn crankshaft spigot bearing
2 Badly worn splines on driven plate hub
3 Loose flywheel

NOTES

CHAPTER 6

THE GEARBOX

6:1 Description

The manually operated gearbox is fitted with four forward speeds, with synchromesh engagement for each speed, and a reverse gear. The gearlever is mounted on the rear extension housing and is connected by a shaft to the selector mechanism in the gearbox top extension. Moving the gearlever sideways rotates the shaft so that pins on the shaft fit into the appropriate selector fork. Pushing the gearlever forwards or pulling it back moves the selector fork to shift the outer sleeve of the appropriate synchromesh unit so that gear is selected, for the forward speeds. For reverse gear, a pin on the selector shaft engages with a lever and movement of the gearlever then operates the reverse lever to slide an idler gear into mesh between the countershaft and mainshaft so that the direction of drive is reversed.

The input shaft of the gearbox is splined to the hub of clutch so that they rotate together. The input shaft meshes with a gear on the countershaft cluster and the remaining gears of the cluster in turn mesh with the gears on the mainshaft. The mainshaft gears are free to revolve about the mainshaft so that when the gearbox is in neutral the mainshaft does not revolve. When the outer sleeve of the synchromesh unit is moved by the selector fork, the synchromesh cup (baulk ring) first takes the drive by the friction of the conical surfaces and when the mainshaft and gear are rotating at the same speed the sleeve can slide over onto the dog teeth of the gear to make the drive positive. The inner hub of the synchromesh unit is splined to the mainshaft and the outer sleeve is splined to the hub so drive is then transmitted to the mainshaft.

A sectioned view of the gearbox is shown in **FIG 6:1**.

Lubrication:

The casing of the gearbox is filled with oil up to the level of the filler plug. The gears, shafts and their bearings rotate in the oil bath and the remainder of the parts are lubricated by splash thrown from the revolving gears. A drain plug is fitted under the gearbox so that the oil can be drained out. Routine or seasonal oil changes are not required and the only time that the oil does need to be changed is after a new gearbox has been run-in. The drain and filler plugs are shown in **FIG 6:5**. Hypoid SAE.90 oil should be used in normal climates but if the temperature regularly drops below —5° (20°F) then Hypoid SAE.80 oil should be used instead. Try to avoid mixing brands, even though each different brand is recommended, as additives in different brands may not always be compatible.

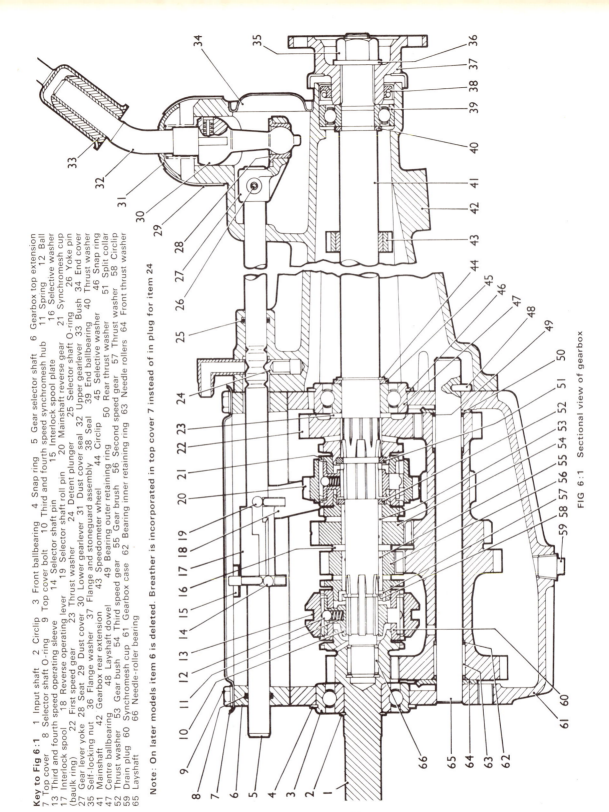

Key to Fig 6:1 1 Input shaft 2 Circlip 3 Front ballbearing 4 Snap ring 5 Gear selector shaft 6 Gearbox top extension
7 Top cover 8 Selector shaft O-ring 9 Top cover bolt 10 Third and fourth speed synchromesh hub 11 Spring 12 Ball
13 Third and fourth speed operating sleeve 14 Selector shaft pin 15 Interlock spool plate 16 Selective washer
17 Interlock spool 18 Reverse operating lever 19 Selector shaft roll pin 20 Mainshaft reverse gear 21 Synchromesh cup
(baulk ring) 22 First speed gear 23 Thrust washer 24 Detent plunger 25 Selector shaft O-ring 26 Yoke pin
27 Gear lever yoke 28 Seat 29 Dust cover 30 Lower gearlever 31 Dust cover seal 32 Upper gearlever 33 Bush 34 End cover
35 Self-locking nut 36 Flange washer 37 Flange and stoneguard assembly 38 Seal 39 End ballbearing 40 Thrust washer
41 Mainshaft 42 Gearbox rear extension 43 Speedometer wheel 44 Circlip 45 Selective washer 46 Snap ring
47 Centre ballbearing 48 Layshaft dowel 49 Bearing outer retaining ring 50 Bearing inner retaining ring 51 Split collar
52 Thrust washer 53 Gear bush 54 Third speed gear 55 Gear brush 56 Second speed gear 57 Thrust washer 58 Circlip
59 Drain plug 60 Synchromesh cup 61 Gearbox case 62 Bearing inner retaining ring 63 Needle rollers 64 Front thrust washer
65 Layshaft 66 Needle-roller bearing

Note: On later models item 6 is deleted. Breather is incorporated in top cover 7 instead of in plug for item 24

FIG 6:1   Sectional view of gearbox

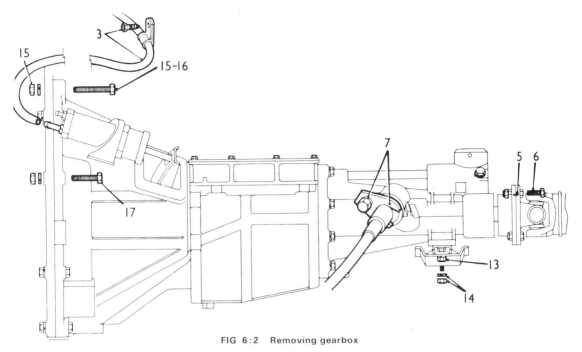

FIG 6:2   Removing gearbox

Key to Fig 6:2   3 Clutch fluid pipe   5 Gearbox and propeller shaft flanges   6 Flange bolts and nuts   7 Speedometer pinion clamp and bolt   13-14 Rear engine mounting bolts and nuts   15-16-17 Flywheel housing bolts and nuts

The level in the gearbox should be checked at intervals of 6000 miles (10,000 kilometres). Stand the car on level ground, preferably checking when the engine has not been run for some time. Unscrew the filler plug 1 and check that the oil level reaches the bottom of the aperture. Top up, if required, using a squeeze bottle and plastic hose and allow any surplus oil to drain out before refitting the filler plug. **Wipe the area clean before removing the filler plug and wipe away surplus oil after the plug has been refitted.**

6:2 Removing the gearbox

The gearbox can be removed leaving the engine in the car as follows:

1 Disconnect the battery and starter leads. Remove the bolts securing the starter to the engine backplate. Draw the starter forward and allow it to rest between the dipstick tube and the cylinder block.
2 Raise the front of the car sufficiently to allow work to be carried out from underneath, or work over a pit.
3 Disconnect the exhaust pipe from the manifold and from the engine backplate.
4 Drain the gearbox oil.
5 After marking the flange relationships 5 in **FIG 6:2** remove the four bolts 6 securing the propeller shaft to the gearbox flange. Tie the shaft up out of the way.
6 Remove the gearlever assembly as follows, referring to **FIG 6:3**. Remove the front carpet and unscrew the gearlever knob 2. Take out the screws 3 and slide the draught excluder and its retaining plate 4 up and off the gearlever. Set the gears to neutral and undo the

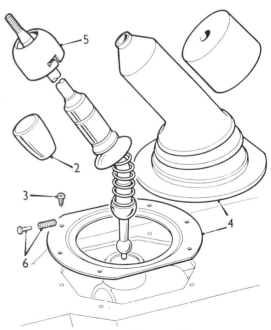

FIG 6:3   Gear lever attachments

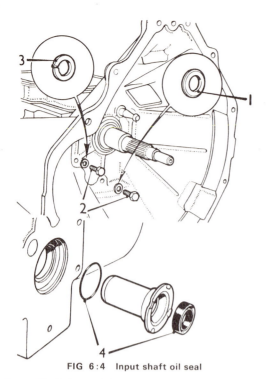

FIG 6:4 Input shaft oil seal

Key to Fig 6:4   1 Sealing washer   2 Securing bolts
3 Spring washer   4 Oil seals

bayonet fitting of the gearlever retainer 5, by pressing it down and turning it anticlockwise. **Carefully collect the anti-rattle plunger and spring 6.** Disconnect the reverse light cable.

7 Place axle stands under the rear of the engine of sufficient height to allow the rear of the gearbox to be lowered about 4 inches. This is important as without such support the engine will descend too far and damage may be caused to fixings and controls.

8 Remove the four bolts securing the gearbox support bracket to the body and lower the unit until the engine rests on the axle stands.

9 Disconnect the clutch slave cylinder by removing the retaining circlip (see **FIG 5:5** in clutch Chapter). Referring to **FIG 6:2** remove the clip 7 and pull out the speedometer drive.

10 Remove the bolts and nuts 15-17 securing the flywheel housing to the engine backplate. Take the weight of the gearbox and ease the flywheel housing off the two locating dowels. Remove the gearbox together with flywheel housing, making sure that the weight of the gearbox does not rest on the clutch splines during the operation.

11 Remove the engine mounting bracket.

Refitting gearbox:

Refitting is a reversal of removal procedures but the following points should be noted. Centralize the clutch drive plate using mandrel 18GA 032. Lubricate the clutch release mechanism with molybond GA 5 grease. Ensure that the weight of the gearbox does not hang on the clutch during fitting. Refill gearbox with recommended grade of oil.

6:3 Input shaft oil seal

The gearbox input shaft oil seal can be renewed without dismantling the gearbox as follows:

1 Remove gearbox as described in previous Section.
2 Remove the clutch release mechanism.
3 Remove the five bolts and washers securing the clutch housing to the gearbox noting that the bottom bolt (see **FIG 6:4**) has a copper sealing washer.
4 Extract the oil seal.
5 Dip the new oil seal in light engine oil and install.
6 Refit remaining parts in reverse order of dismantling, tightening the five bolts securing the clutch housing to a torque of 28 to 30 lb ft.

6:4 Dismantling the gearbox

Rear extension:

1 Referring to **FIG 6:5** pull firmly out the speedometer drive pinion 21 so that it and its housing 23 are withdrawn from the rear extension 12. Withdraw the pinion from its housing and take off seals 22 and 24. Support the gearbox firmly on the bench.

2 Referring to **FIG 6:6** take out the bolts 4, noting that there is a sealing washer fitted under the bottom bolt 4, and remove the clutch housing 5 from the gearbox. Extract the oil seal and remove the O-ring from behind the flange of the front end cover.

3 Hold the drive flange, preferably with the special spanner 18G.1205, and remove the nut and washer that secures the flange, as shown in the inset 6. If the special tool is not available, the gearbox can be locked after removal of the top extension by selecting two gears at once so that the mainshaft cannot turn.

4 Remove the rollpin 7 from the end of the selector rod. Take out the nine bolts and spring washers so that the cover 8 and its gasket can be removed. Lift out the interlock spool plate 9. Turn the selector shaft until the reverse gear position is reached and make sure that the selector shaft pins will clear the interlock spool and gear selector forks. Remove the bolts and washers 11 that secure the rear extension to the main casing and use an extractor, as shown in inset 12, to draw off the rear extension, **making sure that the selector shaft pins do not foul as the shaft is withdrawn.** If the special extractor is not available use a hide-faced hammer to tap gently and carefully on the mounting lugs to drive the rear extension off. Remove the gaskets for the rear extension.

5 Remove the interlock spool 14 and take out the distance washer 15 from the mainshaft. Remove the cover 16 by gently tapping the selector shaft 17 rearwards and then push the shaft further out to expose the gearlever seating yoke. Lightly scribe marks across the end of the shaft and yoke so that they will be correctly reassembled in the right alignment. Drive out the rollpin 18 and remove the socket from the shaft. Withdraw the selector shaft and collect the spring and plunger 19. Take out the bolt and remove the reverse gear lift plate 21.

6 If necessary, extract the oil seal and bearing from the rear end of the extension housing.

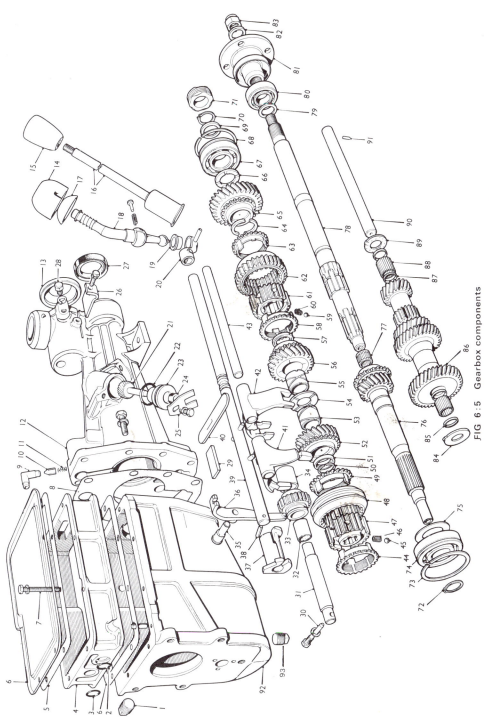

FIG 6:5 Gearbox components

Key to Fig 6:5 1 Filler plug 2 and 3 O-ring 4 Top extension 5 Gasket 6 Cover 7 Bolt 8 Gasket 9 Plug 10 Detent plunger 11 Detent spring 12 Rear extension 13 End cover 14 Dust cover 15 Gear knob 16 Upper gearlever 17 Dust cover 18 Lower gearlever 19 Seat 20 Yoke 21 Speedometer drive pinion 22 O-ring 23 Housing 24 Seal 25 Clip 26 Reverse lift plate 27 Oil seal 28 Screw for reverse light switch 29 Magnet 30 Dowel bolt 31 Spindle 32 Bush 33 Reverse idler gear 34 Pin for lever 35 Reverse operating pin 36 Reverse operating lever 37 Interlock spool 38 Roll pin 39 Selector shaft 40 Interlock spool plate 41 Third/fourth selector fork 42 First/second selector fork 43 Selector shaft 44 Synchromesh cup (baulk ring) 45 Ball 46 Spring 47 Third/fourth synchromesh hub 48 Third/fourth synchromesh sleeve 49 Synchromesh cup 50 Mainshaft circlip 51 Third speed gear thrust washer 52 Third speed gear 53 Bush 54 Selective washer 55 Bush 56 Second speed gear 57 Thrust washer 58 Synchromesh cup 59 Ball 60 Spring 61 First/second synchromesh hub 62 Mainshaft reverse gear and first/second synchromesh sleeve 63 Synchromesh cup 64 Split collar 65 First speed gear 66 Thrust washer 67 Centre bearing 68 Snap ring 69 Selective washer 70 Circlip 71 Speedometer drive 72 Circlip 73 Snap ring 74 Ballbearing 75 Oil flinger 76 Input shaft 77 Needle roller bearing 78 Mainshaft 79 Washer 80 Ballbearing 81 Drive flange 82 Washer 83 Nut 84 Thrust washer 84 and 87 Bearing retaining rings 86 Laygear 88 Needle roller bearing 89 Thrust washer 90 Layshaft 91 Pin 92 Gearbox casing 93 Drain plug

Note: Breather item 9 is now incorporated in cover 6

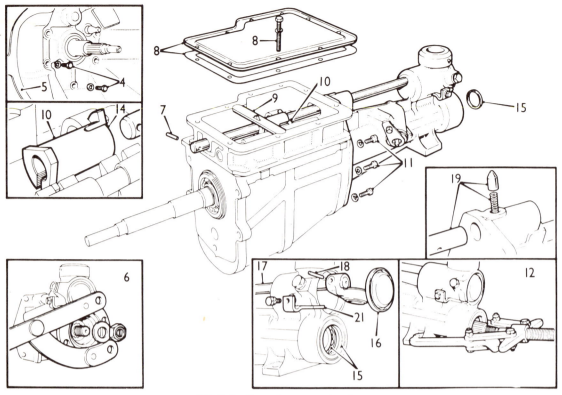

FIG 6:6   Removing rear extension

Input shaft assembly:

Refer to **FIG 6:5**.

1 Remove the rear extension as just described. Drive out the rollpin 91 that secures the layshaft 90. Use the dummy layshaft 18G.1208 to press out the layshaft 90 from the gearbox. The dummy shaft is shorter than the actual one and of the same diameter. When pressing out the layshaft, keep the dummy shaft in contact with it until the dummy is fully in the layshaft 86 and its bearings, and the laygear can slide to the bottom of the main casing, with the dummy shaft still in it.

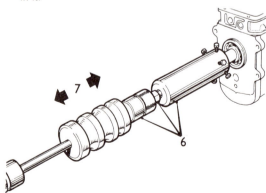

FIG 6:6A   Withdrawing input shaft assembly

2 Use the special impact hammer 18G.284 with adaptors 18G.284.AW and 18G.284.AAA located and secured to the input shaft, as shown in **FIG 6:6A**, and draw the input shaft out of the case by sliding the handle 7 firmly against the end of the tool.

3 Remove the mainshaft spigot roller bearing 77 from the end of the input shaft 76. Remove the securing circlip 72 as well as the locating snap ring 73 and use a press and suitable tools to draw the bearing 74 off the input shaft. Remove the oil flinger 75.

Main case parts:

After the rear extension and input shaft have been removed as described the main case parts are removed as follows:

1 Using service tool 18.GA.034 remove the speedometer drive gear from the mainshaft as shown in **FIG 6:7 (A)**.

2 Referring to **FIG 6:8** remove the circlip 7 and snap ring 8 locating the mainshaft.

3 Using service tool 18GA.034 remove the mainshaft as shown in **FIG 6:7 (B)**.

4 Using a brass drift drive the bearing evenly to remove it from its housing.

5 Remove the mainshaft assembly from the gearbox.

6 Referring to **FIG 6:8** remove the reverse gear idler shaft 9 reverse idler gear 15 and reverse lever 16.

7 Remove the laygear 14 and thrust washers.

Mainshaft assembly:

The parts of the mainshaft are shown in **FIG 6:9**. The parts are removed in the numerical order shown in the figure. The circlip 24 is removed using the special tool 18G.1199, as shown in the inset, with the three long splines inserted between the splines and the thrust washer tabs. **It is advisable to discard the circlip 24 and use a new one on reassembly.**

The synchromesh units 22 and 31 should be removed as an assembly, without sliding the sleeve off the hub. The synchromesh cups (baulk rings) 20, 23 and 29 are very similar in appearance but they should not be interchanged (as they have bedded-in) and they should be stored so that they will be refitted into their original positions.

If the synchromesh units are to be dismantled, mark them across the faces so that the hub and sleeve will be refitted together in their original positions. **Wrap the unit completely in cloth before pushing the inner hub out of the outer sleeve.** If this precaution is not taken the balls and springs will shoot out and be lost.

6:4 Reassembling the gearbox

Wash all parts in clean fuel and examine them for wear or damage. Check all splines for wear. Examine all the teeth on the gears for chipping, wear or fractures. Check the cones on the synchromesh cups (baulk rings) and gears for wear or scoring. Wash the bearings separately

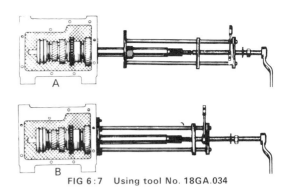

FIG 6:7   Using tool No. 18GA.034

A Removing speedometer gear   **B** Removing mainshaft

in clean fuel to make sure that they do not pick up dirt and examine them for damage or wear, making sure that they rotate smoothly when lubricated with light oil.

The bushes and shafts should not show signs of wear, chatter or fretting. Make sure that the mating faces of all the castings are true and undamaged. Small burrs can be cleaned off by careful use of a fine file. Reject any damaged parts and fit new ones in their place.

Discard all old seals and gaskets, using new ones on reassembly. The reassembling of the gearbox is generally the reverse of the dismantling operations (see previous

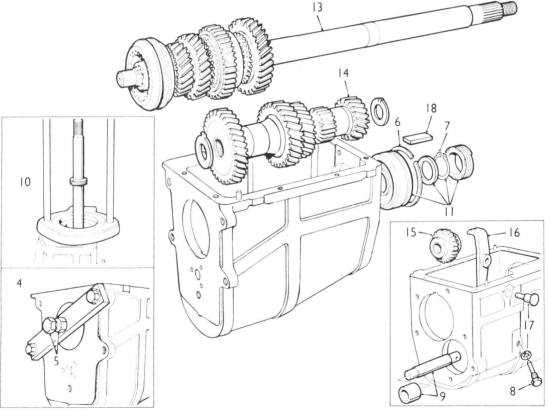

FIG 6:8   Removing parts from main case

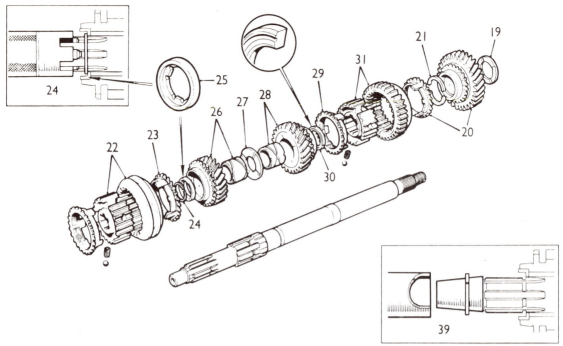

FIG 6:9   Dismantling mainshaft assembly

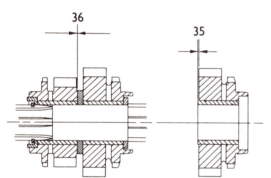

FIG 6:10   Checking mainshaft end float

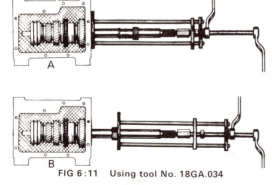

FIG 6:11   Using tool No. 18GA.034

A Replacing mainshaft   **B** Replacing speedometer gear

section) but all end floats should be checked and adjusted as the parts are reassembled. The settings, and the washers available to alter them, are given in **Technical Data**. Washers must be selectively fitted to give the correct end floats. Lubricate the parts with Hypoid oil as they are refitted.

Mainshaft assembly:

The parts are shown in **FIG 6:5** but refer to **FIG 6:9**. The parts are refitted in the reverse numerical order shown in the figure. The third gear circlip 24 should be refitted as shown in the inset 39, using the tool 18GA.039.

If the synchromesh units 22 and 31 have been dismantled, identify the parts and markings made on dismantling. Refit the balls and springs to the hub, holding them in place with grease. Use a large worm-driven hoseclip to compress them into place. Slide the sleeve back onto the hub, so that the previously made marks align, allowing the hoseclip to slide off as the balls all enter the sleeve. Press the sleeve on until the balls click into the detent groove.

Before refitting all the parts check the end floats, shown in **FIG 6:10**. The end float of the gears on their bushes (26 and 28) 37 should be .002 to .006 inch (.05 to .152 mm) and the bushes must be renewed if the end float is outside the limits.

Fit the second gear washer 30 to the mainshaft with its oil groove face away from the shoulder. Fit the gears to their bushes (28 and 26) and slide them back onto the shaft, with the selective washer (27) between them. Slide on the third gear thrust washer (with its oil groove towards the bush as shown) and secure the parts with a broken half of the old circlip (24). Breaking the old circlip and using it this way will make the task easier, rather than trying to fit and remove the new circlip. Measure the clearance 36 with feeler gauges. The end float should be .004 to .006 inch (.101 to .152 mm) and if it is incorrect then the washer (27) must be selectively fitted to bring the end float within limits.

Main case parts:

The use of a dummy layshaft is recommended for assembly purposes. This can be made to the following dimensions:

Length 6.990 +0 —.005
Diam. 0.655 +0 —.005

Fit the inner retainer rings into the laygear, then the dummy shaft. Place the rollers with a liberal coating of grease round the dummy shaft. Fit the outer retainer rings. Attach the front and rear thrust washers to the laygear with grease and carefully lower the assembly into the bottom of the gearbox.

Check the fitting of the reverse idler gear on its bush, noting that it should be flush at one end and the bush should be .010 inch (.254 mm) below the gear face. Place the idler into position and refit the lever and its pivot. Refit the magnet into its location. Fit the mainshaft assembly back into place through the top aperture. Refit the locating snap ring to the centre bearing and press the bearing back into place until the snap ring is tight against the case.

Using service tool No. 18GA.034 draw the mainshaft into the bearing as shown in **FIG 6:11 (A)**. Remove the tool and fit the mainshaft spacer and a new circlip. Check that first gear end float exists. If not, tap gently the end of the mainshaft inward enough to obtain end float.

Using service tool 18GA.034 fit the speedometer drive gear as shown in **FIG 6:11 (B)**.

Input shaft assembly:

Reassemble the parts in the reverse order of dismantling using grease to keep the oil flinger in place when refitting the bearing.

Refit the spindle and distance piece for the reverse gear idler and secure them in place with the dowel bolt. Remove the mainshaft locating tool and press the input shaft assembly back into position so that the locating flange on the bearing is tight against the casing. **Do not forget to refit the roller bearing for the spigot of the mainshaft into the input shaft before refitting the input shaft.**

Lift the laygear cluster assembly up into alignment, making sure that the thrust washers are in place, and press out the dummy layshaft using the countershaft, keeping both shafts in constant contact. Secure the countershaft with its rollpin.

Rear extension:

This is refitted in the reverse order of removal. Make sure that the rollpin for the selector shaft is fitted with an equal protrusion on either side of the shaft, otherwise there may be difficulty in refitting the clutch housing. Make sure that the selector forks are correctly fitted to the outer sleeves of the synchromesh units and that the reverse operating lever engages correctly with the idler. **Do not forget to fit a sealing washer to the bottom bolt that secures the clutch housing.**

Oil seals:

It should be noted that the oil seal on the rear extension and those on the speedometer drive can be renewed without having to remove the gearbox from the car, or remove the rear extension from the gearbox.

Renewal of the speedometer drive oil seals is the same as if the gearbox is on the bench, as the parts can be pulled out once the speedometer cable has been disconnected.

To renew the rear oil seal, disconnect the propeller shaft and remove the gearbox drive flange. The old seal can then be extracted and the new one pressed in using a suitable tube. If the face, on which the seal operates, of the drive flange is damaged or scored then a new drive flange should be fitted. Reconnect the propeller shaft after the flange is in place and check the oil level in the gearbox.

6:6 Fault diagnosis

(a) Jumping out of gear

1 Broken or weak detent spring for selector shaft
2 Excessively worn grooves in selector shaft
3 Wear in appropriate driven gear, bush or synchromesh unit
4 Worn or loose pin in selector shaft

(b) Noisy gearbox

1 Incorrect or insufficient oil
2 Excessive end float
3 Worn or damaged bearings
4 Worn or damaged gear teeth

(c) Difficulty in engaging gear

1 Worn baulk rings
2 Defective clutch release mechanism

(d) Oil leaks

1 Excessively high oil level
2 Damaged joint faces or gaskets
3 Worn or damaged oil seals

NOTES

CHAPTER 7

AUTOMATIC TRANSMISSION

7:1 Description

The automatic transmission available as an alternative to the synchromesh gearbox on 1750 models incorporates a fluid torque converter coupling in place of a clutch. The converter is coupled to a hydraulically operated epicyclic gearbox giving three forward ratios and reverse. All forward ratios are automatically engaged according to accelerator position and car speed. Overriding manual control providing engine braking is available on first and second gear ratios by selecting 1 and 2 positions on the lever.

The torque converter is filled with oil as a drive trans- mitting medium and it gives a smooth take-up of drive (with torque multiplication) from rest, and then acts as a fluid flywheel to transmit direct drive at speed.

An epicyclic gearbox is used instead of the conventional gears in mesh rotating on shafts. The various selections are made by holding the parts of the epicyclic gear train. The parts are held and driven by a combination of brake bands and clutches operated from the hydraulic control system integral in the assembly.

A sectioned view of the automatic transmission is shown in **FIG 7:1** and an exploded view of external components in **FIG 7:3**.

Torque converter:

A schematic view of the torque converter is shown in **FIG 7:2**. The unit is filled with fluid and there is a constant flow through it, from and to the gearbox, to take away heat from friction losses. The unit is sealed on manufacture and cannot be dismantled for repairs, so a defective torque converter must be renewed. The impeller **D** is made up of vanes attached inside the casing of the unit and therefore revolves with the engine, as the casing is bolted to the drive plate of the engine. As the vanes rotate they drag the fluid around with it and the fluid acts on the vanes of the turbine **A** to make it rotate in the same direction. Centrifugal force acts on the oil causing it to have a slightly higher pressure at the outside of the impeller blades than the inside. This difference in pressure sets up a circulatory flow in the cross-sectional plane, so that the combination of this circulation and drag of the fluid makes it follow the path of an imaginary spiral spring laid concentrically into the unit. The stator **B** guides the fluid flow from the inside of the turbine blades so that it impinges on the inside of the blades of the impeller, assisting it to rotate. The turbine will therefore be driven by the fluid flow and because of the stator there will be a torque multiplication effect of up to approximately 2.2:1.

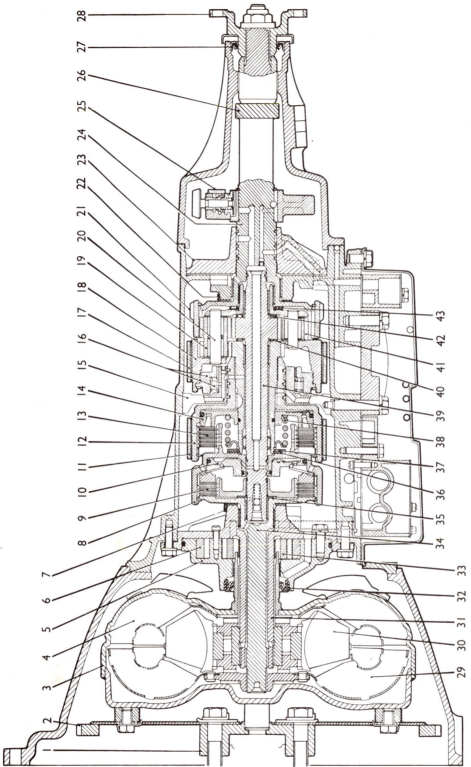

FIG 7:1   Sectioned view of automatic transmission

Key to Fig 7:1   1 Engine crankshaft   2 Converter drive plate   3 Torque converter   4 Impeller   5 Pump housing   6 Pump outer member   7 Thrust washer   8 Front clutch housing   9 Front clutch plates   10 Front clutch piston   11 Front brake band   12 Front drum assembly   13 Rear clutch plates   14 Rear clutch piston   15 Centre support   16 One-way clutch   17 Rear brake band   18 Planet carrier   19 Long planet pinion   20 Pinion shaft   21 Ring gear   22 Thrust washer   23 Rear plate adaptor   24 Driven shaft   25 Governor assembly   26 Speedometer drive gear   27 Rear oil seal   28 Driving flange   29 Turbine   30 Stator   31 Torque converter support   32 Front oil seal   33 Pump inner member   34 Input shaft   35 Thrust washer   36 Bronze thrust washer   37 Steel thrust washer   38 Rear clutch spring   39 Forward sun gear   40 Needle thrust washer   41 Short planet pinion   42 and 43 Needle thrust washer

66

As the impeller and turbine speed up, the fluid flow starts to impinge on the back of the stator blades and this would normally cause power losses. The stator is fitted onto a one-way clutch **C** which allows it to freewheel under the action of the fluid impinging on the back of the stator blades, so that the power losses are minimized. At this point the torque converter acts as a fluid flywheel with a 1:1 drive. Because of the frictional losses the turbine will never rotate at the full speed of impeller and the actual speed is approximately 98 per cent of the impeller speed. The 2 per cent losses are wasted as heat.

The greater the slip, the greater will be the heat produced by churning. In normal driving this does not matter as the heat produced will be radiated and conducted away from the automatic transmission, and a flow of air around the converter (through the stone guards) further assists in cooling. An oil cooler is also fitted to some models so that the fluid is passed through it and cooled by the passage of air. If the car is held stationary with drive selected and the engine speeded up then there will be large amounts of slip and a great deal of heat produced. **This condition should only be used as a test and even then the amount of time taken for the test must be strictly limited.**

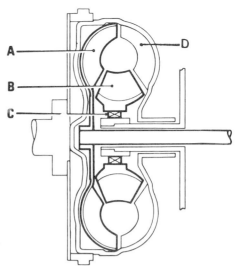

FIG 7:2   A schematic section of the torque converter

Epicyclic gearbox:

The unit consists of an epicyclic gear train and the various ratios are selected by hydraulic pressure acting on internal clutches and brake bands. The actual selection is carried out by a complex valve system which uses both the position of the throttle (through the downshift cable) and a pressure proportional to the road speed. A governor assembly is fitted to the output shaft of the gearbox and it is this unit which supplies the pressure proportional to the road speed of the car. A manually operated selector mechanism overrides the valve assembly as required and also selects the direction of drive.

Oil pressure to lubricate the parts, and to supply the hydraulic pressure for the operation of the unit, is supplied by an oil pump mounted on the input shaft of the gearbox. An oil strainer is fitted to the valve assembly, accessible after the sump has been removed, to ensure that the oil passing through the pump and into the unit is kept clean and free from particles.

The external parts of the automatic transmission are shown in **FIG 7:3**. The internal parts and valve system are not shown as most of them are beyond the powers of the owner to service or dismantle. An inhibiting switch 53 is fitted to the case. This switch prevents the stator from operating when a drive gear is selected, thus ensuring that the car cannot move off accidentally when the engine is started, and it also operates the reverse light when reverse is selected.

A parking pawl is fitted to the output shaft. When the selector is placed to the P position this pawl engages and locks the gearbox. The pawl should and will hold the car on hills but it should always be used in conjunction with the handbrake, as a safety precaution and to ensure that the pawl can easily be disengaged when selecting drive.

The car cannot be tow-started or pushed to start. However, the car can be towed, provided that the automatic transmission is in a satisfactory condition and correctly filled, but the distance of tow must not exceed 40 miles (64 km) and the speed must not exceed 30 mile/hr (48 km/hr). If these conditions cannot be complied with, disconnect the propeller shaft from the rear axle and tie it safely out of the way, or tow the car with the rear wheels on a dolly or hoisted clear of the ground and the steering locked or tied into the straight-ahead position.

The unit is very complicated, requiring many special tools for servicing, and fitters at garages are specially trained for working on automatic transmissions. **If faults cannot be corrected by carrying out the work outlined in this chapter then the car should be taken to an agent specializing in automatic transmissions. Under no circumstances attempt to dismantle the epicyclic gearing parts or valve assembly.**

7:2 Routine maintenance

The level of the fluid in the unit can be checked when the unit is cold or when it has reached its normal operation temperature. Stand the car on level ground and allow the engine to idle for at least two minutes to ensure that the torque converter is full. Select **P** and withdraw the dipstick 3 from its tube, shown in **FIG 7:4**. Leave the engine idling, wipe the dipstick and reinsert it. Immediately withdraw the dipstick and check the level against the marks. The difference between the upper and lower marks represents 1 Imperial pint (1.2 US pint, .57 Litre). If the level is low, top up to the upper mark **using a transmission fluid of recommended grade. Absolute cleanliness is essential. Do not overfill the unit as this will cause frothing of the oil and possible faulty operation.**

Under normal conditions it is not necessary to change the fluid in the transmission. However under severe conditions such as caravan towing in mountainous terrain or in high air temperatures, the fluid should be changed every 12,000 miles or every 12 months.

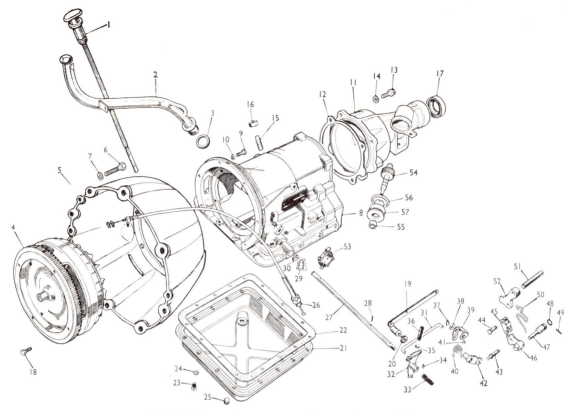

FIG 7:3   External components of automatic transmission

Key to Fig 7:3   1 Dipstick   2 Oil filler and gearbox breather   3 Sealing ring   4 Converter assembly   5 Converter housing
6 Bolt for housing   7 Spring washer for bolt   8 Case assembly   9 Bolt for case   10 Spring washer for bolt   11 Rear extension
housing   12 Gasket for extension housing   13 Bolt for extension housing   14 Spring washer for bolt   15 Rear brake band
adjusting screw   16 Locknut for adjusting screw   17 Rear oil seal   18 Bolt for converter   19 Inhibitor switch operating link and
shaft   20 Oil seal for shaft   21 Oil pan assembly   22 Gasket for oil pan   23 Bolt for oil pan   24 Spring washer for bolt   25 Drain
plug   26 Down-shift cable assembly   27 Manual control shaft   28 Roll pin   29 Circlip   30 Oil seal   31 Manual linkage rod
32 Manual detent lever   33 Spring   34 Clip   35 Ball   36 Spring   37 Clip   38 Washer   39 Torsion lever   40 Spring   41 Clip
42 Toggle arm assembly   43 Toggle pin   44 Toggle link pin   45 Toggle link   46 Toggle lever   47 Toggle pin   48 O-ring for pin
49 Slotted pin   50 Parking brake release spring   51 Parking brake anchor pin   52 Parking brake pawl   53 Inhibitor switch
54 Speedometer pinion   55 Oil seal for pinion   56 Gasket for pinion bush   57 Speedometer pinion bush

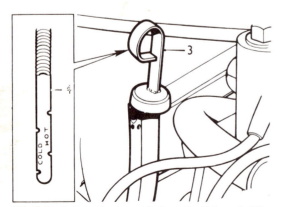

FIG 7:4   Automatic transmission dipstick and filler

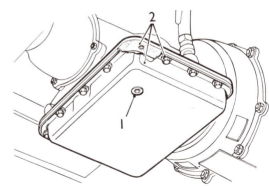

FIG 7:5   Automatic transmission sump and drain plug

Draining:

The sump attachments are shown in **FIG 7:5**. If the unit is drained after the car has been used, **take great care as the fluid will be hot enough to cause serious scalding.** Unscrew the drain plug and allow the fluid to drain out into a suitable container. Note that the unit will not empty completely as some fluid will remain in the torque converter, and oil cooler if one is fitted.

When the fluid has stopped draining, the sump can be removed by taking out the bolts 2. The oil strainer will then be found secured by four bolts. Remove the strainer and wash it thoroughly in clean fuel. Make sure that it is dry and refit the parts in the reverse order of removal, after wiping out and washing the sump. Clean the magnet to remove any metal particles. It is advisable to use a new sump gasket and the drain plug should be sealed with a little Locktite Hydraulic Seal.

Fill the unit with slightly less fluid than is required and run the engine to fill the torque converter. Check the level on the dipstick and add more fluid as required to bring the level to the upper mark. **Do not overfill, and if the unit is accidentally overfilled the surplus should be drained or syphoned out.**

The quantities required to refill the unit are as follows:
Normal draining only, 5 Imp pint (6.5 US pint, 3 Litres)
Torque converter emptied, 9.5 Imp pint (10.7 US pint, 5.4 Litres)
Torque converter and oil cooler emptied, 11 Imp pints (13.2 US pint, 6.2 Litres)

If the oil is black and evil smelling or particles of lining or metal are found in the sump, take the car to an agent for further checks.

Cleanliness:

All operations carried out on the automatic transmission must be done with absolute cleanliness, as even a speck of dirt can block a valve and cause faulty operation. For this reason always use fresh fluid to top up or fill the unit as well as wiping the top of the filler tube clean.

External cleanliness is also important. Periodically wash off the accumulations of mud and road dirt that gather on the casing and make sure that the stone guards in the converter housing are clear and free from mud or stones. If an oil cooler is fitted, blow through the fins with an airline or hosepipe to remove the accumulations of mud and insects. The automatic transmission produces quite a considerable amount of heat and if dirt is left on the outside it will act as an insulator, causing the unit to overheat.

7:3 Adjustments

Inhibitor switch:

The attachments and leads to the switch are shown in **FIG 7:6**. Before checking the action of the switch, chock the rear wheels to prevent the car from moving off. As a further safety precaution, the lead between the distributor and ignition coil can be disconnected at the ignition coil, ensuring that the engine cannot start, but be sure to reconnect the lead when the tests and adjustments are complete.

Disconnect the leads from the switch, **making sure that none of them accidentally earth against a**

FIG 7:6   Inhibitor switch and leads

Key to Fig 7:6   1 Starter/ignition switch leads (white with red trace)   2 Lead to fuse box (green/red trace) (early models) (green) (later models)   3 Lead to reverse lamps (green/brown trace)

metal part of the car. Use a separate supply and test lamp to test the switch (12-volt). Connect the test lamp and battery across the starter terminals 1 and move the selector in the car to each position in turn. The test lamp should only light when the selector is in the **P** and **N** selections. Connect the test lamp and battery across the reverse light terminals 2 and 3 and check the test lamp with the selector in each position in turn. The lamp should only light when the selector is in the **R** selection. If the lamp never lights, either the adjustment is completely wrong or the switch is defective.

Refer to **FIG 7:7** for adjusting the switch. Slacken the locknut 5. Connect the test lamp and battery across the terminals 6 for the reverse light and select '1'. If the light is out, unscrew the switch until the light comes on. Screw the switch back in again until the light has just gone out and make aligning marks 6 on both the switch and case.

Disconnect the test lamp and battery from the terminals 6 and reconnect them across the starter terminals 7, when the lamp should be off. Screw in the switch until the light

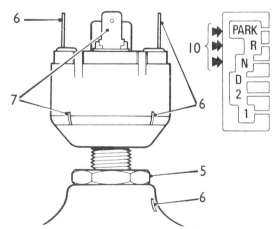

FIG 7:7   Adjusting starter inhibitor switch

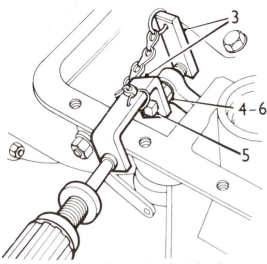

FIG 7:8 Adjusting front brake band

comes on, noting that approximately three quarters of a turn will be required. Make a mark 7 on the switch in line with the previously made mark 6 on the case. Remove the test lamp and battery. Turn the switch until it is midway between the two marks and retighten the locknut 5 without allowing the switch to turn.

Recheck, using the test lamp as described earlier, and then reconnect the leads to the switch. Check that the starter motor only operates in Park and **N** selections and that the reversing lights come on when **R** is selected.

Front brake band:

The method of adjustment is shown in **FIG 7:8**. Drain the fluid out of the unit and remove the sump (see **Section 7:2**). Move the servo lever outwards and fit the gauge block of the special tool BWA.34 between the adjuster and the servo body, as shown at 3. Slacken the locknut 4 and tighten the adjusting screw to a torque load of 10 lb in (.115 kg m). Use a torque wrench or torque screwdriver with the special adaptor BW.548/2 as shown. Hold the adjusting screw in position and retighten the locknut 4. Refit the sump, tightening its

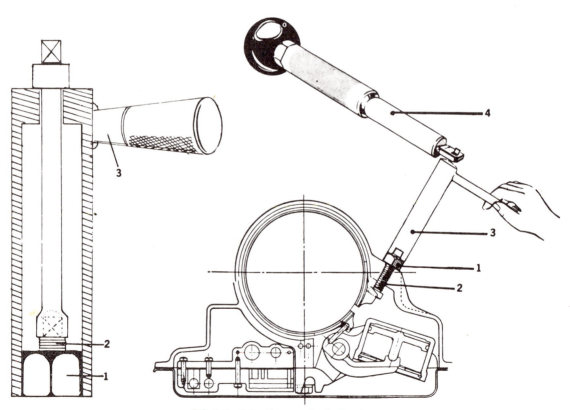

FIG 7:9 Adjusting rear brake band

Key to Fig 7:9   1 Locknut   2 Adjusting screw   3 Adaptor BWA 7196   4 Tension wrench TWA 1

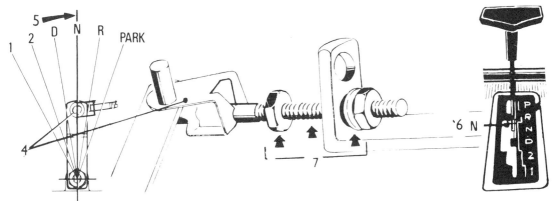

FIG 7:10   Selector rod adjustment

attachment bolts to a torque of 9 to 12 lb ft (1.2 to 1.7 kg m). Refill the unit to the correct level with fresh fluid. Note that if the oil appears black and evil smelling or particles of metal or lining are found in the sump, the car should be taken to an agent for further checks.

Rear brake band:

The method of adjustment is shown in **FIG 7:9**. Using a torque wrench such as TWA-1 shown with adaptor BWA.7196 slacken locknut 1. Tighten the adjusting screw 2 to a figure of 10 lb/ft and back off two turns. Tighten the locknut 1.

Idling speed adjustment:

Correct idling speed is essential to avoid stalling in traffic on the one hand or an excessive thump when engaging gear. A high idling speed will also cause excessive 'creep'. Set the idling to 550 rev/min at working temperature, using an electric tachometer and with the selector in **N** position. For details of carburetter adjustment (see Chapter 2). Note that it is normal for the idling speed to drop 50-70 rev/min when a gear is selected.

Selector rod:

The method of checking and the adjustment point are shown in **FIG 7:10**.

Set the manual selector to the **N** position but allow it to be positioned by the detent in the manual control valve on the gearbox. Check that the lever aligns with the **N** mark on the selector. Move the manual selector to the Park position and check that the gearbox has locked by trying to rock the car backwards and forwards.

If the adjustment of the rod is incorrect, disconnect the rod from the base of the manual selector lever 4. Push the manual selector lever right forward and pull it back by three clicks until it is accurately in the **N** position 5 of the selector. Set the selector lever on the gearbox to the **N** position 6. Slacken the locknut and adjust the nut 7 until the end of the selector rod freely enters the hole in the bottom of the manual selector lever. Reconnect the selector rod after tightening the locknut.

Check the selector in all positions and make sure that the valve on the gearbox is not overriden.

Downshift throttle cable adjustment:

An accurate electronic tachometer and a pressure gauge reading to 300 lb/sq inch are needed for this adjustment. An adaptor 18GA.677B shown at 3 in **FIG 7:11** replacing the plug 2 for test purposes.

Chock the rear wheels and apply the handbrake firmly.

Refer to **FIG 7:11**. Pull down the inner cable by hand and make sure that it is rotating the down-shift cam. If it is not rotating the cam drain the fluid (see **Section 7:2**) remove the sump 3a and make sure that the cable and nipple are correctly in place as shown in 3b. Check the cam in the idling position 3c. Have an assistant open the throttle fully and make sure that the down-shift valve enters the kick-down position of the cam, as shown in 3d, adjusting the cable if necessary. Refit the sump and refill with fluid to the correct level. Note that the checks 3 need only be carried out if the cable is not rotating the down-shift cam and need not be carried out if the cam is rotating.

Start the engine and allow it to idle at 550 rev/min. Check that the crimped stop on the inner cable is $\frac{1}{16}$ inch (1.6 mm) from the outer cable collar 5 and that the trunnion is free to swivel, adjusting as required, by slackening the locknut and turning the adjuster 6. This will give an initial setting for the cable, but the final adjustments should be made with the pressure gauge and tachometer.

Use the car until the transmission has reached its normal operating temperature. Stop the engine and connect the instruments as shown in **FIG 7:11**. **Make sure that the wheels are chocked and the handbrake firmly applied.** Start the engine, apply the foot-brake to make absolutely sure that the car does not move, and select **D** with the engine idling at 550 rev/min. The pressure reading at idling should be 50 to 65 lb/sq inch (3.5 to 4.2 kg/sq cm). Increase the engine speed to 1050 rev/min and if the cable adjustment is correct, the pressure will rise by at least 10 lb/sq inch (1.4 kg/sq cm). If the pressure rise is not correct, stop the engine. If the pressure rise is less than 10 lb/sq inch increase the effective length of the outer cable at the adjuster 6, and if the pressure rise is high then decrease the effective length of the cable.

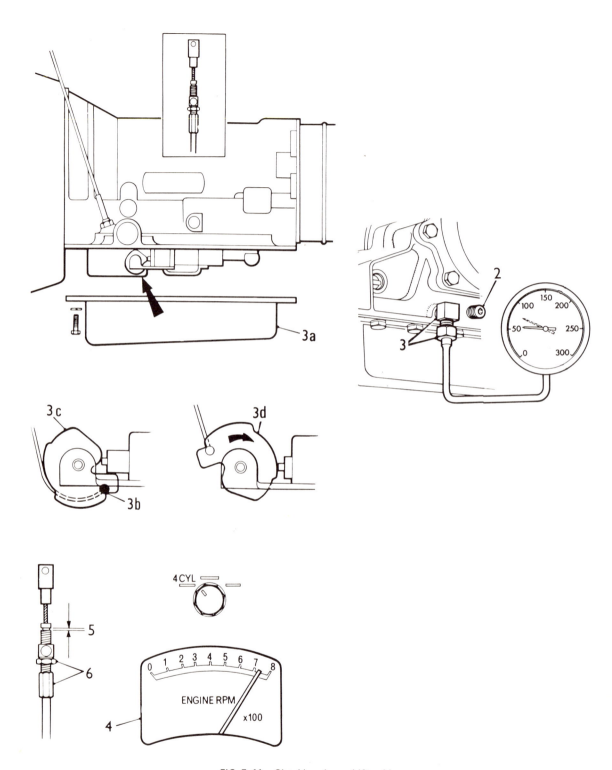

FIG 7:11   Checking downshift cable

Restart the engine and repeat the test, making further adjustments to the outer cable length as required until the pressure rises by 10 lb/sq inch when the speed is raised from idle to 1050 rev/min.

Stop the engine and remove the test equipment, making sure that the blanking plug is refitted and that the locknut on the adjuster is tight.

7:4 Stall speed test

This test provides a quick and accurate guide to the condition of the automatic transmission, and to some degree the condition of the engine. The test, as the name implies, is carried out with the car stationary and the turbine stalled. All the power from the engine goes into churning the fluid in the torque converter and as the energy must be dispersed it is converted into heat. **If the heat is prolonged then the unit will very rapidly overheat and become damaged. For this reason a stall test should not last longer than 10 seconds and if the test has to be repeated, sufficient time must be allowed between tests to allow the unit to cool down.** Allow the unit to cool down by running the engine at idle with **N** selected as this will ensure oil circulation.

Before carrying out the test, make sure that the unit is filled with fluid to the upper mark on the dipstick. Connect an accurate tachometer into the ignition circuit so that it can be seen from the driver's seat. Use the car until the transmission has reached its normal operating temperature. **Chock the wheels and firmly apply the handbrake, using the footbrake as well to prevent the car from moving.** Select either '1' or **R** positions and floor the accelerator pedal, **for a maximum of 10 seconds,** noting the reading on the tachometer. If everything is in order, the maximum speed that the engine will reach is 2100 to 2200 rev/min.

If the maximum speed obtainable is only 1900 to 2000 rev/min then the engine is not producing its full power.

A very low maximum speed, below 1500 rev/min indicates stator slip in the torque converter. The one-way clutch in the torque converter is defective, allowing stator to slip so that the torque multiplication effect cannot take place. The fault will be confirmed by the car having poor acceleration from standstill and having difficulty driving away on steep hills. The only cure is to fit a new torque converter.

If a high maximum engine speed is obtained, over 2300 rev/min, the gearbox is slipping. If the fault is apparent in both '1' and **R** selections then it is most likely caused by low oil pressure or oil starvation. Remove the sump and check the oil strainer for blockage, after making sure that the fluid level in the unit is correct. If the fault occurs in only one selection then it is caused by either a brake band slipping (try adjustment) or a defective clutch.

Road test:

This should when possible be carried out by a qualified mechanic trained on automatic transmissions. The shift speeds should be checked and undue noises listened for. Make sure that the starter motor only operates in Park and **N** selections and check that the reversing lights come on

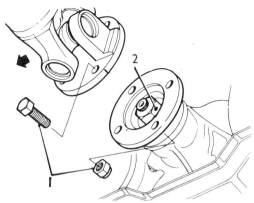

FIG 7:12   Transmission removal—propeller shaft coupling

Key to Fig 7:12   1 Coupling bolts and locknuts (4 off)
2 Output shaft locknut

in-**R** selection. Ensure that the transmission only will hold the car in Park when facing up or down a hill (apply the brake before releasing the selection). Hold the car on the handbrake and see that it attempts to move off in the correct direction in all the drive selections.

It should be noted that the stator clutch can be defective even if the stall speed is correct. If the maximum speed in the gears, particularly top, is reduced and the transmission tends to overheat rapidly and severely then it is likely that the one-way clutch on the stator has seized. This is a rare fault. Usually if the clutch does fail it slips in both directions, but seizing is a fault to be borne in mind.

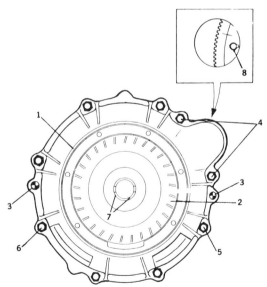

FIG 7:13   Converter housing securing bolts

Key to Fig 7:13   1 Converter housing   2 Converter
3 Locating dowels   4 Starter motor bolts   5 Earth strap
6 Exhaust bracket   7 Pump drive tangs   8 Converter
mounting bolts

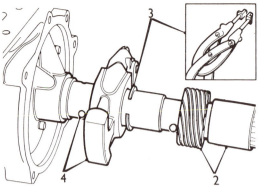

FIG 7:14   The governor attachments

7:5 Removing the automatic transmission

The transmission can be removed together with the engine as described in **Chapter 1 (Section 1:3)** or can be removed separately leaving the engine in the car as follows:

1 Disconnect the battery.
2 Remove the filler tube mounting bolt from the transmission and withdraw dipstick and tube. Disconnect the throttle cable at the heat shield and carburetter linkage.
3 Raise the vehicle to a suitable working height and support firmly or work over a pit. Drain the transmission fluid **noting warning given in Section 7:2.**
4 Disconnect the exhaust pipe at the manifold and rear engine plate.
5 Disconnect the selector lever from the transmission. Disconnect cables from inhibitor switch and reverse light switch where fitted.
6 Disconnect the propeller shaft from the transmission (see **FIG 7:12**) and tie it up to a torsion bar.

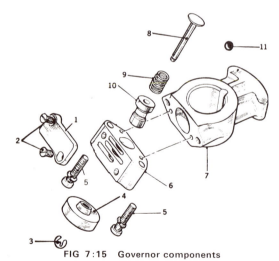

FIG 7:15   Governor components

Key to Fig 7:15   1 Cover plate   2 Cover plate screws
3 Circlip   4 Weight   5 Valve body retaining screws 6 Valve
body   7 Counter weight   8 Valve and spindle   9 Spring
10 Valve   11 Drive ball

7 Support the engine and take the weight of the power unit.
8 Remove the four bolts from the rear crossmember and lower the power unit approximately four inches.
9 Support the transmission and remove the six bolts securing it to the converter housing. Remove the transmission by withdrawing it to the rear clear of the torque converter housing. Do not allow the weight of the transmission to hang on the input shaft in the torque converter. A quantity of fluid will drain from the converter as the transmission is removed.

Refitting transmission:

Refitting is a reversal of the removal procedure but the following points should be noted:
1 Align the front pump drive slots with the drive tangs on the converter horizontal as shown at 7 in **FIG 7:13**.
2 Excercise care when aligning and entering input shaft, stator support and pump drive tangs to prevent damage to pump oil seal. Tighten securing screws to 8 to 13 lb/ft.
3 Refill transmission with correct fluid and check level.

Removing torque converter housing:

After removing transmission as already described, the converter housing can be removed by removing the nine bolts securing it to the engine backplate (see **FIG 7:13**). Two of these bolts secure the starter motor, one the exhaust pipe and one the earth strap. Remove the housing carefully noting the position of the locating dowels. Refitting is a reversal of the removal procedure.

Removing torque converter:

After removing transmission and torque converter housing as already described:
1 Remove the starter motor clear of its aperture in the engine backplate.
2 Referring to **FIG 7:13** remove the four self-locking bolts 8 securing the converter to the drive plate. Access can be obtained through the starter aperture in the backplate as shown.
3 Remove the converter. This will still contain a quantity of fluid.
Refitting the converter is a reversal of the removal procedure noting the following:
1 Fit new self-locking bolts.
2 Tighten the bolts diagonally to 25 to 40 lb/ft.
For attention to starter ring gear/drive plate (see Chapter 1, **Section 1:10**).

7:6 The rear extension oil seal

The rear extension seal can be renewed without having to take the transmission out of the car.

Disconnect the propeller shaft select 'P' take off the nut that secures the drive flange and remove the drive flange using a suitable extractor. Prise out the old oil seal and press a new one back into place. Refit the drive flange, checking that its operating surface is not scored or damaged, and reconnect the propeller shaft.

The seals for the speedometer drive pinion parts can also be renewed without having to remove the rear extension. Disconnect the speedometer cable by removing its securing clip and pull out the drive pinion and housing. Renew the O-ring and seal. Refit the parts in the reverse order of removal.

7:7 The governor

The governor is accessible after the rear extension has been removed, and its attachments are shown in **FIG 7:14**.

To remove the unit, withdraw the speedometer drive gear 2. Remove the circlip 3 and slide off the governor, collecting the drive ball 4.

The governor is refitted in the reverse order of removal. Turn the output shaft until the detent is uppermost and the drive ball can be held in place with a little petroleum jelly (vaseline) and slide on the governor so that the coverplate is away from the gearbox.

The components of the unit are shown in **FIG 7:15**. Remove the cover plate 1. Remove circlip 3 and weight 4. Take out the two screws and separate valve body 6 from counter weight 7. Remove valve spindle 8, spring 9 and valve 10.

Wash the parts in clean fuel and examine them for scoring or wear. Renew worn or damaged parts.

The unit is reassembled in the reverse order of dismantling. The screws 5 must be tightened to a torque of 4 to 5 lb ft (.6 to .7 kg m) and the screws 2 to a torque of 20 to 48 lb in (.23 to .55 kg m) **otherwise there is a danger of the unit leaking in use.**

7:8 Fault diagnosis

This section does not cover all the faults that can be found but only the more common ones that can be cured by the owner. If the fault persists after adjustment or repairs, take the car to a qualified agent.

(a) Transmission overheats

1 Stone guards on converter housing blocked
2 Unit covered in dirt
3 Stator one-way clutch seized (rare fault)
4 Rear brake band incorrectly adjusted
5 Front brake band incorrectly adjusted
6 Oil cooler defective

(b) Noisy operation

1 Incorrect fluid level
2 Incorrectly adjusted selector rod
3 Incorrectly adjusted downshift cable
4 Defective oil sump (screech or whine increasing with engine speed)

(c) Incorrect shift speeds

1 Check 2 and 3 in (b)
2 Governor valve sticking or incorrectly assembled

(d) No drive

1 Check (b)

(e) Poor acceleration

1 Check 3, 4 and 5 in (a)
2 Stator clutch slipping

(f) Jumps in engagement

1 Check 4 and 5 in (a) and also check 2 and 3 in (b)
2 Incorrect engine idling speed

(g) Car does not hold in Park

1 Check 2 in (b)

(h) Incorrect stall speed

1 Check 3, 4 and 5 in (a); 2 in (e). Also check (b) and (c)

(i) Reverse slips or chatters

1 Check 4 in (a) and 2 in (b)

NOTES

CHAPTER 8

THE PROPELLER SHAFT, REAR AXLE
AND REAR SUSPENSION

8:1 The propeller shaft

The attachments of the propeller shaft are shown in FIG 8:1.

Removal and refitting:

1 Jack up the rear of the car so that the propeller shaft can be turned. Make marks 1 across the flanges of the universal joints and those on the gearbox and rear axle drive flanges. These marks should be realigned on reassembly.

2 Take out the nuts and bolts 3 that secure the front propeller shaft to the gearbox and lower the front end of the propeller shaft. When carrying out work on the transmission which requires disconnecting this point, tie the propeller shaft safely out of the way to one of the front suspension torsion bars.

3 Support the rear end of the propeller shaft and remove the nuts and bolts 4 that secure it to the pinion flange of the rear axle.

4 Take out the two sets of bolts and washers 5 that secure the centre bearing to the frame and remove the complete propeller shaft from the car.

Refit the propeller shaft in the reverse order of removal, taking care to align the yokes on the shafts correctly when re-mating the splines, otherwise vibration will occur.

Note that the two yokes on the rear shaft are in the same plane while the two yokes of the front shaft are at 90 deg. to one another. If the self-locking nuts 3 and 4 can be run up and down the threads of their bolts, using only the fingers, the nuts are worn and must be renewed. The nuts 3 and 4 should be tightened to a torque of 28 lb/ft (3.8 kg m) and the bolts 5 should be tightened to 22 lb/ft (3.0 kg m).

Centre bearing:

This can be renewed once the propeller shaft has been removed from the car. Mark the relative positions of internal and external splines. Free the tabwasher 7 and remove the bolt and C-washer 8. Remove the rear propeller shaft from the front one.

The bearing can be pulled off from the front propeller shaft. The new bearing should be driven back into place, preferably using an hydraulic press.

Sliding joint:

Further details of the propeller shaft are shown in FIG 8:2. The rear propeller shaft 2 is fitted with a sliding joint which allows the length of the shaft to alter slightly as the axle moves in its springs. Before separating the

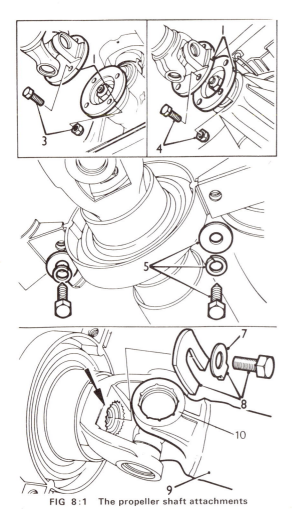

halves of the rear propeller shaft mark them with aligning marks. **It is essential that these marks are again aligned on reassembly, as the two universal joints on the rear propeller shaft must be in the correct phase.** A single universal joint does not give a perfect even drive but, by having the two joints in the correct phase the angular variations in each joint are cancelled out.

Unscrew the cap 9 by hand and separate the two halves of the shaft by pulling them apart. If the splines are worn or damaged a new rear shaft must be fitted.

Lubricate the splines with grease, fit a new cork seal 7, and slide the halves together so that the previously made marks again align. Tighten the cap nut 9 handtight.

Servicing universal joints:

Two alternative locating methods are used for universal joint bearings. Where they are staked in the yokes as at 10 in **FIG 8 : 1** the work of reconditioning is best carried out by a service agent with the necessary special tools, or the complete units can be renewed.

Where the bearings are held by circlips the assembly can be dismantled and a service kit of parts obtained for overhaul. Proceed as follows (see **FIG 8 : 3**):

1 Clean all dirt and paint from around the circlips. Mark yokes and shaft with paint to ensure reassembly in the same relationship. Tap the end of one of the bearings with a brass drift to relieve the pressure on the circlip which can then be removed using circlip pliers.

2 Hold the shaft with the bearing to be removed uppermost and tap the yoke downwards with a lead or copper hammer. Reaction should jar out the bearing upwards. When it projects enough to be gripped, invert the joint and pull the bearing cup out downwards so that the needle rollers come out with it.

3 Remove the opposite circlip and bearing, then the yoke can be detached from the trunnion. Remove the other two bearings and dismantle the other universal joints in the same way.

FIG 8 : 1   The propeller shaft attachments

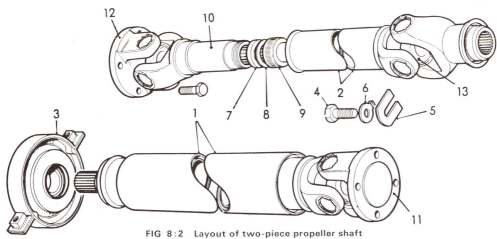

FIG 8 : 2   Layout of two-piece propeller shaft

Key to Fig 8 : 2   1 Propeller shaft front (manual trans.)   2 Propeller shaft rear (both transmissions)   3 Centre bearing mounting   4 Retaining bolt   5 'C' washer   6 Tab washer   7 Seal   8 Seal retainer   9 Screw cap   10 Sliding yoke   11 Front flange (gearbox end)   12 Rear flange   13 Centre universal joint

4 When reassembling universal joints, coat the needle rollers with petroleum jelly to hold them in the races. Ensure that the bearing is one third filled with the recommended grease before assembly. Tap home the races using a flat faced drift slightly smaller in diameter than the yoke bore.

8:2 The rear axle

The rear axle assembly is of the hypoid, semi-floating type of unitized carrier construction. The two pinion, split differential case, which also carries the crown wheel is mounted in opposed taper roller bearings in the carrier. Bearing preload adjustment is provided by varying shim thickness behind the bearing cups. The pinion is also carried in opposed taper roller bearings mounted in the axle housing and are shim adjusted for preload.

The axle shafts which are of unequal length are mounted on ball bearings and held by retainers at the axle housing outer ends. Axle shaft end play is preset and is not adjustable.

An identification tag on the rear axle housing gives the rear axle ratio and part number.

The complete axle unit should be removed from the car for all service operations other than for the removal of axle shafts, pinion flange, oil seals, rear cover and gasket.

Lubrication:

A combined filler and oil level plug is fitted. The level in the rear axle should be checked at intervals of 6000 miles (10,000 kilometres) or 6 months, whichever occurs the sooner. Stand the car on level ground and clean the area around the filler plug free from dirt. Unscrew the plug and check that the oil comes level with the bottom of the aperture. If the level is low, top up using a squeeze bottle and plastic hose. Allow all surplus oil to drain out through the filler hole before refitting the plug. **Do not overfill the axle as this can cause oil to leak past the seals in the hub and contaminate the brakes.** At the same time, check that the breather is clear and not blocked with dirt. A blocked breather can also cause oil leaks, as pressure rises inside the case when the unit gets hot and blows oil past the seals.

Use Hypoid SAE.90 (API GL5) oil. There is no drain plug and if for any reason the axle has to be drained slacken the rear cover bolts allowing the oil to seep out.

Hub and axle shaft:

Removal:

1 Raise the rear of the car and place suitable stands under the rear axle housing.
2 Remove hub caps and rear wheels.
3 Remove brake drums.
4 Remove the four nuts retaining the brake backing plate and outer bearing retainer. Access to these nuts is through the axle shaft flange service hole.
5 Withdraw the axle shaft and wheel bearing assembly using tool 18GA.040 in conjuction with impulse extractor 18GA.284.
6 Remove oil seal if not integral part of bearing.
7 Press wheel bearing and inner bearing retainer from axle shaft.

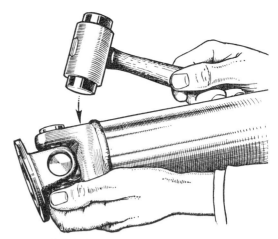

FIG 8:3 Dismantling universal joint

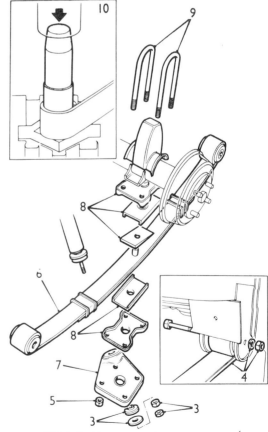

FIG 8:4 Rear suspension components

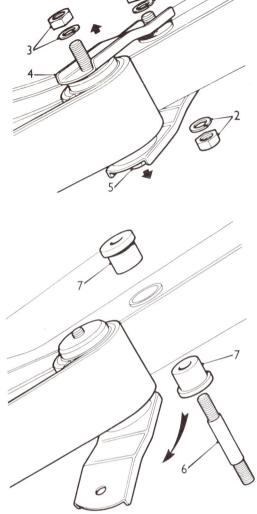

FIG 8:5 Rear spring shackle assembly

8 Examine axle shaft bearing journal and splines for excessive wear or damage. If the axle shaft is in a satisfactory condition it may be re-used.

Bearings and inner bearing retainers which have been removed from an axle shaft should not be re-used.

Refitting:

1 Place the outer bearing retainer on the axle shaft.
2 Press the wheel bearing on the axle shaft until it is hard against the bearing shoulder, ensuring that the oil seal in the bearing faces the splined end of the shaft. If the oil seal is not an integral part of the wheel bearing, fit a replacement seal in the axle housing and make sure that it is seated squarely. Ensure that the bearing is not tilted and is pressed on straight. Pressure must only be applied on the inner track of the bearing race.

3 Place the axle shaft through the brake backing plate and align the axle shaft with the diffetential gear splines.
4 Once the axle splines have been engaged in the differential gears, the axle assembly may be tapped into the axle housing by a soft faced hammer.
5 Secure the brake backing plate and outer bearing retainer, using new nuts.
6 Replace the brake drum and wheel.
7 Lower car to the ground, tighten wheel nuts and replace hub cap.

The differential unit:

Dismantling or servicing the unit should not be carried out by the owner. As the parts of the differential are reassembled they must be set to the correct clearances and mesh, otherwise the unit will not operate quietly and satisfactorily. Special tools, a good selection of shims, and personal skill, are all essential.

Pinion oil seal:

The oil seal can be renewed without having to take out the rear axle or remove the differential.

Disconnect the rear propeller shaft from the drive flange. Hold the drive flange to prevent it from rotating, preferably using the special wrench 18G.1205, and remove the nut and washer after extracting the splitpin which locks the nut. Place a container under the flange to catch oil as it leaks out and withdraw the drive flange, preferably using a two-legged extractor. Prise out the old oil seal. Soak the new seal in light oil for at least one hour before fitting it. Check the face of the drive flange onto which the seal operates for scoring or damage and renew the drive flange if it is defective. Press the new seal back into place so that its lips face into the differential. Refit the drive flange and torque load the nut to a load of 240 to 280 lb/ft (36 kg m) before reconnecting the propeller shaft. Check the level of the oil in the rear axle and top up as necessary.

8:3 The rear suspension

Suspension is by semi-elliptic leaf springs, rubber mounted, and the shackles are fitted with rubber bushes of the flexible type (see **FIG 8:5**).

The rear hydraulic dampers are of the Telescopic type. All working parts are submerged in oil and no adjustment is required or provided.

A radius rod is fitted to the right hand side of the rear axle housing to stabilize the rear axle during acceleration and deceleration.

The radius rod is of cast alloy construction and is fitted with a rubber bush at each end to insulate road noise from the rear axle to the body structure.

A 'U' shaped bracket is welded to the right hand side of the rear axle housing, and a similar bracket is welded to the body structure near the front end of the rear spring.

Road spring:

1 The rear shackle attachment of the spring is shown in **FIG 8:5**. Raise the rear end of the car and place it securely onto stands under the chassis member. Remove the road wheel. Remove the nuts and washers 2 from either side of the shackle pin. Remove the nut

and washer 3 so that the shackle plate 4 can be taken off. Support the axle with a small jack underneath it. Fit a slave nut onto the spring bolt 5, to protect the threads, and partially drift out the bolt in the direction of the arrow so that the outer shackle plate can be released from the shackle pin 6 and swivelled out of the way. Withdraw the shackle pin 6 and its two rubber bushes 7.

2 Refer to **FIG 8:4**. Disconnect the lower damper attachment by removing the nuts, washer and bush 3, carefully noting the position of the rubber bush. Remove the nut, spring washer and bolt 4 that secure the front end of the spring to the frame. Take off the U-bolt nuts 5 while supporting the spring 6. Lower the spring after removing the damper mounting plate 7 and the lower rubber mounting plate and rubber 8. The spring 6 can then be lifted out from under the car, collecting the upper mountings and noting the position of the wedge 8. Withdraw the U-bolts 9 so that the bump rubber can be removed.

The parts are refitted in the reverse order of removal, using new rubber mounts and bushes if the old ones are worn, perished or damaged. Check the spring for cracked leaves or other damage and renew it if it is defective. Make sure that the spring wedge is correctly positioned. Old eye bushes can be pressed out as shown in inset 10 and new ones pressed back into place.

8:4 The dampers

The damper attachment is shown in **FIG 8:6**. The dampers are sealed telescopic units that cannot be repaired if they are defective. The damper is removed by taking off the attachments in the numerical order shown in the figure and is refitted in the reverse order of removal. Check that the rubber bushes are all in good condition before refitting the damper.

Testing:

Specialized test equipment is required to check that the dampers are acting with full efficiency. Equipment is just lately coming into use which will allow the dampers to be tested without removing them from the car, but do not expect every agent to have it and even the test equipment for checking dampers when they have been removed is not always held.

The dampers are weak if the car keeps pitching after going over a bump in the road, and they can be roughly checked by bouncing the suspension and checking that the oscillations are damped out.

The damper must be renewed if it is mechanically damaged, such as with oil leaks, bent ram or dented body.

A check can be made to find a defective damper, though if it passes the test it is no guarantee that it is operating at its full efficiency. Mount the damper vertically in the padded jaws of a vice and pump it up and down, using short strokes about the mid-point. This will ensure that any air is expelled from the fluid and driven to the top of the damper. Gradually increase the length of the strokes until they are reaching the full travel of the damper. If the damper operates noisily, has pockets of weak or no resistance (especially when changing direction) or is too stiff to move by hand it is defective and should be renewed. A rough guide as to condition can be made by comparing the force to that required on a new damper.

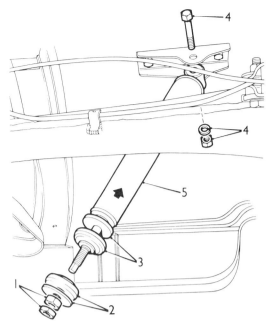

FIG 8:6   Rear damper attachments

Unless a damper is being changed because of mechanical damage, it is advisable to renew dampers in axle pairs.

8:5 Removing the rear axle

The method is shown in **FIG 8:7**.

1 Raise the rear of the car and support it securely on stands positioned under the body forward of the axle. Disconnect the propeller shaft, after making aligning marks 2, by taking out the nuts and bolts 3. Remove both road wheels.

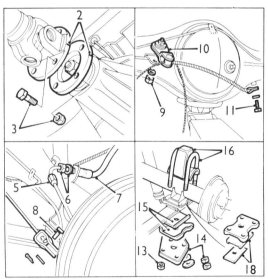

FIG 8:7   Rear axle removal

2 Disconnect the brake pipe. Undo the union nut 5, while holding the flexible hose 7, then unscrew the locknut 6 so that the flexible hose can be freed from the chassis bracket. Hydraulic fluid will drain through, so plug the pipe and use a container to catch spillage. Disconnect the handbrake cables from the levers on the brakes, by removing the clevis pins 8. Remove the nut and washer 9 so that the compensating lever 10 can be freed from the axle. Remove the bolt 11 that secures the handbrake cable clip.

3 Disconnect the radius rod.

4 Support the rear axle, preferably with a trolley jack under the differential. Remove the U-bolt nuts 13 from both sides. The lower damper attachment 14 to the plate need not be disconnected as the damper and plate can be swung to one side. Remove the lower mountings 15. Remove the U-bolts and bump stops 16 from each side and lift the axle up over a spring on one side of the car and out onto the floor. Remove the upper mountings 18, noting the positions of the wedges.

The axle is refitted in the reverse order of removal. Tighten the U-bolt nuts 13 to a torque load of 14 lb/ft (1.9 kg m). Renew any mounting rubbers that are worn or damaged.

Once the axle is in place and the parts reconnected, fill and bleed then adjust the braking system (see **Chapter 11**).

8:6 Fault diagnosis

(a) Noisy axle

1 Incorrect or insufficient lubricant
2 Worn bearings
3 Worn gears
4 Damaged or broken gear teeth
5 Incorrect adjustments on reassembly
6 General wear

(b) Excessive backlash

1 Worn gears, bearings
2 Worn drive shaft splines
3 Worn universal joints
4 Loose wheel attachments

(c) Oil leakage

1 Defective oil seal in hub
2 Defective oil seal in pinion
3 Defective gasket
4 Blocked breather
5 Overfilled rear axle

(d) Vibration

1 Propeller shaft out of balance
2 Worn universal joints
3 Defective centre bearing
4 Propeller shaft assembled out of phase

(e) Rattles

1 Worn damper rubber bushes
2 Dampers loose
3 U-bolts loose
4 Loose spring clips
5 Worn bushes in spring eyes shackles or radius rod
6 Broken spring leaves

(f) Settling

1 Weak or broken spring leaves
2 Badly worn shackles and bushes

(g) Axle knock

1 Badly worn splines on drive shafts
2 Worn universal joints

CHAPTER 9

FRONT SUSPENSION AND HUBS

9:1 Description

The components of the righthand front suspension and hub are shown in **FIG 9:1**. The lefthand side suspension is similar but note that many of the parts are handed and cannot be interchanged between sides.

The road wheel is attached to the hub 48, which also has the brake disc 58 attached to it, by the bolts 59. The hub rotates about the stud axle of the swivel pin 1 on two opposed, tapered bearings 50 and 51 and is secured to stub axle by the nut 53. The swivel pin also carries the dust shield 60 for the disc brake, and the brake caliper 61.

The hydraulic damper 17 is mounted onto the frame of the car and its arm carries at the outer end the ball joint for the top attachment of the swivel pin, so that the damper arm acts as an upper wishbone. The lower end of the swivel pin screws into the lower link 23 which is in turn mounted between the outer ends of the lower arms 30 and 31. The link is mounted on a pivot pin 24 so that the suspension is free to move vertically. Horizontal movement of the suspension is limited by the tie rod assembly 42. The inboard ends of the lower arms are free to pivot about the eye bolt 32 and the rear arm 30 is splined to the torsion bar 37. The rear end of the torsion

bar is attached to the frame and the weight of the car, and road shocks are taken by the restoring force when this bar is twisted. The suspension oscillations are damped out by the damper 17.

9:2 Maintenance

1 At intervals of 6000 miles (10,000 kilometres) grease through all four grease nipples on the front suspension (two per side). Greasing is best carried out with the car jacked up so that the weight is taken off the suspension and the grease can pass through easily. Turn the steering to full lock to make access to the grease nipples easier. Wipe the nipple clean and use a grease gun to pump in fresh grease. Wipe away surplus grease and make sure that none has gone onto the tyres or flexible brake hoses.

2 At intervals of 12,000 miles (20,000 kilometres), the front hub assemblies should be removed, cleaned, checked and refitted after packing with fresh grease. **Removing the grease cap and packing extra grease around the outside bearing is not sufficient as dirt can be forced into the bearing and the inner bearing may be running dry.**

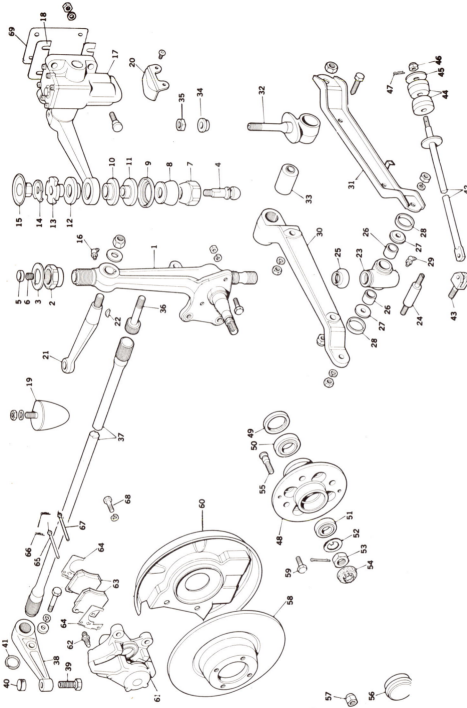

FIG 9:1 Front suspension components

Key to Fig 9:1 1 Swivel pin and stub axle RH 2 Locknut for ball pin 3 Tab washer for ball pin 4 Ball pin 5 Seat for ball pin 6 Spring for ball pin 7 Retaining nut for ball pin 8 Tab washer 15 Reaction pad 16 Grease nipple 17 Clip for dust cover 9 Clip for dust cover 10 Lower bush 11 Housing for lower bush 12 Upper bush 13 Housing for upper bush 21 Steering arm—RH 22 Key for lever 23 Lower link for swivel pin—RH 18 Camber shims 19 Bump rubber for shock absorber 20 Rebound rubber for link 28 Sealing ring 29 Grease nipple for lower link 30 Lower arm—rear 24 Fulcrum pin for link 25 Rubber seal for link 26 Bush for link 27 Thrust washer 36 Splined pivot pin bolt 37 Torsion bar 38 Lever reaction for torsion bar 31 Lower arm—front 32 Eyebolt 33 Bush for eyebolt 34 Bush 35 Nyloc nut tie-bar 44 Pad for tie-bar 45 Plain washer 46 Nut nyloc 39 Adjusting screw 40 Seat for screw 41 Circlip for torsion bar 42 Tie-bar 43 Fork 52 Keyed washer 53 Nut for stub axle 54 Retainer for nut 47 Safety clip for tie-rod 48 Wheel hub 49 Oil seal for hub 50 Inner bearing 51 Outer bearing brake to hub 60 Mud shield for disc 61 Brake caliper—RH 55 Wheel stud 56 Grease retaining cap 57 Wheel nut 58 Front brake disc—RH 59 Bolt for disc for retaining pin 67 Alternative pins for pads 62 Bleed screw for caliper 63 Brake pads 64 Anti-squeal shims 65 Retaining pin for pads 66 Clip 68 Bolts caliper to swivel pin 69 Camber plate (production)

84

9:3 Front hubs

A sectioned view of a hub assembly is shown in **FIG 9:2**.

Removal:

1 Jack up the front of the car and place it securely onto stands, after slackening the road wheel nuts slightly. Remove the road wheel.

2 Disconnect the caliper pipe first from the flexible hose and then from the caliper, using a container to catch the fluid as it drains and plugging the flexible hose to prevent further leakage of fluid. Take out the two bolts that secure the caliper to the suspension and slide the caliper off the brake disc.

3 Carefully prise off the grease cap 1 (see **FIG 9:2**). Remove the splitpin 2 that secures the nut retainer 3. Unscrew and remove both the nut retainer and the nut 4 and then slide off the keyed washer.

4 Pull the hub 6 off the stub axle, collecting the inner race of the outer bearing 8 as it comes free. Remove the oil seal 9 so that the inner race of the inner bearing can be withdrawn. The outer races of the bearings 10 can be drifted out of the hub if required, but if the bearings are satisfactory then they should be left in place.

Cleaning and examination:

Wipe out most of the old grease from the hub and bearings using newspaper or rags. The remainder of the grease can be washed out using petrol or paraffin. Wash the bearing races separately in clean fuel so that they do not pick up any dirt.

Check the circumference of the stub axle, onto which the oil seal acts, for scoring or damage.

Examine the outer races of the bearings, while still fitted to the hub, for any signs of wear, pitting or cracking. Similarly check the inner races. If any defects are found, both bearings must be renewed. **Note that bearings must be renewed completely as the inner and outer races are matched on manufacture.** Lubricate the inner races with light oil and check them in the outer races. Apply firm hand pressure and oscillate the race in its outer race to check for any roughness. If roughness is felt, try cleaning the bearings again and if it is still present after a thorough clean the bearing is defective and must be renewed.

Reassembly:

1 If the outer races 9 have been removed, drift the new ones back into place, preferably using the special tools 18G.134 and 18G.134.DM as shown in inset 12. If the special tools are not available, the races can be driven back using any suitable drift but take care to drive them in evenly and squarely.

2 Pack the inner race of the inner bearing liberally with high-melting point grease and fit it back into the hub. Soak the new oil seal in engine oil and refit it back to the hub, lips facing into the hub, so that it keeps the inner bearing in place.

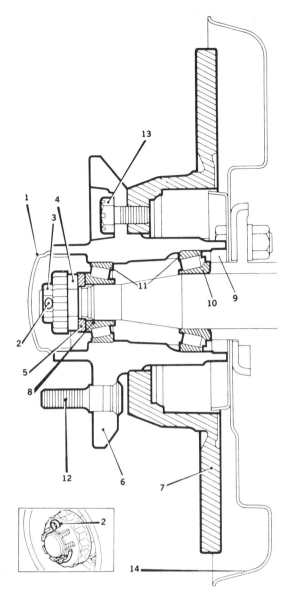

FIG 9:2 Sectional view of front hub assembly

Key to Fig 9:2 1 Hub grease cap 2 Split pin 3 Nut retainer 4 Nut 5 Keyed washer 6 Hub 7 Brake disc 8 Outer bearing cone 9 Oil seal 10 Inner bearing cone 11 Bearing cups 12 Wheel stud 13 Self locking nuts. Hub flange to disc 14 Disc shield

3 Slide the hub back into place on the stub axle. Pack inner race of the outer bearing with grease and slide it back into position on the stub axle. Refit the serrated washer and the stub axle nut followed by the nut retainer. Set the correct end float of .001 to .005 inch (.025 to .127 mm) and lock the nut retainer using a new splitpin. **The splitpin must be locked around the retainer circumferentially,** as shown in inset 12. Refit the grease cap 4, without filling it with grease.

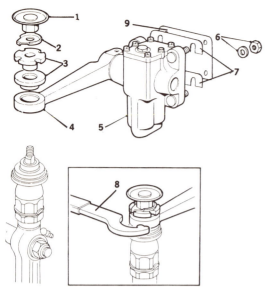

FIG 9:3   Damper removal

Key to Fig 9:3 1 Reaction pad 2 Tab washer 3 Upper bush and housing 4 Shock absorber arm 5 Shock absorber body 6 Locknut and washer (4) 7 Upper and lower camber shims 8 Spanner 18GA 1202 9 One piece production camber plate

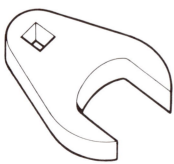

FIG 9:4   Removing swivel balljoint

FIG 9:5   Spanner 18GA 1192 for swivel balljoint

Adjustment:

The most accurate method is to use a DTI (Dial Test Indicator) mounted on the hub, with its stylus resting vertically on the end of the stub axle, and check the end float by pulling and pushing firmly on the hub. The average owner may not have a DTI and the following method will set the end float within limits (.001 to .005 inch).

With the hub fitted in place and secured with the washer 52 and nut 53, spin the hub and gradually tighten the nut to a torque load of 5 lb ft (.69 kg m) or until slight drag is felt on the hub as it rotates. This ensures that the bearings are pressed fully back into position and all clearances taken up. Stop spinning the hub and slacken back the nut until it is just free. Tighten the nut finger tight.

Locate the nut retainer 54 so that the splitpin hole in the stub axle is half covered by one of the arms of the retainer. Slacken back the nut and retainer together until a new splitpin can be fitted to lock the retainer, and the adjustment is then correct.

It should be noted that if the top of the tyre is rocked in and out when the bearing is at its maximum end float a considerable amount of movement will be felt on the wheel. **Do not reduce the hub end float below .001 inch (.025 mm) to ensure that the bearings are not preloaded.**

Once the adjustment has been correctly set, refit the brake parts in the reverse order of removal. On drum brakes it will most likely be necessary to readjust the brake. On disc brakes, the hydraulic system must be filled and bled, and the brake pedal pumped several times to allow the self-adjusting of the brake to take place. Full instructions for dealing with the brakes are given in **Chapter 11.**

9:4 The dampers

The damper attachments are shown in **FIG 9:3.**

Before renewing a damper because it is suspect, check the fluid level in it. The filler plug is fitted to the top cover-plate and should only be removed after the area has been thoroughly cleaned, taking care that dirt is not knocked down from the wheel arch into the damper when the plug is out. Access to the plug is easiest with the road wheel removed. If the level is low, top up using the recommended Armstrong damper fluid to the bottom of the filler plug hole. **Do not overfill as a small air space is essential for correct operation.**

The damper can be checked by bouncing the suspension and seeing that the oscillations are rapidly damped out. When the arm has been disconnected from the upper ball joint, pump the arm up and down to check the resistance. If the movement is erratic, check the fluid level again as air may be trapped in the fluid and only come to the top after filling and operation. If the movement is still erratic, or resistance excessive, the damper is internally defective and must be renewed. **The damper cannot be dismantled or serviced, nor must the arm be removed from the damper.**

Removal:

1 Slacken the road wheel nuts, jack up the car then place it onto stands. Remove the road wheel and support the suspension from underneath on a small jack.

2 Free the tabwasher and unscrew the reaction pad nut 1 while holding the upper bush housing with the spanner 18G.1202, as shown in the inset.

3 Remove the lockwasher 2 upper bush housing and upper bush 3. Support the swivel pin to prevent the hub assembly from falling down, and lift the arm of the damper of the upper ball joint. If the parts are to be left, tie the swivel pin up with a piece of cord to prevent it from leaning over and straining the brake flexible hose.

4 Take off the nuts and washers 6 that secure the damper 5. Retain and note position of any camber shims 7 and camber plate 9. Remove the damper from the car.

The parts are refitted in the reverse order of removal. Check the upper and lower bushes and renew them if they are damaged. Use a new reaction pad lockwasher. Tighten the reaction pad nut 3 to a torque of 35 to 40 lb ft (4.8 to 5.5 kg m), and the attachment nuts 6 to 26 to 28 lb ft (3.5 to 3.8 kg m).

9:5 The upper ball joint

The parts of the upper ball joint are shown in **FIG 9:1** as items 2 to 11 inclusive.

Dismantling:

1 Disconnect the damper arm from the ball joint as described in the previous section. Lift off the lower bush 10 and its housing 11. Remove the dust cover 8 and its retaining clip 9.

2 Unlock the tabwasher 3 and unscrew the retaining nut 7 while holding the locknut 2 as shown in **FIG 9:4**. A special open-ended sprocket spanner 18G.1192, shown in **FIG 9:5**, is designed for holding the locknut while unscrewing the retaining nut.

Remove the ballpin 4, its seat 5 and spring 6. Unscrew the locknut 7 from the top of the swivel pin.

Reassembly:

Wash the parts in clean fuel and examine them, paying particular attention to the ballpin 4 and its seat 5. Renew any defective or worn parts, noting that new tabwashers 3 and 14 will be required even if no other parts are worn. Renew the dust cover 8 if it is damaged or perishing.

1 Screw the locknut 2 back onto the swivel pin 1 and refit the tabwasher 3, spring 6, seat 5 and ballpin 4. Screw the retaining nut 7 down onto the swivel pin after lubricating the parts of the ballpin with grease, but make sure that the locknut 2 is fully slack.

2 Tighten the retainer nut 7 until the force required to produce articulation of the ball joint is 32 to 52 lb in (.38 to .56 kg m). Hold the retaining nut in this position with a ring spanner and prevent the swivel pin from turning. Use the special extension 18G.1202 and a suitable torque spanner to tighten up the locknut 2 to a torque of 70 to 80 lb ft (9.6 to 11.0 kg m). Lock the retaining nut and locknut using the tabwasher.

3 Reconnect the damper arm as instructed in the previous section.

9:6 The tie rods

The attachments are shown in **FIG 9:6**. Remove the spring clip 3, after jacking up the car and removing the road wheel, and undo the nut 4 so that it and its washer

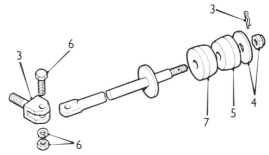

FIG 9:6   Tie rod assembly

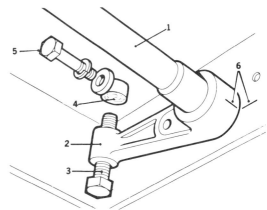

FIG 9:7   Torsion bar adjustment

Key to Fig 9:7   1 Torsion bar   2 Reaction lever
4 Adjusting screw seat   5 Lever locking bolt   6 Alignment marks

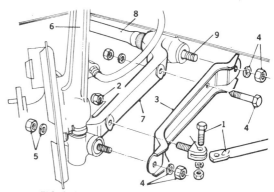

FIG 9:8   Lower suspension arm assembly

Key to Fig 9:8   1 Tie-bar and fork bolt   2 Tie-bar fork and nut   3 Outer arm   4 Bolts, nuts and washers outer arm to rear lower arm   5 Lower link pin nut to rear lower arm
6 Swivel pin assembly   7 Rear lower arm   8 Torsion bar
9 Splined eye bolt pivot pin.

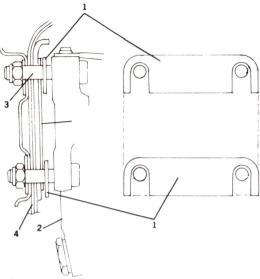

FIG 9:9   Camber shim fitting

Key to Fig 9:9   1 Camber shims   2 Shock absorber
3 Mounting studs   4 Section through valance panel mounting   5 One piece production camber plate

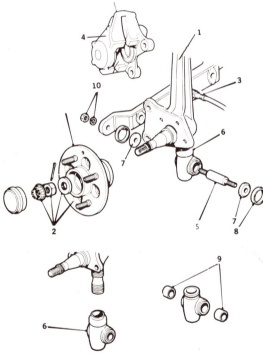

FIG 9:10   Swivel pin and lower link

Key to Fig 9:10   1 Swivel pin   2 Hub assembly removed
(Brake disc and shield removed)   3 Flexible brake pipe
4 Brake caliper   5 Lower link pin   6 Lower link   7 Thrust
washers   8 Sealing rings   9 Bushes lower link   10 Nut
and washer. Rear lower arm to link pin

can be removed as well as the outer pad 5. Remove the
nut, bolt and washer 6 to disconnect the tie rod from the
suspension and remove the tie rod assembly. If necessary,
remove the nut from behind the rear lower arm and take
off the fork 8 from the suspension arms.

Check the inner and outer pads 7 and 5, renewing them
if they are defective or damaged. Refit the tie rod in the
reverse order of removal.

9:7 The torsion bars
Checking trim height:

Stand the car on level ground, with two gallons of fuel
in the tank. The cooling system must be full and the oil
to the correct level in the engine and gearbox.

The measurement from the centre of the hub grease cap
vertically to the underside of the wheel arch should be
14.6 to 15 inch.

Fine trim adjustment:

1 Referring to **FIG 9:7** remove the lever locking bolt 5
   with spring washer and spacer.
2 Turn the adjusting screw 3 clockwise to increase the
   suspension height or anticlockwise to decrease. When
   making an adjustment to increase the height it is
   advisable to lift the vehicle by means of a jack under
   the front chassis member until the wheel is just clear
   of the ground.
3 Lower the vehicle to the ground and rock transversely
   to settle the suspension.
4 Check both sides of the vehicle for trim height. Refit
   and tighten the lever locking bolt.

Coarse trim adjustment:

When a greater range of adjustment is needed the
adjusting lever can be moved on to the next spline in
relation to the torsion bar. This raises or lowers the
suspension approximately 1 inch.

1 Apply the handbrake and chock the rear wheels.
2 Raise the car and fit suitable safety supports under
   the front chassis members.
3 Remove front wheels.
4 Disconnect the steering ball socket from the steering
   arm.
5 Place a jack under lower suspension arm and take the
   weight of the suspension.
6 Unlock the reaction pad nut 1 (**FIG 9:3**) holding the
   upper bush housing 3 with the special spanner
   18GA.1202. Remove the nut.
7 Remove the lockwasher, upper bush housing and bush.
8 Lower the suspension on to a wooden support block.
   **Do not allow the assembly to hang on the flexible
   brake hose.**
9 Referring to **FIG 9:7** remove the lever locking bolt 5
   and mark the lever in relation to the car body as shown
   at 6. **Do not mark the torsion bar.**
10 Turn the adjusting screw 3 to approximately the midway position taking care not to lose the hardened seat
   4.
11 Move the lever 2 forward from the torsion bar splines
   and re-engage one spline up or down as required.
12 Refit all components removed.

13 Check trim height and carry out fine adjustment as previously described.

14 Check and adjust if necessary front wheel camber (see **Section 9:8**) and toe-in (**Section 10:8**).

Torsion bar removal:

Referring to **FIG 9:8** carry out operations 1 to 8 given for coarse trim adjustments. Then proceed as follows:

1 Disconnect the tie bar from the tie bar fork. Remove the fork from the lower arms.

2 Remove the front lower outer suspension arms 3.

3 Remove the nut and spring washer 5 securing the lower link pin to the rear lower arm 7.

4 Remove the swivel pin assembly from the lower arm and suspend it by the steering arm from a convenient point on the valance panel box section using a wire hook.

5 Using a soft faced hammer knock the lower arm backward to release it from the splined eyebolt pin 9.

6 Remove the lever locking bolt 5 (**FIG 9:7**) at the rear of the torsion bar. Withdraw the torsion bar complete taking care not to lose the adjusting screw seat 4 (**FIG 9:7**). **Do not mark the torsion bar with punches chisel or file marks as these can cause failure. Use only coloured crayon or paint.**

Refitting is the reversal of the removal procedure but before tightening the nut on the splined eyebolt pivot pin or the bolts securing front lower arm to rear lower arm lower the vehicle to the ground, bounce the suspension several times and recheck trim height.

9:8 Camber adjustment

Provision is made for adjusting camber but this work should where possible be carried out by a service agent having the specialized equipment for checking steering geometry as a whole.

Suspension height must first be checked as described in the previous Section. **FIG 9:9** shows how shims of .062 thickness are fitted in pairs with their slots downwards between the damper body and the valance panel. The same number of shims must be fitted to top and bottom bolts up to a maximum of two pairs. Each shim fitted or removed alters the camber $\frac{1}{2}$ deg. A one-piece camber plate 5 is fitted in production. This can also be seen at 69 in **FIG 9:1**. To fit or remove shims:

1 Apply the handbrake. Jack up the car under the lower suspension arm and place a safety stand under.

2 Slacken all four damper retaining nuts just sufficiently to allow the damper to be pulled away from the valance panel.

3 Add or remove shims in pairs as required.

4 Tighten the retaining nuts evenly to a torque of 30 to 45 lb ft.

9:9 Swivel pin lower link

Dismantling (see FIG 9:10):

1 Jack up the front suspension under the front lower arm and fit suitable safety supports. Remove the road wheel.

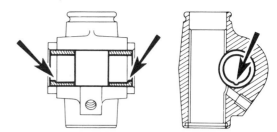

FIG 9:11 Showing correct position of bushes in lower link

2 Disconnect the flexible pipe 3. Plug the pipe to minimize fluid loss.

3 Remove the brake caliper 4 and the hub grease cap. Remove splitpin, nut retainer, hub nut 2 and keyed washer. Remove the hub assembly complete with disc and shield.

4 Remove the remaining nut and spring washer from the lower link pin 5. Swing the swivel pin 1 forward and remove the rubber sealing rings 8 and thrust washers 7 from the lower link 6.

5 Remove the lower link pin. Unscrew the lower link from the swivel pin. Drive out the lower link bushes 9.

Examination:

Discard all the old seals and dust covers, fitting new ones on reassembly. Thoroughly clean the threads on the swivel pin and lower link so that they can be checked for wear. If the threads are worn then both the lower link and swivel pin must be renewed (disconnect the damper arm from the upper ball joint to remove the swivel pin assembly).

Examine the thrust washers and renew them if they are worn.

If the bushes 14 are worn, drift them out and press in new bushes, making sure that the grooves are aligned as shown in **FIG 9:11**. Once the new bushes have been fitted they must be line-reamed to .688±.0005 inch (17.48±.013 mm).

Check the pin 12 for wear or scoring and renew it if it is defective.

Reassembly:

The parts are reassembled in the reverse order of dismantling. Screw the lower link 13 fully back into place on the swivel pin then unscrew it one complete turn and fit the parts to it in this position.

Bleed and adjust the brakes after refitting the hub and setting it to its correct end float.

9:10 Fault diagnosis

(a) Wheel wobble

1 Worn hub bearings
2 Weak front torsion bars
3 Uneven tyre wear
4 Worn suspension linkage
5 Loose wheel attachments

(b) Bottoming of suspension

1 Check 2 in (a)
2 Rebound rubbers worn or missing
3 Dampers defective

(c) Heavy steering

1 Neglected swivel pin lubrication
2 Incorrect suspension geometry (caused by damaged components)

(d) Excessive tyre wear

1 Check 4 in (a); 3 in (b) and 2 in (c)

(e) Rattles

1 Neglected lubrication
2 Damper mountings loose
3 Worn bushes

CHAPTER 10

THE STEERING SYSTEM

10:1 Description

All the components of the steering system are shown in
FIG 10:1.

As can be seen from the figure, rack and pinion steering
is fitted as standard. Though the figure may look complicated the system is simple with the minimum of moving
parts and the most direct connections possible. As a result
the steering is precise and the driver has good 'feel'.

The steering wheel 1 is splined to the upper inner
column 12 and the column 12 is in turn connected to the
lower column 30 by a flexible coupling 29. A flexible
joint connects the lower cloumn to the pinion of the
steering unit. Rotation of the steering wheel will then act
to rotate the pinion by the same amount. The teeth of the
pinion mesh with those of the rack so that rotation of the
pinion drives the rack from side to side in the housing.
Tie rods and ball joints connect the ends of the rack
directly to the steering arms on the suspension swivel pins.

Shims are fitted so that wear in the parts can be taken
up by removing some of the shims from the pack.

10:2 Maintenance

There are no lubrication points in the system as the
parts are lubricated on manufacture. The tie rod ends are
sealed after manufacture and require no greasing.

When carrying out the 6000 mile service, the system
should be checked through for excessive play or worn
gaiters and security of parts. Any gaiters that are damaged
must be renewed before they actually split and allow dirt
to enter. If dirt has entered a tie rod end there is no method
of flushing out the dirt and the only cure is to fit a new tie
rod end. If the gaiter is renewed before it has actually
split, pack a little extra grease into the tie rod end before
fitting a new gaiter.

10:3 The steering wheel and steering column lock

The steering wheel and its attachments are shown in
FIG 10:1.

Steering wheel:

Remove the safety pad 2 by carefully prising it out of
the steering wheel 1. Take out the five screws 39 which
secure the cowls 40 and 42 so that the cowls can be
removed. Unscrew the nut 4 and remove it with its lockwasher 6. Mark the steering wheel hub and end of the
inner column 12, so that the steering wheel can be refitted
in the correct alignment. It may be possible to remove the
steering wheel by giving firm and even blows, with the
palm of the hand, at the base of the spokes. If the steering
wheel cannot be removed by hand, use a universal
steering wheel puller.

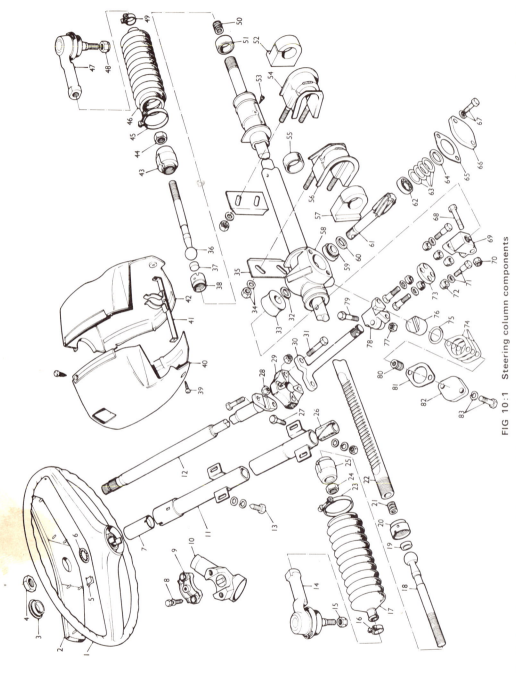

FIG 10:1   Steering column components

Key to Fig 10:1 1 Steering wheel 2 Safety pad 3 Motif 4 Nut 5 Clip 6 Lockwasher 7 Upper bush 8 Shear-head bolt 9 Clamp plate 10 Steering lock 11 Upper outer column 12 Upper inner column 13 Bolt for upper clamp 14 Tie rod end 15 Self-locking nut 16 Small clip 17 Bellows 18 Tie rod 19 Ball seat 20 Locknut 21 Thrust spring 22 Rack 23 Large clip 24 Locknut 25 Ball housing 26 Lower bush 27 Bolt 28 Nut 29 Flexible coupling 30 Lower column 31 Bolt 32 Cowl half 33 Sealing washer 34 Nut and plain washer 35 Locating plate 36 Tie rod 37 Ball seat 38 Locknut 39 Screw 40 Cowl half 41 Cowl support 42 Cowl half 43 Ball housing 44 Large clip 45 Large clip 46 Bellows 47 Tie rod end 48 Self-locking nut 49 Small clip 50 Thrust spring 51 Rack bearing 52 Mounting rubber 53 Screw for rack bearing 54 Rack clamp 55 Sealing rubber 56 Rack clamp 57 Mounting rubber 58 Pinion housing 59 Pinion bearing 60 Washer 61 Pinion 62 Pinion bearing 63 Shim 64 Shim .60 inch (1.524 mm) 65 Shim gasket .010 inch (.254 mm) 66 End cover 67 Bolt and spring washer 69 Flexible joint half 70 Nut 71 Shouldered bolt 72 Rubber bush 73 Joint plate 74 Shim 75 O-ring 76 Support yoke 77 Nut 78 Flexible joint half 79 Bolt 80 Thrust spring 81 Joint 82 End cover 83 Bolt and spring washer For alternative type parts (items 75 and 80) see **Fig 10:6**

Refit the steering wheel in the reverse order of removal. Make sure that the previously made marks align or, if a new steering wheel is being fitted, set the front wheels in the straight-ahead position and refit the steering wheel so that the spokes are level. Tighten the steering wheel nut 4 to a torque of 32 to 37 lb ft. When refitting the safety pad 2, locate it by the outer pins first as this will ensure that the pad has an even gap on both sides.

Steering column lock (see FIG 10:2):

The lock is secured to the column by special shear-bolts. Remove the steering wheel followed by the lower facia and instrument panel (see **Chapter 13**). Disconnect the battery (which should already have been done when removing the instrument panel). Disconnect the switch harness from the loom at the connector 4. Drill out the old shear screws 5, or drill them and use a suitable proprietary tool to unscrew them. **In either case take great care not to damage the threads of the switch itself.** Remove the clamp plate and switch.

For electrical details (see **Section 12:11**).

The switch is refitted in the reverse order of removal, using new shear-head screws 5. Refit the switch, tightening the shear-head screws 5 just sufficiently to hold the switch in place, and locating it using the grub screw of the clamp plate seating into the recess in the column. Check the full operation of the switch. When satisfied that the switch is operating satisfactorily, tighten the shear screws 5 until their heads break off at the waisted portion.

Refit the lower facia, instrument panel and steering wheel in the reverse order of removal.

10:4 Upper steering column

The attachments of the upper steering column are shown in **FIG 10:3**.

Removal:

1 Remove the steering wheel (see previous section) as well as the lower facia panel and instrument panel (see **Chapter 13**). Slacken the screw that retains the combined switches, see insert 4, disconnect their

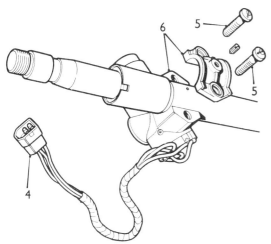

FIG 10:2 Steering lock attachments

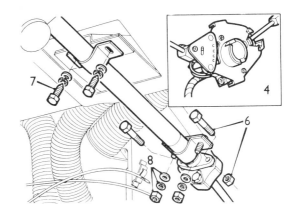

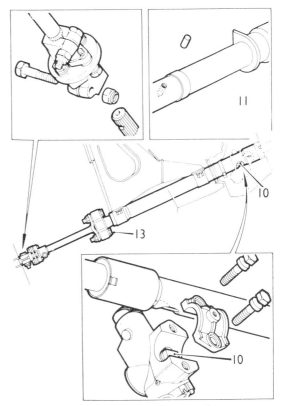

FIG 10:3 The upper column attachments

leads from the harness at the connector and remove the switches. Disconnect the harness for the steering column lock switch at its connector.

2 Remove the two sets of nuts and washers 6 that secure the inner upper column to the flexible coupling. Remove the two sets of bolts and washers 7 that secure the upper clamp of the outer column. Support the column and take off the two sets of nuts and washers 8 that secure the lower clamp. The upper steering column assembly can then be removed from the car.

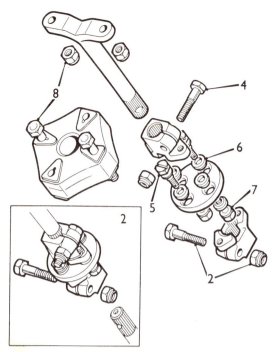

FIG 10:4   The steering column coupling

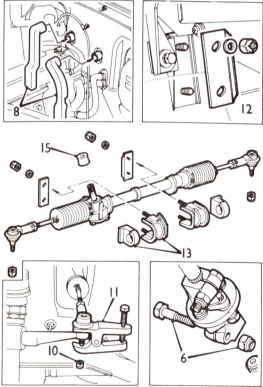

FIG 10:5   Removing the steering rack unit

Refitting:

The parts are refitted in the reverse order of removal. Engage the steering column lock 10 to lock the column. Centralize the steering rack as shown in inset 11 and reconnect the parts. Tighten the coupling bolts 6 to a torque load of 20 to 22 lb ft (2.77 to 3.04 kg m). The nuts 8 and bolts 7 are tightened to 14 to 18 lb ft (1.94 to 2.49 kg m).

If the lower bush (item 26 in **FIG 10:1**) is worn or damaged, it can be renewed when the upper column assembly has been removed from the car.

If a new coupling has been fitted, break and remove the band by compressing the coupling.

Upper bush:

This can be renewed without having to remove the upper column assembly. Disconnect the battery, remove the steering wheel (see previous section), slacken the screw which secures the combined switch assembly and slide the switch assembly off, over the top of the inner column.

If care is taken the old bush can be hooked out and the new one pressed back into place with a suitable piece of pipe as a sleeve. If hand pressure is not sufficient, use a large washer and nut to draw the bush back in. When refitting the new bush, make sure that the chamfered end enters first and that the slots in the bush align with the depression in the outer column.

10:5 Steering column couplings

The parts are shown in **FIG 10:4**.

Remove the upper steering column assembly, as described in the previous section. Remove the pinch bolt and nut 2 that secure the lower coupling to the pinion shaft on the steering rack unit. The lower steering column assembly complete can now be removed from the car.

Remove the pinch bolt and nut 5, and pull the flexible joint assembly complete free from the lower column splines. The lexible coupling can be freed from the column by taking out the bolts 8.

Unlock and remove the four shouldered bolts 5 from the flexible joint. Remove the rubber eashers 6, noting how their conical faces mate with the countersunk face of the joint plate. Collect the plain washers 7 from the bolts.

The parts are reassembled and refitted in the reverse order of removal, after cleaning and renewing worn parts. If a new flexible coupling (item 29 in **FIG 10:1**) is fitted, leave the band on the coupling until the coupling has been bolted back into place. Once the coupling is in place, break the compressing band and discard it.

When aligning the parts, lock the steering column with its lock and centralize the rack unit, as described in the previous section. Leave the steering rack unit centralized when refitting the steering wheel, so that the spokes are horizontal in the straight-ahead position. **Remove the centralizing pin before attempting to drive the car or check the action of the steering column lock.**

10:6 Removing the steering rack unit

1 Remove the lower facia and instrument panel (see **Chapter 13**). Disconnect the leads for the steering column lock switch and combined switch at their connectors with the harness.

2 Remove the nuts and bolts that secure the upper steering column outer case (items 7 and 8 in **FIG 10:3**) while supporting the column. Remove the pinch bolt and nut that secures the lower flexible joint to the steering rack pinion shaft (item 2 in **FIG 10:4**). Lift out the steering column assembly.

3 Raise and firmly support the front of the car or work over a pit. For the remainder of the removal operation, refer to **FIG 10:5**. Remove the two heater drain pipes 8. Take off the nuts 10 from both of the tie rod ends and disconnect the tie rod ends from the steering arms on the suspension, using an extractor such as that shown at 11. **Never hammer directly on the end of the threaded pin of the tie rod end as even with a slave nut fitted to protect the threads internal damage will be caused to the tie rod end.**

4 Remove the nuts 12 which secure the rack clamp brackets to the bulkhead. Mark and note the position of the packing piece in relation to the bulkhead and remove the packing pieces. Remove the clamp brackets and mounting rubbers 13, and slide out the rack unit through a wheel arch opening. Remove the pinion seal 15.

The unit is refitted in the reverse order of removal. When all the parts are in place and reconnected, check the front wheel alignment as described in **Section 10:8**.

10:7 Servicing the steering rack unit

The components of the unit are shown in **FIG 10:1**. Remove the unit as described in the previous section.

Dismantling:

1 Slacken the locknuts 24 and 44. Unscrew the tie rod ends 14 and 47 from the tie rods 18 and 36 and then screw off the two locknuts 24 and 44. Free the clips 16, 23, 45 and 49 then slide the bellows 17 and 46 off from the rack housing and tie rods (catching the oil in a container).

2 The locknuts 20 and 38 are staked down into the slots of the housings 25 and 43. Prise out the locking from the slot, noting that it will be necessary to fit new locknuts 20 and 38 on reassembly. Hold the locknut and unscrew the housing. Special spanners 18GA.580/1, are made for holding the locknut and undoing the housing. Remove the tie rods 18 and 36, collecting their ball seats 19 and 37 as well as the springs 21 and 50. Prise out the locking indents that secure the locknuts 20 and 38 to the rack 22 and unscrew the locknuts from the rack.

3 Take out the pan-headed screw 53 and remove the rack bearing 51 from the housing. Remove the two sets of bolts and washers 83 so that the cover 82, joint washer 81 and shim pack 74 can be removed from the housing. Withdraw the rack support yoke 76 and remove the spring 80 and O-ring 75 from it.

4 Remove the two sets of bolts 67 securing the pinion cover 66. Remove the pinion cover followed by the shim gasket 65, shim 64 and shim pack 63. Push out the pinion shaft 61 so that the pinion bearing 62 is removed with it. Take out the oil seal 32 and extract the pinion bearing 59 with its washer 60. Slide the rack 22 out of the housing.

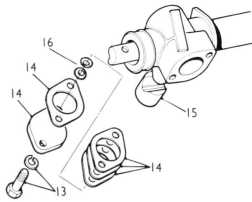

FIG 10:6   Rack support yoke. Alternative type

Key to Fig 10:6   13 Rack yoke cover plate bolts   14 Cover plate, shims and joint washer   15 Rack support yoke   16 "O" ring and thrust washer

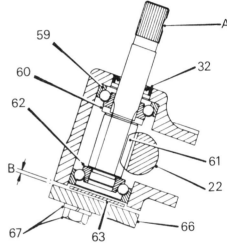

FIG 10:7   Sectional view of rack unit

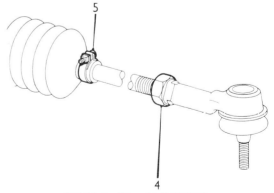

FIG 10:8   Tie rod adjustment

Examination:

Thoroughly clean all the components by washing them in fuel. Examine the rack and pinion for cracks, wear or damage, paying particular attention to the teeth. Check the bellows for signs of splitting or cracking. Renew any components that are damaged or badly worn.

Reassembly:

1 Refit the bearing 51 to the housing and secure it with the screw 53. Coat the screw with sealing compound before refitting it and **make sure that it does not protrude through into the bore of the bearing.** If a new bearing is being fitted, position it so that its flats are offset to the retaining screw hole. Use a .119 inch (3.0 mm) drill through the retaining hole in the housing to drill through the new bearing, for the attachment screw. **Remove all swarf and burrs from the inside of the bearing.**

2 Refit the rack 22 into the housing. Fit the bearing 59 and washer 60 to the pinion 61 and slide the assembly back into the housing. The rack should be centralized by inserting a peg through the housing and rack (through the hole in the housing normally covered by the sealing rubber 55). Insert the pinion assembly so that when the teeth are meshed the locating groove **A** in the pinion is parallel to and on the same side as the rack teeth, as shown in **FIG 10:7.**

3 Refit the bearing 62. Fit sufficient shims 63 and 64 to ensure that the shim pack stands proud of the end of the housing. Refit the coverplate 66, omitting the shim gasket 65, and tighten the bolts 67 by hand only. Use feeler gauges to measure the gap **B** between the cover and housing, shown in **FIG 10:7.** Remove the cover and bolts and adjust the shim pack thickness, by selective fitting of shims, until the gap **B** (still without the shim gasket 65 fitted) is correct at .011 to .013 inch (.279 to .330m). When the shim pack has been correctly adjusted, remove the cover and refit it with the shim gasket 65 in place, making sure that the shim 64 is nearest to the end cover end. Dip the threads of the bolts 67 into sealing compound and use them, with their spring washers fitted, to secure the cover 66. Tighten the bolts 67 to a torque of 15 to 18 lb ft. Fit a new pinion seat 32 back into place. Remove the centralizing peg.

4 Refit the rack support yoke 76, joint 81 and cover 82. Secure the parts in place with the bolts 83. While turning the pinion backwards and forwards through an angle of 180 degrees tighten the bolts 83 until it is just possible to rotate the pinion using a force of 12 to 14 lb in. Use feeler gauges to measure the clearance between the housing and the cover. Remove the cover and its attachment bolts. Refit the spring 80 and O-ring 75 to the yoke 76. **FIG 10:6** shows alternative type in which thrust spring and large O-ring are replaced by thrust washer and small O-ring 16. Make up a shim pack 74 which is .002 to .005 inch (.05 to .13mm) greater in thickness than the gap measured with feeler gauges. Refit the cover and secure it by tightening the bolts 83 to a torque of 15 to 18 lb ft, not forgetting to refit the lockwashers. Check the force required to start the pinion rotating. **The force required must not exceed 25 lb in (.28 kg m).**

5 Screw new locknuts 20 and 38 back onto the ends of the rack, right to the ends of the threads. Refit the springs 21 and 50. Slide the tie rods 18 and 36 back through the housings 25 and 43 and fit the seats 19 and 37 back into place. Screw the housings 25 and 43 back onto the rack 22 until the tie rod is pinched. Screw the locknuts 20 and 38 outwards until they contact the housings 25 and 43, **making sure that the tie rods are still pinched.** Hold the locknuts and slacken the housings outwards by $\frac{1}{8}$ turn each to allow the tie rod to articulate. Hold the housing firmly, so that it does not turn about the rack, and tighten the locknut up to it to a torque of 33 to 37 lb ft (4.6 to 5.6 kg m). The tie rod should now articulate smoothly and require a force of 32 to 52 lb in (.37 to .6 kg m) to make it move. Punch the edges of the locknuts into the slots in the rack and housings to lock the parts.

6 Slip the bellows 17 and 46 into place over the tie rods. Screw the tie rod end locknuts 24 and 44 back onto the tie rods. Screw back on the tie rod ends 14 and 47 so that the dimension between the ball centres of tie rod end and tie rod ball are equal at 43.7 inch (110.9 cm, then tighten the locknuts 24 and 44 up to them to secure them.

7 Attach the bellows 46 to the housing and rack using the clips 45 and 49. Make sure that the sealing rubber 55 is in place over the centralizing hole in the case. Stand the unit up on end and pour in $\frac{1}{3}$ pint (190 cc) of Hypoid oil SAE.90 (API-GL.5). With the unit still standing upright, refit the other bellows 17.

10:8 Front wheel alignment

This should always be checked after the steering rack unit has been removed and refitted as well as when major work has been carried out on the front suspension. Incorrect front wheel alignment will show by excessive tyre wear, which leaves the edge of the tread worn to a characteristic feathered edge.

It is most advisable to take the car to an agent, who will check the alignment accurately using optical equipment or special gauges.

The front wheel alignment will be near the correct limits if both tie rod ends are set so that the length between ball centres on each tie rod is 43.7 inch (110.9cm).

The adjustment point for each tie rod is shown in **FIG 10:8. Both tie rods must be adjusted by an equal amount,** to ensure that the steering wheel spokes are horizontal when the wheels are straight-ahead.

If the owner wishes to check the alignment then a level piece of ground must be found. Some form of trammel will also make the task easier. The trammel rests on the ground and has two pointers mounted on it, at wheel centre height, which are just slightly less far apart than the inner wheel rims on the front wheels. Instead of measuring the total dimension only the gap between one pointer and the wheel rim need be measured, while making sure that the other pointer is in contact with the other wheel rim.

Drive the car onto level ground and set the front wheels to the straight-ahead position. The rack can be locked using a suitable peg. Push the car forwards to settle the bearings. Measure, as accurately as possible, the distance between the inner wheel rims at the front of the wheel and at wheel centre height. Mark the positions with chalk and push the car forwards so that the wheels turn exactly half a revolution and the chalk marks are again at wheel centre height, but at the rear of the wheels. **Never push the car backwards while checking the track.** Again measure the distance between the wheel rims at the chalk marks. The difference between the two measurements represents the front wheel alignment.

The correct setting is $\frac{1}{16}$ inch (1.6 mm) toe-in. If the setting is incorrect, slacken the locknuts 4 and the bellows clips 5. Screw the tie rods in or out of the tie rod ends so as to alter their effective length and the front wheel alignment. **Both tie rods have a righthand thread and they must both be of the same effective length between ball centres when the adjustments are complete.**

When the adjustment is correct, tighten the locknuts 4 to a torque of 40 to 45 lb ft and tighten the clips for the bellows.

10:9 Fault diagnosis

(a) Wheel wobble

1 Unbalanced wheels and tyres
2 Slack steering connections
3 Incorrect steering geometry.
4 Excessive play in the steering rack unit

5 Weak torsion bars on suspension
6 Worn or loose front hub bearings
7 Loose wheel attachments

(b) Wander

1 Check 2, 3 and 4 in (a)
2 Uneven tyre pressures
3 Uneven tyre wear
4 Weak dampers or rear springs
5 Body distorted so that front suspension not in line with rear axle

(c) Heavy steering

1 Check 3 in (a)
2 Very low tyre pressures
3 Neglected lubrication
4 Wheels out of alignment
5 Steering rack unit incorrectly adjusted
6 Steering column bent or misaligned
7 Steering column bushes tight
8 Steering flexible coupling or joint defective
9 Defective ball joints or tie rod ends

(d) Lost motion

1 Check 8 and 9 in (c)
2 Loose steering wheel or worn splines
3 Worn rack and pinion teeth
4 Worn suspension system or swivel pin swivels

NOTES

CHAPTER 11

THE BRAKING SYSTEM

11 : 1 Description

On all models disc brakes are fitted to the front and drum brakes at the rear. All four wheel brakes are operated by hydraulic pressure from the master cylinder when the brake pedal is pressed. The hydraulic pressure generated in the master cylinder is led to the brakes by a system of metal and flexible pipes.

The handbrake lever operates the rear brakes only using a system of cables to operate the brakes mechanically. **FIG 11 : 1** shows the layout of the braking system.

The disc front brakes, are of the standard fixed caliper type. Each half of the caliper contains a piston and under hydraulic pressure these two pistons move towards each other. As the pistons come together they clamp the rotating disc, attached to the wheel hub, between friction pads to exert the retarding force on the disc and consequently on the wheel and tyre. Seals are fitted between the piston and bore and these seals deform slightly when the piston moves to apply the brake. As soon as the hydraulic pressure is released, the seals return to their original shape and draw back the pistons to give a running clearance between the pads and disc. If the pads wear, the piston can slide through the seal, allowing wear to be taken up.

The drum rear brakes have one brake cylinder in each operating a leading and a trailing shoe. The shoes are automatically adjusted by application of the handbrake.

11 : 2 Maintenance

Fluid level:

At regular intervals check the level of the fluid in the master cylinder reservoir. **Wipe the top clean before removing the filler cap. Ensure that the level never falls to the danger mark on the outside of the reservoir.** Disc brakes being fitted, the level in the reservoir will slowly drop as the pads wear. Any sudden drop or increase in the rate of dropping indicates a leak in the system. **Check the system thoroughly and rectify and leaks found with the utmost urgency.** Use fluid to specification Leyland Australia HBF.6 or SAE.J.1703b (minimum boiling point 260°C). **The use of the incorrect fluid in the system can be extremely dangerous as some fluids will attack the material of the seals in the system, causing them to fail.**

Front brakes:

These are self-adjusting. At intervals of 6000 miles (10,000 kilometres) they should be checked for pad wear

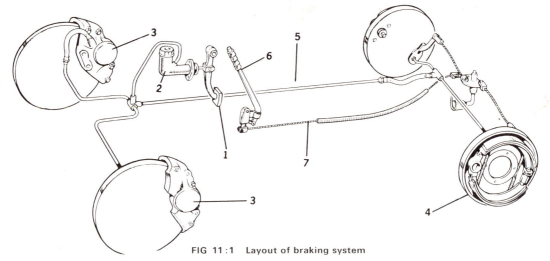

FIG 11:1   Layout of braking system

Key to Fig 11:1   1 Brake pedal   2 Master cylinder   3 Front brake calipers   4 Rear drum brakes   5 Brake pipes   6 Handbrake lever   7 Hand brake cables

and other defects. New pads must be fitted when the friction material on them has worn down to $\frac{1}{16}$ inch (1.6 mm).

The handbrake:

If handbrake retardation is poor, check through the system for defects before adjusting the cable. Make sure that the rear linings are not excessively worn, the cables and levers moving freely and that clevis pins on attachments are not excessively worn or sticking.

Handbrake cable adjustment:

1 Raise the rear of the car and support on axle stands. Adjust the rear brake shoes by applying the handbrake several times. Set the handbrake lever on the fourth notch of the ratchet and check for braking effect on rear wheels.
2 If braking effect is insufficient release the handbrake and referring to **FIG 11:2** slacken locknut 3. Turn the adjusting nut 4 clockwise to tighten the cable, holding the outer cable to prevent that from turning. Tighten the locknut.

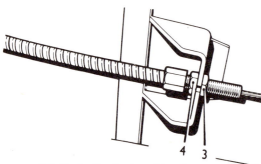

FIG 11:2   Handbrake cable adjustment

3 Check braking with handbrake on fourth notch and repeat operation 2 as necessary.
4 Release the handbrake and check that the wheels rotate freely.

Brake servo:

Where a servo unit is fitted (see **Section 11:9**) the servo air filter should be cleaned every 12,000 miles using compressed air at low pressure. Do not use cleaning fluid or lubricant of any kind on the filter. To remove the filter lever the dome 1 in **FIG 11:3** off the valve cover with a screwdriver. When refitting, ensure that the air valve spring 3 is securely located on to the valve, refit the filter 2 and snap fit the dome 1 on the valve cover.

Preventative maintenance:

Never use any fluid in the system except the type recommended. Fluid that has been drained or bled from the system is best discarded.

Absolute cleanliness is essential when working on any part of the hydraulic system.

When carrying out the 6000 mile service, check the brake pipes and flexible hoses for damage, leaks or corrosion. Have an assistant apply heavy pressure to the brake pedal, with all the parts assembled, and check through the system for leaks or weak spots. Corroded metal pipes or defective flexible hoses should be renewed as they will be a weak point that may fail under the stress of heavy braking. The brake pedal must not be pressed when the brake drums are off, or a disc brake caliper removed, otherwise the pressure will force out the pistons.

It is recommended that the fluid is drained out of the system at intervals of 18 months or 18,000 miles and the system refilled and bled using fresh fluid. Brake fluid absorbs moisture from the air which lowers its boiling point, and it is for this reason that the fluid should be renewed, otherwise it may boil in the brakes under the stress of heavy braking and cause brake fade.

It is also recommended that the system is flushed through with methylated spirits at intervals of 3 years and all the components dismantled and checked for wear, followed by reassembly using all new seals. Any components found to be worn or defective should be renewed.

11 : 3 Flexible hoses

When removing or refitting a flexible hose, the flexible portion must never be twisted or strained.

The attachment of a typical flexible hose is shown in **FIG 11 : 4**. To disconnect the hose, hold it at its hexagons 3 with a spanner and undo the union nut 1 with another spanner, taking care not to twist the metal pipe.

Still holding the hose with a spanner, undo the locknut 2 and remove it complete with its lockwasher. The hose can then be withdrawn from its bracket. Refit the hose in the reverse order of removal, noting that the system must be filled and bled.

If a hose is blocked and cannot be cleared by blowing through it, it is defective. **Do not attempt to clear blocked hoses by poking wire through them.**

The average safe life of a flexible hose is 5 years. For this reason it is advisable to renew the flexible hoses after $4\frac{1}{2}$ years (when changing the hydraulic fluid).

11 : 4 Renewing the friction pads

The method of renewing the friction pads on the disc brakes is shown in **FIG 11 : 5**.

1 Jack up the front of the car and remove the road wheel.
2 Remove the spring clips 3 and withdraw the pad retaining pins 4. On some cars long splitpins 4A are used instead of pins and clips. The pads and anti-squeal shims 5 can then be withdrawn from the caliper. If the pads are difficult to withdraw, pass a length of wire or cord through the holes in the pad and use a wooden handle through the wire to give good purchase so that the pads can be pulled out. The pads must be renewed if the friction material has worn down to $\frac{1}{16}$ inch (1.6 mm). The correct friction material for all models is BENDIX BM.78.
3 Brush out all dust and grit from inside the caliper. If washing is required, only methylated spirits (denatured alcohol) or hydraulic fluid may be used. Any other solvent will attack the material of the seals.
4 Press the pistons back into the cylinders. **The level of the fluid in the master cylinder will rise during this operation so syphon off any surplus to prevent it from overflowing. Hydraulic fluid will quickly remove paint, so avoid any spillage.** It may help to open the bleed screw on the caliper when pressing back the pistons, as surplus and old fluid will then be ejected, but it may then be necessary to bleed the brakes after the new pads have been fitted.
5 Refit the new pads and old anti-squeal shims in the reverse order of removal, making sure that the arrows on the anti-squeal shims are pointing upwards. Secure them with the retaining pins 4 and new clips 5. If long splitpins 4A are used fit new splitpins head to outside of caliper and bend the long leg of the splitpin upwards to secure. Refit the road wheel and lower the car back to the ground.

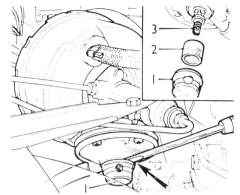

FIG 11 : 3   Servo air filter maintenance

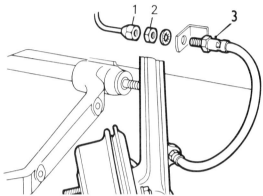

FIG 11 : 4   Typical brake hose attachment

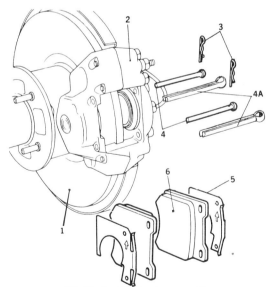

FIG 11 : 5   Disc brake assembly

Key to Fig 11 : 5   1 Brake disc   2 Caliper   3 Spring clip
4 Pad retaining pin   4A Pad retaining splitpins   5 Anti-rattle spring and squea shim   6 Brake pad

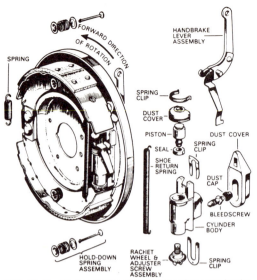

FIG 11:6   Components of self-adjusting reat brake

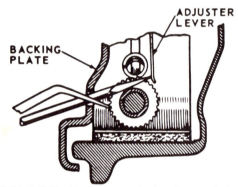

FIG 11:7 Self-adjusting rear brake. Access hole in backplate

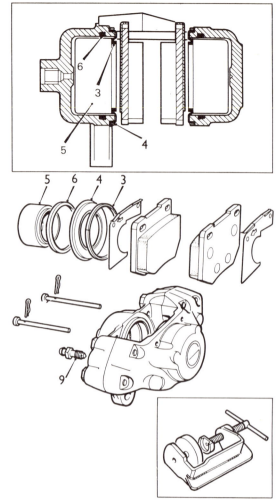

FIG 11:8   Servicing a disc brake caliper

6 Renew the pads on the other front brake in a similar manner. **Before driving the car, pump the brake pedal hard several times to take up the adjustment in the disc brakes.**

11:5 Renewing drum brake linings

The rear drum brakes are of the self-adjusting type. The components are shown in **FIG 11:6**.

A lever mechanism incorporated in the wheel cylinder adjusts the shoes automatically when the handbrake is applied. An arm attached to the lever engages a ratchet wheel which drives the adjustment screw of the wheel cylinder body. When the shoe lining wears, the increased handbrake lever movement results in rotation of the adjustment screw, thus extending the length of the wheel cylinder body.

A safety factor is incorporated in the automatic adjustment mechanism as the adjustment screw is prevented from unscrewing completely from the ratchet wheel. This ensures the linings do not wear down to the rivets and score the drum. Consequently, when the linings are worn to a predetermined minimum thickness, the rear brakes no longer self-adjust and this is an indication to replace the brake shoes.

Although the self adjustment of the rear brakes will not continue beyond a certain point, the brakes will still operate.

However, the brake pedal position when the brakes are firmly applied will become progressively lower. At this point the brake linings must be replaced to prevent scoring of the drums.

In cases where the brake drum is excessively scored it may not be possible to remove the drum without releasing the brake adjustment.

The correct procedure to release the brakes is as follows:

1 Raise the rear of the car and place suitable stands under the rear axle.
2 Remove the rear wheels.

3 Release the hand brake.

4 Insert the screwdriver through one of the holes and lift the actuating lever away from the ratchet wheel (see **FIG 11 : 7**).

5 Using a second screwdriver, turn the ratchet wheel to retract the brake shoes from the drum.

6 Remove the countersunk head screw retaining the brake drum and pull off the drum.

If the linings are contaminated, do not waste time trying to wash or bake out the oil or grease. Some oil will always remain, unless the treatment is so drastic as to ruin the lining, and will creep out under the stress of heavy braking.

In all cases fit genuine maker's replacement shoes where available. These are supplied complete with linings ground to the correct drum contour.

Checking brake drums:

Blow out loose dust and dirt. Wash off any oil or grease with fuel or methylated spirits. Check the operating surface for scores or cracks. Light scores can be turned out in a lathe but if they are deep or the drum is cracked a new drum must be fitted. The drum can be checked for cracks by hanging it on a wooden handle through the centre and tapping it with a light metal tool. If the drum rings it is satisfactory but a flat note indicates a crack.

11 : 6 Servicing disc brakes

The renewal of friction pads has been dealt with in **Section 11 : 4**.

Caliper removal:

1 Raise the front of the car and place stands under the lower suspension arms.

2 Remove front wheels.

3 Disconnect the brake flexible hose from the fixed pipe (see note **Section 11 : 3**) and plug the fixed pipe to prevent fluid loss.

4 Remove the two bolts retaining the caliper to the swivel arm.

5 Remove caliper complete with brake pads.

Refit the caliper in the reverse order of removal. Tighten the bolts to a torque of 40 to 45 lb ft. When the caliper is in place and the pipe reconnected, fill and bleed the hydraulic system.

Brake disc:

The brake disc can only be removed after the front hub assembly has been withdrawn from the stub axle on the front suspension (see **Chapter 9, Section 9 : 3**). Mark the relative positions of the hub and disc before taking out the four bolts that secure the disc to the hub. Gently tap the disc free from the hub.

Refit the brake disc in the reverse order of removal, tightening the four bolts that secure it to the hub to a torque of 40 to 45 lb ft.

When the hub has been refitted, mount a DTI (Dial Test Indicator) onto the suspension so that its stylus is resting vertically on the outer operating face of the disc at a radius of 4.75 inch (120.7 mm) and check that the runout of the disc does not exceed .006 inch (.152 mm) through one revolution of the hub assembly.

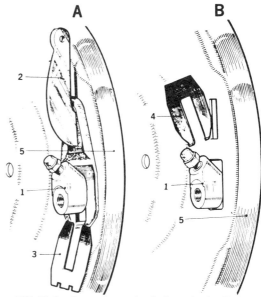

FIG 11 : 9   Removing and refitting wheel cylinder

Key to Fig 11 : 9   1 Wheel cylinder   2 Hand brake lever
3 Retaining plate   4 Spring plate   5 Backplate

If the runout is excessive, remove the disc and make absolutely sure that the mating faces of the disc and hub are scrupulously clean, as specks of dirt will alter the runout. If dirt is not the cause, try rotating the disc relative to the hub to see if the runout is minimized in the new position. If excessive runout cannot be cured, a new disc must be fitted.

In normal use slight concentric scoring will build up on the discs. If the scoring is deep or radial, braking efficiency will be affected and a new disc must be fitted.

Deposits on the disc can be cleaned off by soaking with trichlorethylene and gently scrubbing with worn emery-cloth. **Carry out this operation in a well-ventilated space (or out of doors) as the fumes from trichlorethylene are harmful, especially if inhaled through a cigarette.**

Mudshield and brake caliper bracket:

These can be removed from the suspension, after the hub assembly has been removed, by taking out the bolts that secure them to the swivel pin.

Caliper servicing:

Remove the caliper from the car and take out the brake pads with their anti-squeal shims. **Under no circumstances separate the two halves of the caliper.** The components are shown in **FIG 11 : 8**.

Carefully prise out the dust cover retaining rings 3 and remove the dust covers 4. Fit a piece of cloth into the caliper and use compressed air through the inlet port to blow the pistons out of their bores. If a piston sticks, clamp the other piston back into place and reconnect the caliper to the hydraulic system. Bleed the brake through the bleed screw 9. Wrap the caliper in cloth, to catch fluid

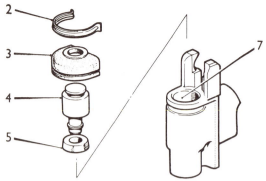

FIG 11:10   Rear brake wheel cylinder components

Key to Fig 11:10   2 Clip   3 Dust cover   4 Piston
5 Seal   7 Body

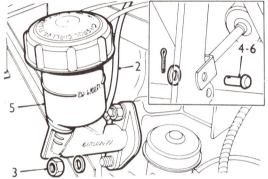

FIG 11:11   Attachments of master cylinder

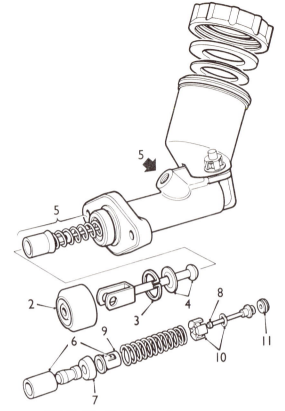

FIG 11:12   Master cylinder components

which will spurt when the piston comes free, and apply steadily increasing pressure to the brake pedal until the piston frees. **Do not press the brake pedal if the other caliper is free or the drums removed from the rear brakes.**

Remove the pistons 5 and then take out the seals 6 from their recesses in the bore, using a small tool but **taking great care not to damage or score the bore.**

Wash all the parts, except the brake pads, in methylated spirits or Girling Cleaning Fluid. **Do not use any other solvent.** Discard the old seals 6 and dust covers 4. Check the pistons 5 for scoring or wear and renew them if they are defective. If the cylinder bore shows signs of corrosion, scuffing, scoring or wear a complete new caliper assembly must be fitted.

Wet the new seals 6 in hydraulic fluid and insert them back into the bores, using only the fingers and making sure that the seal is fully seated and not twisted. Wet the pistons with hydraulic fluid and press each one in turn back into the bore, using the fingers first and then pressing them in with the special tool 18G.590, shown in the inset, until each piston protrudes by .31 inch (.8 mm). **When first entering the piston into the bore, take great care not to cock it and jam it in the bore.**

Refit the dust cover 4 onto the piston and secure it to the caliper with the clip 3.

The caliper is then ready for refitting.

11:7 Drum brake wheel cylinders

These can be removed from the brake backplate after the brake drums and shoes have been removed (see **Section 11:5**). If the brake backplate itself needs to be taken out, the hub must be removed first. See **Chapter 8, Section 8:2**.

Removal:

Remove the brake drum and shoes as described in **Section 11:5**. Disconnect the flexible brake hose (see note **Section 11:3**) and plug the pipe to minimize fluid loss. Referring to **FIG 11:9**.

1 Disconnect the handbrake cable from the lever 2. Remove the external rubber boot, retaining plate 4 and spring plate 3.
2 Withdraw the wheel cylinder 1 from the backplate. Separate the handbrake lever from the wheel cylinder.

Refitting:

1 Smear the slot in the backplate and wheel cylinder face with Girling Brake grease.
2 Locate the handbrake lever on the wheel cylinder engaging the spindles of the lever in the recess on the cylinder arms.

3 Referring to **FIG 11 : 9A** position the handbrake lever
  and neck of the wheel cylinder through the slot in the
  backplate.
4 Referring to **FIG 11 : 9B**, slide the spring plate 4
  between the wheel cylinder and backplate.
5 Slide the retaining plate 3 between the spring plate
  and the wheel cylinder ensuring that the pips of the
  spring plate engage in the holes in the retaining plate.
6 Refit the remaining parts in the reverse order of
  dismantling.
7 Fit the road wheels. Operate the handbrake lever
  several times to set the brake adjusters.
8 Bleed the brake system (see **Section 11 : 10**).

Servicing a wheel cylinder:

The components of a rear wheel cylinder are shown
in **FIG 11 : 10**.

Remove the dust cover, after freeing the clip if fitted.
Withdraw the piston assembly from the bore, collecting
the spring if fitted. Remove the cup seal from the piston.

Discard the old dust seal and cup seal, fitting new parts
on reassembly. Wash the parts in any suitable solvent but
give them a swill in methylated spirits or Girling Cleaning
fluid before reassembly. This ensures that there are no
traces of other solvents left to attack the material of the
seals.

The unit is reassembled in the reverse order of dismantling. Dip the cup seal into hydraulic fluid and refit
it while it is wet to the piston. The lips of the seal must
face into the bore of the cylinder. Use only the fingers to
refit the seal, making sure that it is fully and squarely
seated in its recess. When refitting the piston into the bore,
take great care not to bend back or damage the lips of the
seal.

11 : 8 The master cylinder

Removal:

The master cylinder attachments to models fitted without a servo are shown in **FIG 11 : 11**. On the models fitted
with a servo, the unit is bolted directly to the servo and
the reference to withdrawing the clevis pin 4 can be
ignored, otherwise the removal is the same.

Remove the filler cap and syphon out the hydraulic
fluid from the reservoir. Disconnect the metal pipe 2 from
the master cylinder, **using rags to catch any spillage.**
Remove the nuts and washers 3 securing the master
cylinder. From inside the car, remove the clevis pin 4 that
secures the pushrod to the brake pedal and from inside the
engine compartment withdraw the master cylinder.

Refit the master cylinder in the reverse order of removal,
noting that on models without a servo the clevis pin must
be passed through the upper hole in the brake pedal. Fill
and bleed the hydraulic system.

Dismantling:

The components of the unit are shown in **FIG 11 : 12**
and a sectional view in **FIG 11 : 13**.

1 Pull back the dust cap 2. Lightly press the pushrod
  down the bore and remove the circlip 3. The pushrod
  with its integral stop washer 4 can then be removed
  from the unit. Apply air pressure at the port 5, or shake
  out the internal parts by tapping the open end of the
  cylinder onto the palm of the hand.

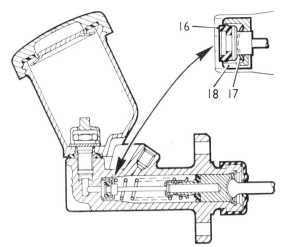

FIG 11 : 13   Master cylinder sectional view

2 Use a small screwdriver through the coils of the return
  spring to lift up the lip on the spring retainer so that the
  retainer can be slid off the piston 6. Remove the
  cup seal 7 from the piston. Lightly compress the
  return spring and slide the head of the valve stem 8
  sideways in the retainer so that it can pass out
  through the larger parts of the keyhole in the end of
  the retainer 9.
3 Slide off the valve spacer 10 and washer from the
  valve stem. Remove the valve seal 11 from the end of
  the stem.

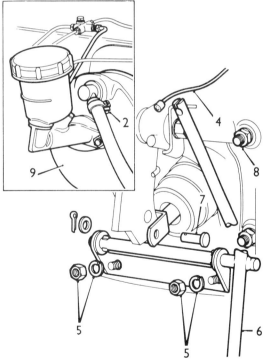

FIG 11 : 14   Servo unit attachments

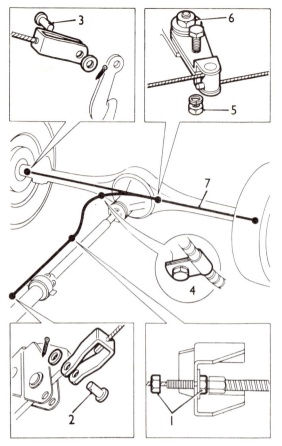

FIG 11:15 Handbrake cables and attachments

Examination:

Discard the old seals and fit new ones on reassembly (available in service kits). Wash the parts in methylated spirits and allow them to dry. Check the bore of the cylinder and renew the complete unit if the bore is at all scored, ridged or worn.

Check that the ports are clear, cleaning them out with a blunt-ended piece of wire if they are blocked or dirty.

Reassembly:

The internal parts should be dipped into clean hydraulic fluid and reassembled and refitted while wet.

Refer to **FIG 11:13**. Refit the valve seal 16 (see item 11) to the valve stem so that its smallest diameter is seated on the valve head. Slide on the curved washer 17 (see item 10) with its curved side towards the shoulder as shown. Refit the spacer 17 (see item 10) with its legs towards the curved washer.

Refer to **FIG 11:12**. Refit the return spring followed by the retainer 9. Centralize the stem of the valve in the retainer to locate it. Use the fingers only to refit the new seal 7 to the piston, so that its lip will face into the bore of the cylinder, and make sure that it is fully and squarely seated in its·recess. Press the retainer 9 back onto the piston, making sure that the tongue on the retainer is pressed fully and squarely down behind the lip of the piston.

Again wet the internal parts with hydraulic fluid. Press them back down the bore of the master cylinder, **taking great care not to bend back or damage the lips of the seal as they enter the bore.** Insert the pushrod and use it to press the internal parts down the bore while refitting the circlip 3. Check that the internal parts return freely under the action of the return spring before refitting the dust cover 2. The end of the pushrod and inside of the dust cover should be smeared with Girling Brake Grease (supplied in the kit).

11:9 The brake servo

The attachments of the unit are shown in **FIG 11:14**. Note that when a servo is fitted, the servo pushrod is always attached to the lower of the two mounting holes on the brake pedal.

The renewal of the servo filter is dealt with in **Section 11:2**.

Removal:

Remove the brake master cylinder as described in the previous section. Disconnect the vacuum hose from the non-return valve 2 on the unit. The non-return valve can be removed from the case and renewed if it is defective.

From inside the car, remove the parcel shelf. Disconnect the throttle cable 4 from the throttle pedal. Remove the nuts 5 and take off the throttle pedal assembly 6. Disconnect the servo pushrod from the brake pedal by taking out the clevis pin 7. Remove the nuts 8 which secure the unit and then withdraw the unit from the engine compartment.

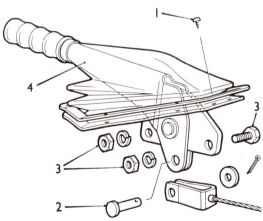

FIG 11:16 Handbrake lever assembly

Servicing:

The filter should be renewed if it is choked. The non-return valve can be renewed, lubricating its sealing washer lightly with Girling Grease 64949009. A seal and end plate assembly is fitted around the pushrod that connects to the master cylinder. The seal and plate can be carefully prised out and new parts pressed back into position, after lubricating them with Girling grease.

If the unit shows any other defects it must be renewed.

Reassembly:

The unit is refitted in the reverse order of removal, making sure that the pushrod attaches to the lower hole. Refit the master cylinder then fill and bleed the braking system.

11:10 Bleeding the hydraulic system

This is not routine maintenance but it must always be carried out when air has entered the hydraulic system, either through allowing the fluid level in the reservoir to fall so low that air is drawn into the system, leaks in the system, or after dismantling and reassembly.

Before starting the operation, remove the filler cap from the reservoir and fill it as far as it will go without spilling. During the operation, keep a constant check on the level, topping up as required to keep the level above the danger mark. Use fluid to Specification HBF.6 or SAEJ.1703b (minimum boiling point 260°C).

Fluid that has been bled from the system should be discarded. Only if the fluid is perfectly clean may it be used again, after storage in a clean sealed container for 24 hours to allow all air to disperse. **Never return fluid directly from bleeding to the master cylinder reservoir.**

Start bleeding at the front brake furthest from the master cylinder, followed by the other front brake and finally the lefthand side rear brake (noting that only one bleed screw is fitted to the rear brakes).

Attach a short length of small-bore plastic or rubber tube to the bleed screw of the brake to be bled and dip the free end of the tube into a little clean hydraulic fluid in a glass container. An assistant will now be required. Open the bleed screw by $\frac{1}{2}$ turn. The assistant presses the brake pedal fully down to the floor and then gives three short rapid strokes before allowing the pedal to fly back on its own. Carry on this sequence until the fluid coming out of the bleed tube is perfectly clear and free from air bubbles. Tighten the bleed screw as the pedal is being pressed down on the first slow long stroke of the sequence.

Bleed the remaining brakes using the same method. Check that the bleed screws are sufficiently tight to prevent leaks. If the system has been fully dismantled and the pedal still feels spongy after bleeding, use the car for a day or so and then rebleed the system. The tiny air bubbles will have had time to coalesce and will be easier to bleed out.

After brake bleeding is completed, top up the reservoir to the correct level and refit the filler cap.

11:11 The handbrake

The attachments of the cables are shown in **FIG 11:15** and the attachment of the handbrake lever is shown in **FIG 11:16**.

Removing cables:

1 Slacken the adjuster nut and locknut 1 so that the cable is released from its bracket. Remove the splitpin, washer and clevis pin 2 that secure the front end of the cable to the handbrake lever.
2 Disconnect the cables from the levers on the rear brakes by removing the splitpins, washers and clevis pins 3. Free the clip that secures the handbrake cable clip to the axle case by taking out the bolt 4.
3 Remove the nut, washer and bolt 5 that hold the compensating levers together and secure the trunnion off the cables. Slacken the nut 6 so that the trunnion can be removed from the compensating levers. Remove the cable from the car.

The parts are refitted in the reverse order of removal. Renew all clevis pins that are worn and use new splitpins to secure the clevis pins.

Adjust the cable, at the point 1, as described in **Section 11:2**.

The lever assembly:

Ease back the floor covering and take out the four screws 1 that secure the gaiter 4 in place. Remove the clevis pin 2 which secures the cable to the lever. Slide the gaiter up and off the lever. Remove the nuts and bolts 3 that secure the assembly and lift out the handbrake lever parts from the car.

Refit the handbrake lever in the reverse order of removal and check the handbrake adjustment.

11:12 Fault diagnosis

(a) Spongy pedal

1 Leak in the fluid system
2 Air in the fluid system
3 Worn master cylinder
4 Leaking wheel cylinders
5 Gaps between shoes and linings on drum brakes
6 Excessive hub end float (disc brakes only)

(b) Excessive pedal movement

1 Check 1 and 2 in (a)
2 Excessive lining or pad wear
3 Very low fluid level in reservoir

(c) Brakes grab or pull to one side

1 Seized piston in wheel cylinder or caliper
2 Seized handbrake cable or compensator
3 Wet or oily friction linings
4 Broken shoe return springs
5 Mixed linings of different grades
6 Unbalanced shoe adjustment
7 Scored, cracked or distorted brake drums or discs
8 Uneven tyre pressures or uneven tyre wear
9 Defective suspension or steering

NOTES

CHAPTER 12

THE ELECTRICAL SYSTEM

12:1 Description

All the versions covered by this manual are fitted with a 12-volt electrical system in which the negative terminal of the battery is earthed. **Care must be taken to ensure that the correct polarity is observed when connecting up circuits, as some components will be irreparably damaged if they are connected with the wrong polarity.**

An alternator is fitted as standard in place of the conventional generator. The alternator has its own in-built rectifier pack, to change the AC current to DC which is acceptable to the battery, as well as its own regulator. The alternator will charge at a slower speed and provide a higher current as compared with a generator, so it is most useful where much stop-start driving and short journeys are carried out. The alternator also has greater reliability by virtue of its design and construction.

Wiring diagrams are shown in **Technical Data** at the end of this manual, to enable those with electrical experience to trace and rectify wiring faults. A test lamp or any 0 to 20 voltmeter will do for testing the continuity of circuits, by connecting the tester between the suspect terminal and a good earth on the car. **Cheap and unreliable instruments must not be used when checking performance or adjusting components, as they cannot measure to the accuracy required.**

For accurate checks, high grade instruments must be used, preferably instruments of the moving-coil type.

Special care is needed when dealing with alternator systems as even a momentary wrong connection can cause considerable damage. In particular, do not disconnect the battery terminals or make or break any connection in the charging circuit when the engine is running. If in doubt the work should be entrusted to an auto electrical specialist.

Remove battery leads and alternator connections before carrying out electric arc welding on any part of the car as stray induced currents may damage the alternator.

Instructions are given in this chapter for servicing the components of the system but it must be realized that it is a waste of time and money to attempt to repair items which are seriously defective, either electrically or mechanically. In such cases, advantage should be taken of the exchange scheme to fit new or reconditioned units in their place.

12:2 The battery

The battery is the heart of the electrical system and if it is in poor condition the operation of the whole electrical system will suffer. The battery is also the component that will suffer first from neglected maintenance.

Maintenance:

Always keep the top of the battery clean and dry. Wipe away any dampness, spillage or dirt from the top of the battery. If acid has spilt, or dirt allowed current to leak, the metal surrounds around the battery can become corroded. Take out the battery and wash the area with dilute ammonia or baking powder dissolved in warm water. When the acid has been neutralized, flush the area with plenty of clean water and allow to dry. Use anti-sulphuric paint to prevent further corrosion.

Keep the battery connectors clean and tight. Poor contact here is one of the commonest causes of the starter motor failing to operate satisfactorily. Wash away corrosion with dilute ammonia followed by clean water. Oxides can be gently scraped away with a sharp knife, though it should be noted that special tools are made for cleaning the posts and connectors. Smear the posts and connectors with petroleum jelly to prevent further corrosion.

At regular intervals check the electrolyte level in the battery, topping up with pure distilled water only. Do not add acid, electrolyte or additives.

Charging:

If it becomes necessary to recharge the battery from an outside source, the best charging rate is 4 to 5 amp. If charging with the battery still in the car, disconnect both leads to avoid damage to alternator circuit. If using boost charger also disconnect the alternator leads.

Electrolyte:

Electrolyte, of the correct specific gravity, should only be added to replace spillage or leakage.

Concentrated sulphuric acid is a very dangerous chemical so buy electrolyte ready-mixed. Electrolyte of the correct specific gravity should only be added to the battery to replace spillage or leakage.

If electrolyte is spilled, it should be immediately neutralized with baking powder or dilute ammonia and then flushed away with plenty of clean water.

Testing:

Single-cell heavy-duty testers cannot be used on either make of battery.

Provided that the battery has not been just topped up, the charge of the cells can be checked with a hydrometer. If the battery has just been topped up the car should be used for a short while to mix the electrolyte (this should also be done after topping up in very cold weather). Draw sufficient electrolyte from each cell in turn into the instrument to ensure that the float is clear of the sides and bottom. Take the reading at eye level and at the same time note the condition of the electrolyte. Dirt, specks or a cloudy appearance indicate a defective cell and this will be confirmed if the reading of that cell differs radically from the other five cells.

The readings give the following indications:

For climates above 27°C (80°F):

1.270 to 1.290	..	..	Cell fully charged
1.1190 to 1.210	..	..	Cell half charged
1.110 to 1.130	..	..	Cell discharged

Replace spillage with electrolyte of 1.270 specific gravity.

For climates below 27°C (80°F):

1.120 to 1.230	..	..	Cell fully charged
1.130 to 1.150	..	..	Cell half charged
1.050 to 1.070	..	..	Cell discharged

Replace spillage with electrolyte of 1.120 specific gravity.

The figures are given assuming a standard electrolyte temperature of 16°C (60°F). If the actual temperature is different from the standard, then convert by adding .002 to the reading for every 3°C (5°F) rise in temperature and subtract for every 3°C (5°F) drop in temperature.

Storage:

Short-term storage provides no problems provided that the battery has been well maintained. If the battery is to be stored for long periods, make sure that it is fully charged, the top dry and the posts well covered with petroleum jelly. Keep the battery stored in a cold dry place, well away from extremes of temperature.

At monthly intervals give the battery a freshening-up charge and at three-month intervals discharge it, using a lamp bank, and fully recharge it. If this is not done the battery will slowly self-discharge and the plates sulphate up, to the ruination of the battery.

12:3 Servicing electrical motors

All the motors fitted to the car operate on the same principles and are basically very similar in constructional detail. It should be noted that a generator can be considered as a specialized form of motor in which mechanical energy is fed in and electrical energy taken out.

For a detailed description of alternator and special precautions necessary, refer to **Section 12:5**.

The removal and dismantling of the various motors will be dealt with in the relevant sections, but to save constant repetition, general instructions for dealing with all motors are collected into this section.

Brush gear:

Dismantle the motor sufficiently to expose the brush gear. **Great care must be taken not to damage the brushes on the edge of the commutator as they are withdrawn or refitted,** and on some motors it will be necessary to partially withdraw the brush from its holder and secure it in this position with the spring resting on the side instead of on the top of the brush. The assembly can then be slid off the commutator, or refitted, without damaging the brushes. Once the assembly is back in place use a rod or hook to lift the spring onto the top of the brush.

Renew the brushes if they are excessively worn. On motors where the connectors are soldered into place, grip the connector with a pair of pliers to prevent solder from creeping up them and making them stiff. On the starter motor, cut the old connector so that approximately $\frac{1}{4}$ in of old connector is left and pass this tag through the loop of the new connector before soldering the new connector into place. The old tag can be bent over but make sure that there is no danger of the tag or new connector earthing against the yoke of the motor.

Check that the brushes move freely in their brush holders. If the brushes stick, remove them and polish their sides on a smooth file. Clean the brush holders with a piece of cloth moistened with fuel or methylated spirits

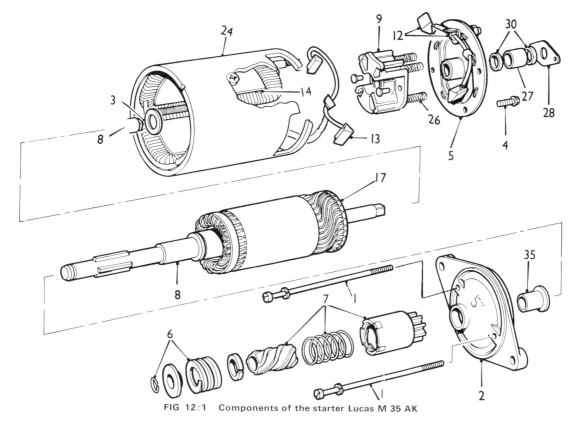

FIG 12:1   Components of the starter Lucas M 35 AK

Key to Fig 12:1   1 Through bolts   2 Drive end bracket   3 Thrust washer   4 Commutator end bracket screws   5 Commutator end bracket   6 Inertia spring and retainer   7 Starter drive assembly   8 Armature shaft   9 Brush holder   12 End bracket brushes   13 Field brushes   14 Field windings   17 Commutator   24 Yoke   26 Brush springs   27 Bush (commutator end bracket)   28 End plate   30 Felt seals   35 Bush (drive end bracket)

before refitting the brush. If the original brushes are being refitted, make sure that they are refitted into their original positions and facing the same way as before removal. This ensures that the bedding-in is not lost.

Use a suitably-modified spring balance to check the pressure of the brush springs. Fit new springs if the old ones are weak or broken.

Brushes are usually supplied ground to shape on the end. If further bedding-in is required, make up a wooden rod the same diameter as the commutator (or use the commutator itself) and wrap it with a fine grade of glasspaper. Fit the brush holder complete with brushes over the mandrel and rotate the mandrel inside the brushes for a few turns. Bedding-in in use will then finally fit the brushes accurately.

Before reassembling the motor, brush and blow out all dust and dirt. Wipe the commutator over with a piece of cloth moistened in methylated spirits or fuel.

Commutator and armature:

If the commutator is worn or scored the armature assembly must be removed from the motor. Light score or burn marks can be polished off using a fine grade of glasspaper. Never use emerycloth as this will leave abrasive particles embedded in the copper.

If the damage is deep it can be skimmed off in a lathe, provided that the minimum diameter of the commutator is not reached. Use the highest speed possible and a very sharp tool. Starter motor commutators must never be undercut. On generators and motors where the insulation is undercut between the segments, grind a hacksaw blade so that it is the exact width of the insulation and use it to undercut the insulation to a depth of $\frac{1}{32}$ inch. Take a light final skim cut using a diamond or carbide-tipped tool. Failing such a tool, polish the commutator, as it rotates, using a fine grade of glasspaper. Remove all swarf and metal dust from the commutator before reassembly.

Very little can be done to the remainder of the armature, apart from checking it for physical damage. A special tester is required for checking shortcircuits in the coils, though they may be suspected if individual commutator segments are burnt. Check that there are no loose laminations, segments or wiring, as well as checking the laminations for scoring. Scoring all round the laminations indicates excessively worn bearings or loose polepieces, while scoring on one side only indicates a bent armature shaft. **A defective armature shaft cannot be repaired and it must not be machined or an attempt made to straighten it.** The only cure is to fit a new armature.

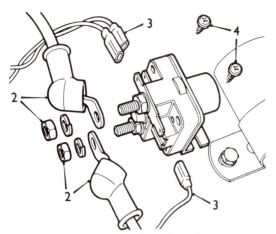

FIG 12:2   Starter solenoid attachments

Field coils:

On some of the smaller motors, permanent magnets are fitted in place of field coils. Care must be taken when dismantling such motors as the magnet, attached inside the cover, will draw the armature out with it, to the possible damage of the brushes.

The field coils can be checked by connecting a test lamp and 12-volt battery across the terminals and between a terminal and the yoke. In the first case the lamp should light, showing continuity, and in the second case it should not light, showing that the insulation is satisfactory. A more accurate test is to connect an ammeter in place of the test lamp and measure the current flow. The resistance can then be calculated using Ohms law (Voltage divided by Current equals Resistance). Obviously a resistance meter will give a direct reading of resistance and should therefore be used in preference.

The field coils on starter motors and generators are held in place by the polepieces, which are in turn secured by large screws to the yoke. The screws must be tightened to a high torque using a wheel-screwdriver and then locked by staking or punch dots. An ordinary screwdriver cannot exert the torque required to slacken or tighten these screws so renewal of field coils should be left to an agent.

Bearings:

Either ballbearings or bushes may be used. Ballbearings are usually held in place by a riveted retainer plate. To remove rivets use a drill larger in diameter than the stem but smaller than the head. File a flat on the rivet head and then centre punch it as a guide. Drill carefully until the head is so weakened that it can be tapped off with a small cold chisel, then use a suitable punch to drive out the rivet stem. Before refitting ballbearings, make sure that they are packed with grease.

Porous bronze bushes are used on some larger motors. Sometimes they can be extracted by driving them out

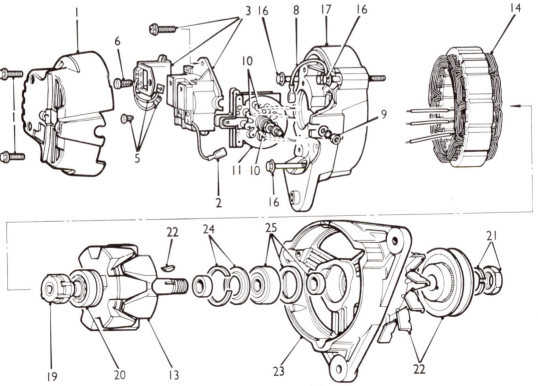

FIG 12:3   Exploded view of alternator

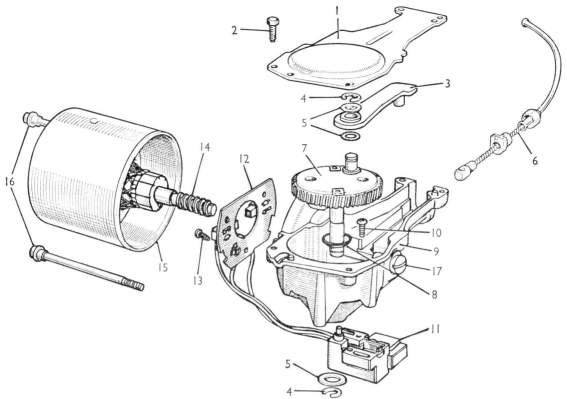

FIG 12:4   Windscreen wiper motor components

Key to Fig 12:4   1 Gearbox cover   2 Screws   3 Connecting rod   4 Circlip   5 Washers   6 Cable rack assembly
7 Shaft and gear   8 Dished washer   9 Gearbox   10 Screw   11 Limit switch assembly   12 Brush gear   13 Screw   14 Armature
15 Cover assembly   16 Through bolts   17 Armature adjusting screw

using a suitable punch. If the bushes are fitted in blind holes, screw a tap of the correct size into the bush and use the tap to draw the bush out. Soak the new bush in oil for 24 hours before fitting it. The period can be reduced by heating the oil over a bath of boiling water for two hours, leaving the oil to cool before taking the bush out of it. Press the new bush back into place, using a stepped mandrel whose spigot is just longer than the bush and has a highly finished surface of the same diameter as the armature shaft. **Do not machine or bore the bush.**

Smaller motors are fitted with spherical self-aligning bushes, usually held to the end cover by a riveted spring clip plate. Spares may not be readily obtainable and if the bush is worn the complete end cover must usually be renewed. Check that such bushes move freely in their clips and that their bores are not worn. Lubricate them with a few drops of oil before reassembly.

Insulation:

Clean away all metal and carbon dust from the inside of the motor. Use an air-line or tyre pump as well as a small brush. Oil or grease can be washed away using methylated spirits or clean fuel. The field coils and armature must not be wetted with solvent but only wiped over with a moistened cloth.

The best method of testing resistance is to use a resistance meter, though not the type known as a 'megger' which generates a high voltage. A test lamp and 12-volt battery can also be used but if the method is to be employed it is better to have a neon test bulb and 110 AC volt supply.

12:4 The starter motor

All models are fitted with inertia-type starter Lucas M.35.AK of which the components are shown in **FIG 12:1**. The starter is operated through a solenoid shown in **FIG 12:2**.

Starter motor fails to operate:

1 Check the condition of the battery terminals, making sure that they are clean and firmly held down by the screws. At the same time check that the battery is charged. If, when operated, the horn sounds weak or the lights are dim then it is likely that the battery is low in charge.

2 Switch on some lights which can be seen from the driving seat and again operate the starter switch. If the lights go dim then the starter motor is taking current. One cause of the motor failing to rotate at all is that it is jammed in mesh. Select a gear and rock

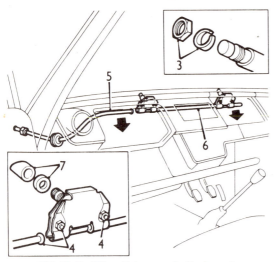

FIG 12:5 Wiper linkage and attachments

the car backwards and forwards. If this fails to free the starter motor, use a spanner on the squared end of the armature shaft, exposed at the end of the motor, to try to rotate the motor backwards and so free it. If all methods of freeing the motor fail, or the motor is free but does not rotate, then it must be removed for further examination. Broken or worn pinion teeth are a cause of jamming and the teeth on the flywheel should also be checked, by examining them through the starter motor aperture while slowly turning the engine over. Dirt on the drive pinion will also cause it to jam (either keeping it in engagement or preventing it from engaging).

3 If the lights do not go dim when the starter is operated then the motor is taking no current. Disconnect the single control wire from the solenoid and check that current is reaching the terminal of the wire when the switch is operated, using a test lamp or voltmeter. If current is not reaching the terminal, trace back through the system until the fault is found and can be rectified. If current is reaching the control terminal for the solenoid, listen for the click as the solenoid operates. If there is no click the coils are defective and a new solenoid must be fitted. On the separate solenoids, the starter can still be operated by pressing in the rubber covered end of the solenoid plunger. Burning of the contacts in the solenoid can be another cause of starter motor failure. If the solenoid clicks and the motor does not operate (similarly when the solenoid is operated manually), try shorting across the heavy-duty terminals with a thick piece of metal. The starter motor now operating shows that the contacts are burnt and again the only cure is to fit a new solenoid.

Removal:

1 Disconnect the battery
2 Remove the lead from the terminal on the starter motor
3 Remove the bolt attaching the engine dipstick guide to the cylinder block

4 Loosen the nut locking the dipstick guide tube to the sump and turn the tube 180 deg.
5 Remove the two bolts securing the starter motor to the engine backplate.
6 Withdraw the starter motor

Testing:

The motor can be roughly checked by mounting it in the padded jaws of a vice. If the motor is hand-held the starting torque will make it kick heavily. Use heavy duty leads and connect the positive terminal of the battery to the terminal on the motor. Firmly hold a heavy duty lead, connected to the negative terminal of the battery, against the yoke of the motor. If the motor is satisfactory, it will rotate at high speed in its normal direction of rotation. Note that the current even under free-running can reach 65 amps on some motors.

Dismantling M35AK starter motor:

The components are shown in **FIG 12:1**. This type of starter motor has a commutator where the brushes act on the vertical face instead of on the circumference as is more usual.

1 Remove the through bolts 1 so that the drive end bracket complete with armature 2 and pinion assembly can be withdrawn from the yoke. Collect the thrust washer 3 from the end of the shaft 2.
2 Take out the two screws 4 and remove the commutator end bracket 5 complete with brushgear assembly 9.
3 Compress the mainspring and remove the snap ring 6. The pinion parts 7 can then be removed from the armature shaft 2.

The components are checked following the instructions in **Section 12:3**. The spring tension of the brushes is checked, using new brushes and a push-type spring gauge with the brushes pressed in until they protrude by approximately $\frac{1}{16}$ inch (1.6 mm). If the spring pressure is weak, the complete end bracket assembly 5 must be renewed. When checking the insulation of the field coils, unrivet the terminal 21 and keep it well clear of the yoke, checking between each field coil brush and yoke in turn. The place 28 must be unriveted before the bush 27 and felt seals can be renewed, using a $\frac{1}{2}$ inch tap to withdraw the bush. The bush 35 can be pressed straight out and a new bush pressed straight in.

The motor is reassembled in the reverse order of dismantling.

12:5 The alternator

The components of the alternator are shown in **FIG 12:3**. The unit is dismantled in the numerical order of the parts shown in the figure, noting the following points:

1 When unsoldering the stator leads from the rectifier pack at 10, note their positions so that they can be resoldered back to their original terminals. **When unsoldering any wires connected to the diodes in the rectifier pack, use a hot iron so that the solder melts rapidly and grip the diode pin with a pair of long-nosed pliers to act as a heat-sink and prevent heat from reaching the diode.** This also applies when resoldering the leads.
2 Before removing the stator 14, mark its position in relation to the end brackets.

3 If the rotor bearing 25 has to be removed the slip rings 19 must first be taken off, after unsoldering their connections to the stator.

The alternator is reassembled in the reverse order of dismantling, after checking and cleaning the parts.

Precautions:

The following precautions must be carried out when an alternator is fitted:
1 Never make or break the charging circuit while the engine is running.
2 Always ensure that the system is at the correct polarity, as reverse voltages can damage the alternator.
3 When carrying out arc-welding repairs to the body-work or charging the battery on a heavy duty boost charger, always disconnect the charging circuit to prevent the alternator from picking up stray induced voltages.

Servicing:

Generally servicing can be carried out following the instructions given in **Section 12:3**. The field coil resistance is measured between the rotor slip rings. The stator windings have a very low resistance and need not be checked for resistance, but they should be checked for continuity and insulation. Check between any pair of stator leads then repeat the test using one of the original leads and the third lead.

The slip rings must not be machined and usually wiping with a cloth moistened with methylated spirits is sufficient though they may be lightly polished with fine glasspaper if required.

Diodes:

These are tested with a 12-volt battery and 1.5 watt test lamp. Connect the lamp and battery in series across the diode pin and its heat sink, then repeat the test with the polarity reversed. If the diode is satisfactory the bulb will light when the current flows in one direction but it will prevent current flowing in the reverse direction and the lamp will not light. If the lamp lights in both directions, or fails to light at all then the diode is defective and the rectifier assembly 11 must be renewed.

Driving belt adjustment:

For method of adjustment (see **Chapter 4**). The use of a high quality belt with a top width of $\frac{3}{8}$ inch is essential.

12:6 The windscreen wipers

A Lucas 12AUW two-speed wiper motor is fitted as standard, and the components of the motor are shown in **FIG 12:4**.

Poor or no operation:

Check the fuse and if it has blown trace through the circuit for faults such as defective insulation.

If the wipers operate sluggishly, first check through the wiring for points of high resistance. Use a voltmeter to check that all points in the circuit give battery voltage. A test bulb can be used, in which case it should glow as brightly when connected between terminals (with the motor disconnected) and earth as it does across the battery. Clean up and tighten any loose or poor contacts.

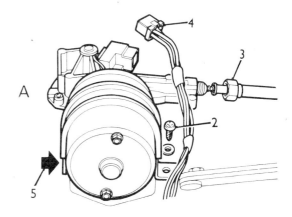

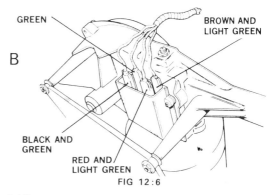

GREEN

BROWN AND LIGHT GREEN

BLACK AND GREEN

RED AND LIGHT GREEN

FIG 12:6

A Wiper motor attachments **B** Wiring connections for wiper motor

Remove the gearbox cover 1 from the motor and disconnect the connecting rod 3 from the cable rack by removing the circlip 4. Connect an accurate ammeter into the circuit and measure the operating current after the motor has been running for a minute. At normal speed the motor should take 1.5 amps and at high-speed it should take 2 amps. The normal speed is 46 to 52 cycles/minute while the high-speed is 60 to 70 cycles/minute.

If the motor does not operate satisfactorily on its own then the fault lies in the motor. Abnormal current demands by the motor can be caused by faulty brush gear or defective armature, while high currents will be caused by internal shortcircuits or excessive internal resistance. No field coils are fitted as the exciter field is produced by a permanent magnet in the cover 15.

If the motor operates satisfactorily on its own, check the linkage, shown in **FIG 12:5**. Remove the wiper arms from the spindles of the wheel boxes and use a spring balance to check that the pull required to move the cable operating rack (after disconnection from the motor) does not exceed 6 lb (2.72 kg). If this force is exceeded then the tubes are damaged or misaligned or the wheel-boxes are damaged. The parts of the linkage can be removed following the numerical order given in **FIG 12:5**, after the instrument panel and glove box have been taken out (see **Chapter 13**) and the wiper arms and cable rack removed.

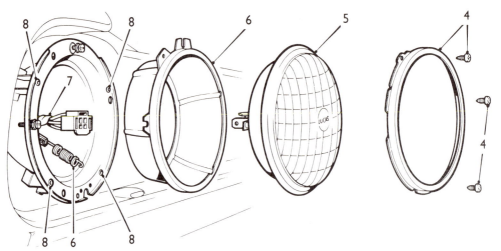

FIG 12:7 Headlamp components (sealed beam)

Removing the motor:

The attachments of the motor are shown in **FIG 12:6A** and the wiring connections in **FIG 12:6B**. Take out the screw 2 which secures the motor strap. Undo the cable union nut 3 and disconnect the connector 4. Remove the wiper arms from the wheelbox spindles. Press the motor clamp strap into its release slot 5 and lift out the motor. Withdraw the cable rack with the motor.

Refit the motor in the reverse order of removal, guiding the cable rack through the tubing of the linkage. When the motor is in place, operate it and switch it off so that it is in the park position. Refit the wiper arms so that they are also correctly in their parked positions.

Dismantling the motor:

1 Disconnect the cable rack by removing the circlip 4 and lifting out the connecting rod, carefully collecting the washers 5. Check that the end of the gearshaft is free from burrs and damage, polishing it with emery-cloth if necessary. Withdraw the shaft and gear 7, noting the position of the dished washer 8. Do not remove the crankpin mounting plate from the gear unless it is essential, and if it must be removed carefully mark the relation of the pin to the gear.

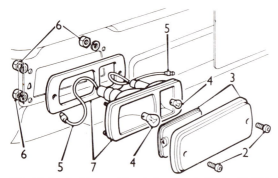

FIG 12:8 Parking and front direction indicator lamps

2 Indelibly mark across the cover 15 and gearbox flange 9, noting that if the cover is assembled 180 deg. out the motor will run in reverse. Take out the two through-bolts 16 and withdraw the cover by **no more** than $\frac{3}{16}$ inch. Ease the brushes off the commutator and then completely withdraw the parts, **taking care to prevent grease from getting onto the brushes.**

3 Remove the screws 10 and 13 to free the limit switch 11 and brush gear assembly 12.

Servicing and reassembly:

The parts are serviced following the instructions given in **Section 12:3**. Wipe out any old grease and lubricate the bearings and shafts with zinc oxide grease on reassembly. The gearbox and cable rack should also be packed with zinc oxide grease.

Reassembly is the reverse of the dismantling operation, but take care when refitting the cover not to damage the brushes or contaminate them with grease. The screw 17 controls the armature end float, and it should be adjusted to give a float of .004 to .008 inch (.1 to .21 mm). Packing washers can be fitted under the head to increase the end float but the underside of the head must be turned down in a lathe if the end float is excessive. On some models a locknut and screw will be found and these can be used to set the adjustment without any trouble.

12:7 The headlamps

The attachments of a headlamp are shown in **FIG 12:7**. Sealed beam units are used, where the whole light unit 5 is a bulb with the filaments sealed into it.

Removal:

Disconnect the battery. Remove the four screws securing the front grille at the top of the body. Lift out the grille. Remove the three rim securing screws 4 and lift out the light unit 5 and disconnect it as shown in the appropriate inset.

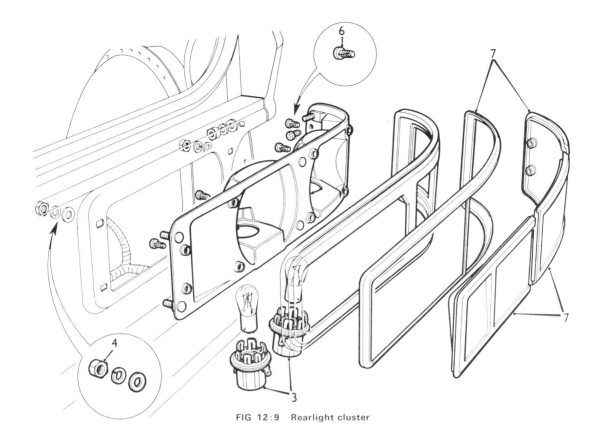

FIG 12:9   Rearlight cluster

If more parts require removal, disconnect the spring 6 and lift out the shell, freeing it from the two adjusting screws. Free the snap connectors at the wing valance for the leads 7. Drill out the rivets 8 and detach the lamp shell complete with wiring from the body.

The parts are refitted in the reverse order of removal.

Beam setting:

Remove the grille in order to gain access to the two adjusting screws on each headlamp. The beams can be set by standing the car a little distance from, and squarely to, a plain vertical wall. The upper adjusting screw controls the vertical alignment and the screw on the side the horizontal alignment.

It is more accurate to take the car to an agent who will set the beams precisely, and within the legal limits, using special beamsetter equipment.

12:8 Direction indicators. Parking and rear lamps

If the flash rate on one side alters or stops, check the bulbs on that side as a blown filament will badly affect the flashing rate. The attachments of the front lights are shown in **FIG 12:8** and the bulbs are accessible after the two screws 2 and lens parts 3 have been removed. The attachments of the rear lights are shown in **FIG 12:9**. The bulbs are accessible after the holders 4 have been freed from inside the luggage compartment. **Check that the bulb holders or connections have not accidentally been displaced by luggage or items in the boot.**

If the flashers fail to operate, disconnect the leads from the flasher unit and use a suitable tester to check that battery voltage is reaching the unit. Connect the two leads together and operate the direction indicator switch. The lamps should operate correctly, but without flashing. If lamps do not operate, trace through the wiring to find the fault and at the same time make sure that the earth points of the lamps are satisfactory. If the lamps do operate correctly, the flasher unit itself is at fault and must be renewed. Unclip the old unit from its holder and fit a new one back into place. Handle the unit with care and do not plug it back into a live circuit.

12:9 Temperature and fuel gauges

Both these instruments operate from a special voltage stabilizer, and the whole system uses the expansion and contraction of bi-metallic springs, as they heat and cool when current is passed through them. If either instrument is defective, trace through the wiring and check for faults. If both instruments fail then it is likely that the voltage stabilizer unit itself is defective. Ordinary instruments cannot be used for testing the systems. The voltage stabilizer opens and closes its contacts so that over a period of time the current flow through the system is exactly the same as if the systems were connected to a stable 10-volt supply. If a voltmeter is used to take the reading it will give alternating periods of full battery voltage and no voltage. Special test instruments are essential and for this reason the car should be taken to an

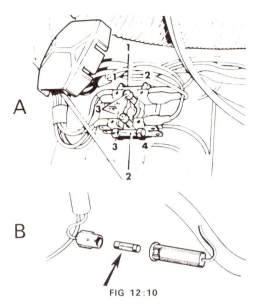

FIG 12:10

A Fuse block   B Line fuse

agent who can then pinpoint the fault and change the defective unit, without the process of trial and error that the owner would have to carry out. **Never connect parts of the system across full battery voltage.**

12:10 Fuses:

A fuse holder is mounted on the righthand valance panel in the engine compartment as shown in **FIG 12:10**. Circuits protected by fuses are as follows:

Fuse 1 connects terminals 1-2. This fuse protects the interior lamp, horn push and luggage compartment lamp (when fitted) circuits.

Fuse 2 connects terminals 3-4. This fuse protects the circuits which function when the ignition is switched on. The circuits are—direction indicators, windscreen wiper motor, heater blower motor, brake stop warning lamps and reversing lamps.

Two spare fuses are provided. The fuses are blow rated 35 amperes.

Line fuse. The Line fuse protects the park, tail and number plate lamp circuit.

It is located in a cylindrical fuse holder adjacent to the instrument wiring connector near the fuse box and is rated at 15 amperes. A line fuse also protects the radio when fitted.

The units protected by each fuse may be identified by referring to the wiring diagram (see **Appendix**).

12:11 Steering lock switch

The vehicle is equipped with a combined steering column lock, ignition and starter switch, operated by a key.

The lock face is marked O (off) I (ancillary) II (ignition) III (start).

To remove the key from the lock, turn the key to the I position, press the key in and while maintaining pressure, turn anti-clockwise to position O and withdraw the key.

The steering lock is set during withdrawal of the key, and rotation of the steering wheel engages the lock bolt making it impossible to steer the car.

When the steering wheel is in the locked position it will be necessary to disengage the locking mechanism before the engine can be started. This is accomplished by fully inserting the key and turning it in a clockwise direction, and simultaneously turn the steering wheel slightly to release the lock bolt from the inner steering column. The key may be now turned to the start position.

The steering column lock works in conjunction with and is integral with the ignition-starter switch. The designed operating sequence prevents the engine being started with the steering locked. **Serious consequences may result from alteration or substitution of the ignition-start switch which would allow the engine started with the lock engaged. Under no circumstances must the ignition switch or the ignition-start function be separated from the steering lock.**

Instructions for removal of the switch and steering lock are given in **Section 10:3** of the Chapter on steering.

12:13 Fault diagnosis

(a) Battery discharged

1 Terminals loose or dirty
2 Shortcircuit in part of system not protected by fuse
3 Alternator/generator not charging
4 Battery internally defective

(b) Battery will not hold charge

1 Low electrolyte level
2 Battery plates sulphated or distorted
3 Electrolyte leakage from cracked case
4 Plate separators ineffective

(c) Alternator output low or nil

1 Loose or broken drive belt
2 No battery supply to field coils (in rotor)
3 Defective wiring
4 Control unit failed (defective diodes)
5 Brushes excessively worn or slip rings dirty

(d) Suspected alternator noise

(Note: A slight hum is normal. Otherwise check the following:)

1 Glazed drive belt
2 Drive belt too tight
3 Alternator mounting bolts loose
4 Defective water pump
5 Worn alternator bearings

(e) Starter motor lacks power or will not operate

1 Battery discharged, loose or dirty connectors
2 Starter jammed in mesh
3 Starter switch defective
4 Starter solenoid defective
5 Brush gear defective
6 Armature or field coils defective
7 Engine abnormally stiff

(f) Starter motor runs but does not turn engine

1 Dirt jamming pinion open
2 Broken teeth on pinion or flywheel ring gear

(g) Starter motor rough or noisy

1 Loose mountings
2 Damaged pinion or flywheel teeth
3 Weak or broken pinion spring
4 Motor mechanically defective

(h) Lamps inoperative or erratic

1 Battery low
2 Bulb filaments blown
3 Defective wiring
4 Faulty earth points
5 Defective lighting switch
6 Blown fuse

(i) Fuel or temperature gauges do not register

1 No battery supply to voltage stabilizer
2 Defective voltage stabilizer
3 Broken cable
4 Defective gauge
5 Defective transmitter
6 Poor earth on transmitter unit

(j) Fuel or temperature gauges erratic

1 Defective wiring
2 Defective voltage stabilizer
3 Defective transmitting units
4 Defective gauges

NOTES

CHAPTER 13

THE BODYWORK

13:1 Bodywork repairs

On cars fitted with an alternator remove the battery leads and alternator connections prior to carrying out electric arc welding on any part of the car as stray induced currents can damage the alternator.

Large scale repairs to bodywork are best left to experts. Even small dents can be tricky as too much or injudicious hammering will stretch the metal and make the dent worse instead of better. Gentle tapping to reduce the dent will help but the best method available to the owner is filling and spraying, particularly when self-spraying cans of exactly matching paint are readily available. Minor dents and scratches should be touched in with a retouching kit before the metal underneath has a chance to corrode.

As the car gets older the surface finish will lose its lustre and fade slightly so there may be a slight difference between new paint and the old finish. Spraying a complete wing or panel will make any difference in colour far less obvious. Original lustre and colour can be partially restored using a mild cutting compound type cleaner, but this must not be used too often as it removes paint to expose a new layer underneath.

If an area is to be sprayed or filled, wash it thoroughly with white spirits to remove all traces of wax polish. Even more drastic treatment will be required to remove silicone-based polishes. If possible, take off any trim or handles in the area as a better result will be obtained with these removed. Lightly scuff the whole area to give a good key for the new finish and rub down any corrosion to bare metal. Apply a coat of primer over bare metal areas. Build up the damaged area to just proud of the surface, using filler or paste stopper as required. When the surface is hard, rub it down using 400 grade 'Wet and Dry' paper and clean water. Wash off slurry and apply further coats of filler or stopper if required. Spend plenty of time and patience at this stage in removing all blemishes and obtaining a perfect surface, as any marks at this stage will stand out glaringly on the final polished surface. When the surface is smooth, wash it down with plenty of water and let it dry and then wash off the slurry that was missed in the first wash.

Mask off surrounding areas using newspaper and masking tape.

Spray a complete panel evenly all over, including the edges, but if only a patch is being sprayed the paint

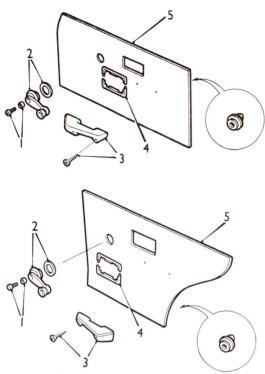

FIG 13:1   Door trim attachments

upper and lower bezels from the remote control handle. Use a steel rule or flat-bladed screwdriver to carefully lever out the clips and remove the trim panel from the door.

Refit the trim panel in the reverse prder of removal.

Door trim capping:

Remove the arm rest interior handle, bezels and trim panel. Take out the screws that secure the capping and unclip it from the door.

Refit the capping in the reverse order of removal, making sure that the door glass seal and wiper are correctly positioned.

13:4 Door glass and regulator

The parts are shown in **FIG 13:2**.

Removal:

1 Remove the door interior trim pad as described in the previous section. Lower the glass until the glass regulator channel 14 is accessible through the aperture in the inner panel.

2 Remove the four screws and washers 3 that secure the regulator 4. The inset shows the regulator fitted to rear doors. When removing the regulator, free the arm from the channel 14 and withdraw the unit through the aperture in the inner door panel. Hold the glass up by hand or support it with rubber wedges between it and the door.

3 On front doors lower the glass right down to the bottom, but on rear doors raise it to the top and support it. If a finisher strip is fitted, remove it. Spring off the six clips 6 securing the outer weatherstrip and remove the strip 6. Similarly remove the wiper strip 7 by freeing its six clips 7. Remove the window channel rubber 8.

4 Drill out the pop rivet 9, remove the screw and washer 10 securing the bottom of the centre window channel, and remove the channel 11 by turning it through 90 deg. and aligning the narrowest section with the glass aperture in the door. Remove the quarter light assembly 12.

5 The window glass can now be removed, if necessary taking off the regulator channel and its rubber 14 from the glass.

Refit the parts in the reverse order of removal, making sure that the regulator channel is fitted centrally on the glass. Grease regulator and pivot points.

13:5 Door locks

The front door lock components are shown in **FIG 13:3** and the rear door lock components in **FIG 13:4**.

Removal:

1 Remove the door trim panel as described in **Section 13:3**. Remove the three screws and shakeproof washers that secure the remote control assembly 3 and remove the lock screw. Disconnect the long remote control rod 4 from the safety locking lever. On front doors, disconnect the remote release rod 16 from the clip 18 (rod 15 from clip 17 on rear doors). Remove the remote control unit.

should be 'feathered' at the edges. Apply two or more thin coats, rubbing down between each coat, rather than one thick one which may run.

Remove the masking and leave the paint to dry for at least a night. Use a mild cutting-compound to lightly polish the surface and remove any spray dust. Leave the paint to fully harden for a period of weeks, not days, before applying wax polish.

13:2 Seat belts

All models are fitted with five seat belts. The individual front bucket seats have lap and sash (lap-diagonal) type belts. The rear seat has three belts, that in the centre being of lap type while the outside belts are lap and sash.

Do not attempt to alter the attachments of the belts and periodically check that the attachments are tight and secure. If the belts become soiled, they may be washed by gently sponging with non-detergent soap and warm water and then allowed to air dry naturally. **Do not apply any cleaning chemicals, bleaches or dyes to the belts.**

If in any doubt about the condition, attachments or details of the seat belts, consult an agent.

13:3 Door interior trim

The trim pad attachments are shown in **FIG 13:1**. Take out the screw and spacer 1 from the regulator handle 2 and remove the handle with its seal. Remove the arm rest 3 by taking out its attachment screws. Slide the

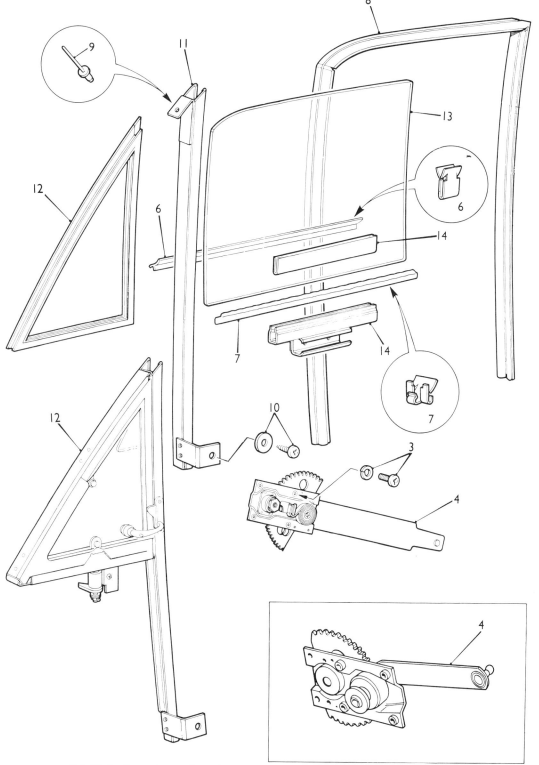

FIG 13:2   Door glass and regulator components. Inset shows rear door regulator

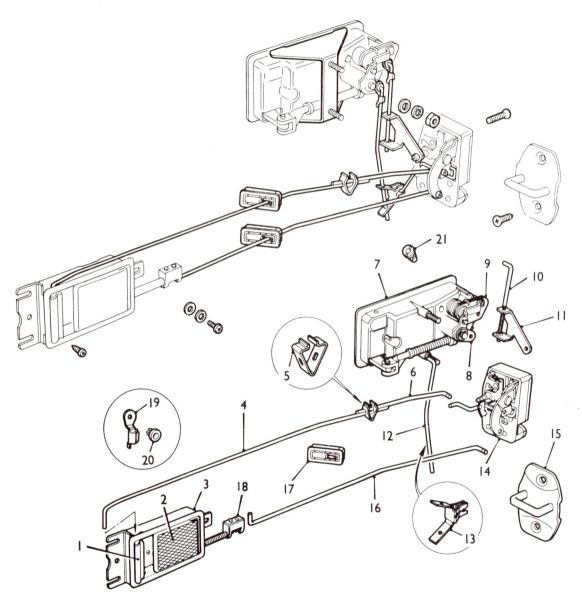

FIG 13:3   The front door lock components

Key to Fig 13:3   1 Safety locking lever   2 Remote release handle   3 Remove control assembly   4 Remote lock rod—long
5 Remote lock rod clip   6 Remote lock rod—short   7 Outside handle   8 Lock barrel freewheel lever   9 Outside handle release lever
10 Screwed rod   11 Transfer lever   12 Lock rod (outside handle)   13 Lock rod clip   14 Disc lock assembly   15 Lock striker
16 Remote release rod   17 Door rod guide   18 Retaining clip   19 Rod clip   20 Rod bush   21 Rod bush (cross control lever)

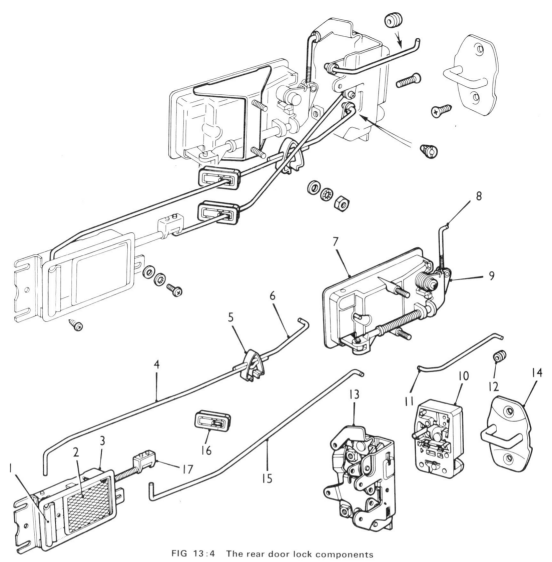

FIG 13:4   The rear door lock components

Key to Fig 13:4   1 Safety locking lever   2 Remote release lever   3 Remote control assembly   4 Remote lock rod—long
5 Remote lock rod clip   6 Remote lock rod—short   7 Outside handle   8 Screwed rod   9 Outside handle release lever
10 Disc lock assembly   11 Child safety lever rod   12 Door grommet   13 Freewheel assembly   14 Lock striker
15 Remote release   16 Door rod guide   17 Retaining clip   18 Rod bush

2 On the front door only, remove the screw that secures the bottom of the centre window channel (see item 10 in **FIG 13:2**), and disconnect the outside handle transfer lever 11 from the lifting stud on the cross control lever.

3 On the rear doors only, disconnect the screwed rod 8 from the cross control lever.

4 Disconnect the remote release rod 16 from the operating lever on the front lock. On the rear lock disconnect the rod 15 from the freewheel assembly on the lock.

5 On the front door, disconnect the lock rod clip 13 from the lock rod 12. On both doors disconnect the short lock rod 6 from the lock assembly. Mark the position of the lock assembly relative to the door, take out the attachments screws and remove the assembly.

The parts are refitted in the reverse order of removal. Lightly lubricate pivot points before refitting the parts. The operation of the remote control unit can be adjusted by altering the lengths of the control rods.

Exterior handle and private lock:

The attachment of the parts are shown in **FIG 13:5**. Remove the door trim pad, as described in **Section 13:3**. Remove the screws or nuts 2 that secure the clamp plate 3 and take out the plate.

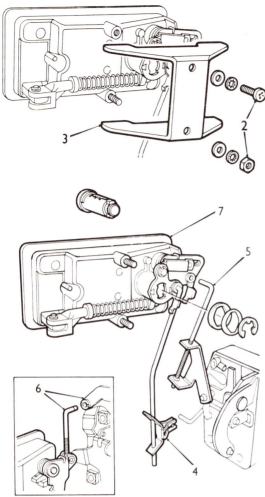

FIG 13:5 Outside door handle attachments

Striker plate :

This is secured to the pillar by two countersunk screws. **Do not slam the door if the striker is out of adjustment.**

Tighten the striker screws sufficiently to hold the striker in place while allowing it to move under pressure. Gently shut the door and pull or push on the door until it is in line with the body. Carefully open the door so as not to move the striker. Make lines around the striker so that it can be aligned horizontally. Make vertical adjustments of the striker until the door can be closed easily, without rattling, dropping or having to be lifted. Tighten the striker adjustment screws fully in this position. When correctly adjusted, it should be possible to press the door in slightly against the compression of the door seal.

13:6 Door attachments

The door attachments are shown in **FIG 13:6**. Remove the door trim panel. Mark the position of the stiffening plates inside the door at 2. Support the door and remove the nuts 3, with their washers, and the stiffening plates 4. The door 5 can then be lifted off.

Refit the door in the reverse order of removal.

The remainder of the figure shows the attachments of the hinges to the body. Note that the front parcel tray must be removed and the trim pulled back to remove the front hinges, and the trim must be removed from the B post to remove the rear hinges.

13:7 The bonnet

The bonnet hinge attachments are shown in **FIG 13:7**. To remove the bonnet, open it and support it open on its stay. Mark around the hinges and bonnet at 4 so as to make refitting easier. Have an assistant support the bonnet and remove the screws 5 that secure the hinge to the bonnet. Lift off the bonnet, **taking great care to prevent its corners from scratching the paintwork on the body.**

Refit the bonnet in the reverse order of removal. If the bonnet does not line up accurately, leave all screws just tight enough to prevent the bonnet from moving under its own weight and pull or push it into alignment. Once the bonnet is in place, do not overtighten the attachment screws.

The bonnet lock components are shown in **FIG 13:8**. If the parts require removal, they are freed in the numerical order shown in the figure.

When refitting the lock parts, the release cable should be located in the clip 4 and trunnion 3 so that a minimum movement of $\frac{1}{2}$ inch (13 mm) is required on the control before the bonnet is released, and the bonnet should release before the control has been pulled out by 2 inch (50 mm) of movement.

The lockpin on the bonnet should be set to the dimension A at 2 inch (50.8 mm). Some adjustment on the bolts 6 is possible to ensure that the pin enters the lock centrally. When the bonnet is closed check if it rattles, in which case shorten the dimension A. If the bonnet is difficult to close, slightly lengthen the dimension A.

On the front door, disconnect the private lock control rod from the locking bar cross-shaft at the clip 4 and disconnect the screwed rod 5 from the exterior handle.

On the rear door, disconnect the screwed rod 6 from the cross lever. In both cases the exterior handle can now be renewed.

The private lock is secured by the circlip shown in the figure and can be taken out after removing the circlip, spring washer and special washer.

The parts are refitted in the reverse order of removal. The screwed rod 5 or 6 should not be altered when dismantling or reassembling the parts. Check the adjustment before refitting the trim panel.

Close the door and partially operate the outside handle and check that there is free movement of the lever before transfer lever and screwed rod move. Fully operate the exterior handle and check that the lock is released before the handle is fully operated. If the settings are not correct, alter the effective length of the screwed rod 5 or 6 to correct.

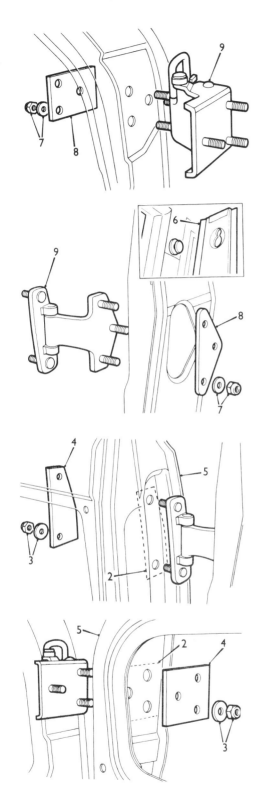

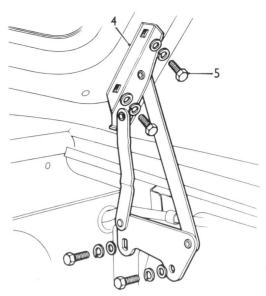

FIG 13:7   The bonnet hinge

FIG 13:6   Door hinges and door attachments

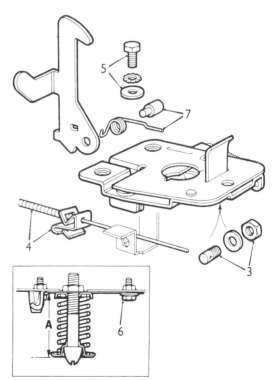

FIG 13:8   The bonnet lock

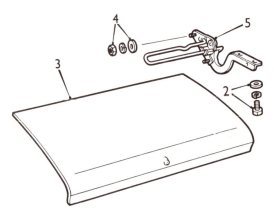

FIG 13:9 Luggage compartment lid

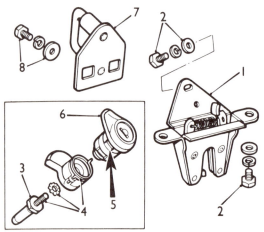

FIG 13:10 Luggage compartment lock

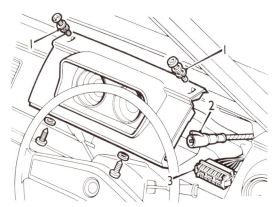

FIG 13:11 The instruments panel attachments

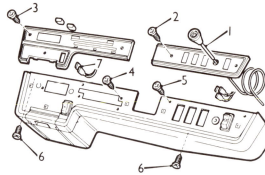

FIG 13:12 Lower facia attachments

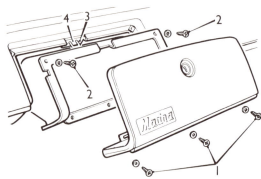

FIG 13:13 The glove box attachments

13:8 The luggage compartment lid

The attachments of the lid are shown in **FIG 13:9**. The lid alone can be removed by taking out the bolts 2 that secure the hinge to the lid, after marking the position of the hinge relative to the lid. The hinges can then be removed from the car by taking off the nuts and washers 4.

The holes are slotted to allow the lid to be accurately aligned with the body when it is refitted. Do not over-tighten the attachment bolts when refitting the lid.

The lock components are shoen in **FIG 13:10**. Mark the position of the catch plate 1 relative to the lid and remove the lock catch by taking out the three screws and washers 2. Slacken the locknut and unscrew the spindle 3 on that the spindle striker, shakeproof washer and spring 4 can be removed. Break off the ears 5 on the retaining clip and remove the seal and lock barrel 6. The striker 7 on the body can be removed, after marking its position, by removing the bolts 8.

Refit the parts in the reverse order of removal, using a new retaining clip on the barrel housing.

13:9 The windscreen

The method of attaching the backlight and quarter light is the same as for the windscreen, but references to the wiper arms and cleaning out the ventilation system can beignored. If a heated backlight is fitted, the leads must be disconnected before removing the glass.

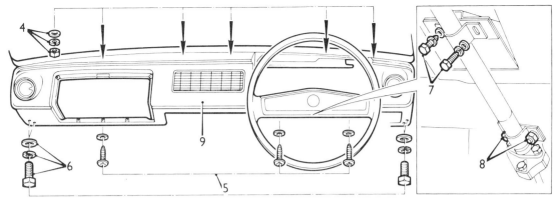

FIG 13:14   The facia attachments

If the glass has broken and fallen away, take care to remove all particles from the car. **If a windscreen has broken it is particularly important to ensure that there are no particles left in the ventilation system, even if it means dismantling the system, as the action of the heater can blow the particles into the front seat occupants' faces.** If the glass has broken but not fallen out, it will be easier to remove if sheets of paper are stuck on both sides.

If the glass has to be removed in an unbroken state, press on it firmly from inside the car with a padded hand or foot. Start at the top corner and have an assistant outside to take the glass as it comes free. **Remove the wiper arms before working on the windscreen.**

Once the glass has been removed, check the flange in the body aperture for damage or distortion. Dress out dents with a block of metal and hammer and file down any protrusions with a smooth file. If the flange is left distorted, it can set up stress points which will cause the new glass to break in service.

Lay the glass onto a padded bench and refit the weather seal to it. Apply sealer between the glass and rubber. Apply a bed of mastic sealer to the body flange. **It should be noted that as the glass is sealed into place, it is unlikely that the old weatherseal will be in good condition after removal and it is always advisable to fit a new one on reassembly.**

Lay a length of cord around the groove in the weatherseal into which the aperture flange will fit, making sure that the cord is long enough to overlap at the ends leaving enough hanging out to get a good grip on.

Pass the ends of the cord through the aperture and have an assistant accurately and firmly press the glass and weatherseal assembly against the aperture. Grip the ends of the cord and pull them out of the groove, parallel and towards the centre of the glass, so that the lip of the rubber is lifted over the flange and into place.

Refit the embellisher or insert. Wipe away surplus sealant with a cloth moistened with white spirits. **Avoid the excessive use of white spirits otherwise the solvent will creep between the glass and rubber and wash out sealant.**

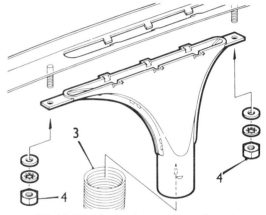

FIG 13:15   The demister vent attachments

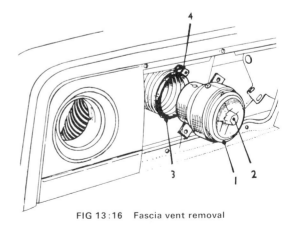

FIG 13:16   Fascia vent removal

Key to Fig 13:16   1 Fascia vent   2 Control knob   3 Air hose   4 Hose clip

13:10 The facia and instrument panel

Instrument panel:

The attachments are shown in **FIG 13:11**. It should be noted that the panel must be removed to change the instrument bulbs or the voltage stabilizer for the fuel and temperature gauges.

Disconnect the battery. Take out the four screws 1 which secure the panel in place. Partially withdraw the panel. Press the release lever and disconnect the speedometer drive cable from the back of the instrument. Disconnect the multi-connector 3 and if a tachometer is fitted, disconnect the lead at the back of the instrument. The panel can then be removed from the car.

Refit the panel in the reverse order of removal, noting that the longer screws are fitted above the instruments.

Lower facia panel:

The attachments are shown in **FIG 13:12**. Free the choke cable 1 from the carburetter and pull out the inner cable. Remove the screws 2 and 3 securing the switch panels and remove the panels. Note that the battery should be disconnected before removing switch panels. Remove the two screws 4 securing the heater controls. Remove the three screws 5 and the two screws 6. Move the panel slightly forward so that the heater switch and lighting switch connections can be freed. Remove the panel, at the same time withdrawing the choke outer cable.

Refit the parts in the reverse order of removal.

Glove box:

The attachments are shown in **FIG 13:13** and the parts are removed in the numerical order shown in the figure. Refit the parts in the reverse order of removal.

The facia:

The facia attachments are shown in **FIG 13:14**. Remove the instrument panel, lower facia and glove box. The parts are then removed in the numerical order shown in the figure. The bolts 7 securing the upper steering column upper clamp must be removed but the nuts for the lower clamp 8 need only be slackened.

The parts are refitted in the reverse order of removal.

13:11 The heater

The attachment of a demister vent is shown in **FIG 13:15** The instrument panel and glove box must be removed as already described to gain access to the nuts which secure the duct. **FIG 13:16** shows the method of removing one of the facia vents fitted to Super de Luxe and TC models. After removal of glove box or instrument cluster as the case may be slacken the hose clip 4 and detach the flexible hose. Remove the two screws securing the vent assembly to the facia and withdraw the vent.

Heater removal:

1 Disconnect battery. Remove wiring from fan switch. Disconnect the two Black/Green wires from the fan.
2 Drain the radiator (see **Chapter 4**).
3 Remove both demister tubes, disconnect the interior-screen-off control at heater. Disconnect the hot-warm-off control at heater.
4 Remove parcel tray if fitted.
5 Remove nuts and washers from support bracket at lefthand side of heater, at rear lower part of heater and from righthand side of heater.
6 Remove screw nut and washer from top support bracket.
7 Remove screw and flat washer securing inlet pipe to heater.
8 Remove heater hose support clips. Loosen both hose clips and remove heater hoses from thermostat housing and water pump (see **Chapter 4**).
9 Apply low pressure air to either hose after opening the control valve and force the water from the heater.
10 Withdraw hoses through the bulkhead and remove heater. Loosen both hose clips and remove hoses.

Refitting is a reversal of removal procedure. Fill up the cooling system, top up after the engine has reached working temperature and check for water leaks.

APPENDIX

TECHNICAL DATA

Engine   Fuel system   Ignition system   Cooling system
Clutch   Transmission   Suspension   Steering   Brakes
Electrical   General dimensions   Weights   Wheels and tyres

WIRING DIAGRAMS

FIG 14:1 General wiring diagram
FIG 14:2 Printed circuit de luxe models
FIG 14:3 Printed circuit super & TC

CONVERSION TABLES

HINTS ON MAINTENANCE AND OVERHAUL

GLOSSARY OF TERMS

INDEX

NOTES

TECHNICAL DATA

Dimensions are in inches unless otherwise stated

Engines:

1500 models

Capacity	1485 cc
Bore and stroke	76.2 x 81.28 mm
Compression ratio	8.6:1

1750 models

Capacity	1748 cc
Bore and stroke	76.2 x 95.75 mm
Compression ratio	8.6:1 (TC 9.0:1)
Cranking pressure	165 to 180 lb/sq in
Idling speed	550 rev/min
Firing order	1,3,4,2

Crankshaft:

Type	Forged steel, 5 main bearings
Main journal diameter	2.503 to 2.251
Crankpin journal diameter	1.8751 to 1.8764
End float	.002 to .003
End float adjustment	Selective thrust washers
Main bearing length	.811 to .812
Main bearing diametrical clearance	.001 to .0029
Main bearing material	Steel-backed, reticular tin/aluminium
Undersizes (main and crankpin)	—.010, .020, .030 and .040

Connecting rods:

Type	Big-end split horizontally, small-end solid
Big-end bearing material	Steel-backed, reticular tin/aluminium
Length between centres	5.828 to 5.832
Small-end bore	.811 to .8115
End float on crankpin (nominal)	.006 to .01

Gudgeon pin:

Type	Press-fit in small-end
Outside diameter	8.124 to .8125

Pistons:

Type	Aluminium, solid skirt W-slotted
Oversize	.020
Clearance in cylinder (bottom of skirt):	.0006 to .0013
Gudgeon pin bore	.8128 to .8130

Compression height (centre of gudgeon to top of piston):

1500 models	1.687 to 1.695
1750 models	1.403 to 1.411
TC models	1.403 to 1.411

Piston rings:

Number per piston	3
Top ring, type	Molybdenum torsional
Second ring, type	Plain torsional
Oil control ring, type	Circumferential expanding (SR.70) with top and bottom segments

	1500 models	
Width, top ring	1.97 to 1.98 mm	(0.0775 to 0.078 in)
second ring	1.97 to 1.98 mm	(0.0775 to 0.078 in)

Groove clearance, top ring	..	..	..	0.05 to 0.089 mm	(0.002 to 0.0035 in)
second ring		..	..	0.05 to 0.089 mm	(0.002 to 0.0035 in)
Ring gap (fitted), top ring	..	..	..	0.20 to 0.40 mm	(0.008 to 0.016 in)
second ring		..	..	0.20 to 0.40 mm	(0.008 to 0.016 in)

1750 and TC models

Width, top ring	..	..	..	1.58 to 1.60 mm	(0.062 to 0.063 in)
second ring	..	..	..	1.58 to 1.60 mm	(0.062 to 0.063 in)
Groove clearance, top ring	..	..	..	0.038 to 0.089 mm	(0.0015 to 0.0035 in)
second ring		..	..	0.038 to 0.089 mm	(0.0015 to 0.0035 in)
Ring gap (fitted), top ring	..	..	..	0.203 to 0.432 mm	(0.008 to 0.017 in)
second ring		..	..	0.203 to 0.432 mm	(0.008 to 0.017 in)
Top, second and third	..	..	..	..	.012 to .022 in
Oil control	..	..	..	..	.015 to .045 in

Camshaft:

Type	..	..	..	..	..	..	Single, overhead, three-bearing, chain driven

Journal diameters:

Front	..	..	..	..	..	..	1.9370 to 1.9375
Centre	..	..	..	..	..	..	1.9683 to 1.9688
Rear	..	..	..	..	..	..	1.9995 to 2.000
End float	..	..	..	..	..	..	.007 max.
End thrust taken	..	..	..	..	..	..	On front locating plate
Adjustment	..	..	..	..	..	..	Renew locating plate
Drive	..	..	..	..	..	..	Chain, .375 pitch x 108 pitches
Bearings	..	..	..	..	..	..	3 direct in aluminium carrier

Tappets:

Type	..	..	..	..	..	..	Bucket, spherical base, internal shims for adjustment

Valves:

Seat angle	..	..	..	..	..	..	$45\frac{1}{2}$ deg. (cylinder head 45)

Head diameter:

Inlet	..	..	..	..	..	..	1.500
Exhaust	..	..	..	..	..	..	1.217

Stem diameter, later engines:

Inlet	..	..	..	..	..	..	.3115 to .3120
Exhaust	..	..	..	..	..	..	.3115 to .3120

Stem to guide clearance:

Inlet	..	..	..	..	..	..	.001 to .002
Exhaust	..	..	..	..	..	..	.001 to .002
Valve lift	..	..	..	..	..	..	.36

Running clearance (adjust if less than .012):

Inlet	..	..	..	..	..	..	.018
Exhaust	..	..	..	..	..	..	.022

Valve springs:

Free length	..	..	..	..	..	..	1.797
Fitted length	..	..	..	..	..	..	1.375
Load at fitted length	..	..	..	..	..	..	52 lb
Load at top of lift	..	..	..	..	..	..	96 lb

Valve timing marks

..	..	..	..	..	..	On boss of camshaft sprocket and camshaft housing. On crankshaft pulley

Oil pump:

Type	..	..	..	..	..	..	Concentric (serviced as a unit)

Oil filter:

Type	..	..	..	..	..	..	Tecalemit fullflow

Oil pressure:

Idling	..	..	..	..	..	..	20 lb/sq in at 500 engine rev/min
Running	..	..	..	..	..	..	60 lb/sq in at 4000 engine rev/min

FUEL SYSTEM

	1500 models	1750 models	TC models
Carburetter(s):			
Make ..	Single-SU HS4	Single-SU HS6	Twin-SU HS6
Type ..	20 deg. semi downdraught	20 deg. semi downdraught	20 deg. semi downdraught
Choke diameter	38.10 mm (1½ in)	44.45 mm (1¾ in)	44.45 mm (1¾ in)
Jet diameter	2.286 mm (0.090 in)	2.54 mm (0.100 in)	2.54 mm (0.100 in)
Needle type	AAE (STD)	BAN (STD)	XBAD or BAD (STD)
Spring colour ..	yellow	red	blue
Damper oil	S.A.E. 20 or 10/30 multigrade	S.A.E. 20 or 10/30 multigrade	S.A.E. 20 or 10/30 multigrade
Air cleaner(s)			
Type ..	Pressed metal air box with tapered tube	Pressed metal air box with tapered tube	Twin— Lynx Ramflo
Element(s)	Impregnated paper element	Impregnated paper element	Polyurethane foam

Fuel pump:	All models
Make and type	Goss—vertical
Delivery pressure	9.23 to 20.85 KPa (1½ to 3¼ lb/sq in)
Delivery rate, maximum	6.24 litre (110 pt/hr) at 6000 engine rev/min
Pushrod length	73.15 to 73.41 mm (2.88 to 2.89 in)
Type of filler cap	Non-vented

IGNITION SYSTEM

	1500 models	1750 models	TC models
Coil	Lucas ALH, oil filled	Lucas ALH, oil filled	Lucas ALH, oil filled
Distributor	Lucas 29D4	Lucas 29D4	Lucas 29D4
Distributor service number	AYH.0724	AYH.0726	AYH.0728
Contact point gap ..	.355 to .406 mm (.014 to .016 in)	.355 to .406 mm (.014 to .016 in)	.355 to .406 mm (.014 to .016 in)
Cam dwell angle	60 ± 3 deg	60 ± 3 deg	60 ± 3 deg
Condenser capacity ..	.18 to .24 (mF)	.18 to .24 (mF)	.18 to .24 (mF)

Distributor test data (decelerating rev/min)	Distributor rev/min	Degrees	Distributor rev/min	Degrees	Distributor rev/min	Degrees
	2250	12½° to 14½°	2250	8° to 10°	2250	9° to 11°
	1900	12½° to 14½°	1750	8° to 10°	1650	9° to 11°
	1400	9½° to 11½°	1250	6° to 8°	1200	7½° to 9½°
	750	5½° to 7½°	750	4° to 6°	700	6° to 8°
	600	3° to 5°	625	2° to 4°	550	3° to 5°
	425	0° to 2°	450	0° to 2°	425	0° to 2°
	375	no advance	375	no advance	375	no advance

Vacuum advance commences	16.95 KPa (5 in hg)	19.34 KPa (6 in hg)	
Vacuum advance finishes	61.02 KPa (8 in hg)	30.91 KPa (9 in hg)	Not applicable
Maximum vacuum advance	10 deg.	6 deg.	Not applicable
Stroboscope ignition timing	10 deg BTDC at 500 engine rev/min	10 deg BTDC at 500 engine rev/min	10 deg BTDC at 500 engine rev/min
Spark plug type	Champion N9Y	Champion N9Y	Champion N9Y
Spark plug type	.635 mm (.025 in)	.635 mm (.025 in)	.635 mm (.025 in)

COOLING SYSTEM

Type	Pressurized. Spill-return to expansion tank. Pump- and fan-assisted
Pressure in system	13 lb/sq in
Thermostat:	
Type	Western Thompson
Opening temperature:	82°C (179°F)
Fully open	94°C (201°F)

CLUTCH

Make and type	Repco 7½ in
To suit gearbox model	12V or 18V (see below for number of splines)

	1500 models	1750 models	TC models
Clutch linings	AMCO 3271	AMCO 3271	MINTEX BM 79 or AMCO 3271
Damper springs	4	4	4
Number of splines	12V (23)	12V (23)	
	18V (20)	18V (20)	18V (20)

Release bearing	Ballbearing RHP6/W 1,5057
Master cylinder bore size	.875
Slave cylinder bore size	.875
Free travel	Nil
Clutch fluid	Leyland Australia HBF-6

MANUAL GEARBOX

	12V	18V
Type	12V	18V
Number of forward gears	4	4
Synchromesh on	All forward gears	
Gear ratios:		
Fourth ot top	1.00:1	1.00:1
Third or intermediate	1.43:1	1.31:1
Second	2.11:1	1.92:1
First or low	3.41:1	3.11:1
Reverse	3.75:1	3.42:1
Overall ratios:		
Fourth or top	3.89:1	3.89:1
Third or intermediate	5.55:1	5.10:1
Second	8.20:1	7.50:1
First or low	13.25:1	12.10:1
Reverse	14.60:1	13.30:1

Road speed in top gear at 1000 rev/min:

12V	18V
26.7 km/h 16.6 mile/h	26.7 km/h 16.6 mile/h

AUTOMATIC TRANSMISSION

Type	Borg Warner 35
Number of forward gears	3
Maximum converter torque multiplication	2:1
Gear ratios:	converter 1.00:1
Top	1.00:1
Intermediate	1.45:1
Low	2.39:1
Reverse	2.09:1
Overall ratios:	
Top	3.89:1
Intermediate	5.65:1
Low	9.30:1
Reverse	8.10:1
Road speed in top gear at 1000 rev/min	26.7 km/hr 16.6 mile/hr

PROPELLER SHAFTS

Type	Front and rear tubular with centre bearing
Diameter	
Front	3 (76.2 mm)
Rear	2 (50.8 mm)
Universal joints	GKN needle roller bearings

REAR AXLE

Type	BW model 68 Hypoid semi-floating
Number of teeth:	
Pinion	9
Crown wheel	35
Ratio	3.89 to 1

REAR SUSPENSION

Type	Semi-elliptic leaf spring with telescopic shock absorbers
Number of spring leaves	2
Width of leaves	2 (50.8 mm)
Working load	270 lb (122.7 kg)
Free camber	5 (126.9 mm)
Camber at working load	2.30 (58.42 mm)

FRONT SUSPENSION

Type	Independent with handed torsion bars
Torsion bar identification	Righthand—red dot
	Lefthand—green dot
Torsion bar adjustment	Vernier bracket and bolt assembly on centre crossmember
Trim height	14.6 to 15 from wheel centre to underside of wheel arch
Shock absorbers	Armstrong York lever type
Camber angle, unladen	1 deg.
Castor angle, unladen	2 deg.
Kingpin inclination	$7\frac{1}{2}$ deg.
Turning circle	31.5 feet between kerbs

STEERING

Type	Rack and pinion
Oil capacity	$\frac{1}{3}$ pint (0.2 litre) HYPOID S.A.E.90
Rack damper setting	Spring loaded and shims
Toe-in	$\frac{1}{16}$
Toe-out on turns	Outer wheel 20 deg. with inner at 19 deg.

BRAKES

Make and type	'Girlock' hydraulic, front and rear
Type, front	Disc with opposed pistons
rear	Drum, self adjusting
Disc diameter	248.92 mm (9.80 in)
Disc thickness	9.652 mm (0.380 in)
Disc permissible run out when assembled on suspension	0.152 mm (.006 in) at 121.7 mm (4.79 in) radius
Disc faces, minimum regrind	0.635 mm (0.025 in) max. from each face
Total disc pad area, four pads	113.5 cm² (17.6 in²)
Minimum pad thickness	1.58 mm (1/16 in)
Disc pad material	'Bendix' BM78
Drum diameter, rear	203.20 mm (8.00 in)
Drum surface, width	43.69 to 44.2 mm (1.72 to 1.74 in)
Rear brake lining material	'Bendix' BM79
Brake lining, area, four brake shoes ..	243.8 cm² (37.8 in²)
Master cylinder bore diameter	17.78 mm (0.70 in)
Master cylinder stroke, maximum ..	36.32 mm (1.43 in)
Caliper bore diameter	48.01 mm (1.89 in
Rear wheel cylinder bore	19.05 mm (0.75 in)
Brake fluid	Leyland Australia—HBF-6
Handbrake cables	Polyethylene lined. No lubrication required

ELECTRICAL

System	12V
Polarity	Negative Earth
Battery	9 plate
Capacity	40 amp/h at 20 hour rate or 46 amp/h at 20 hour rate

Alernator:

Type	Lucas 15ACR-2D
Maximum output	28 amp at 14.2 volts
Cut in speed	500 engine rev/min
Resistance of rotor windings ..	3.5 ohms±5% per phase at 20°C
Resistance of stator windings ..	0.198 ohms±5% per phase at 20°C
Slip ring brushes length (new) ..	12.70 mm (0.5 in)
Voltage regulator, part of alternator ..	(13 ATR) transistorised unit— non adjustable

Starter motor:

Make	Lucas M35AK
Type	88.9 mm (3.5 in) End face commutator
Current draw	325 amp
Starter terminal voltage	7.5 volt
Running torque at 1000 rev/min ..	6.7 Nm (5 lbf/ft) minimum
Brushes, length	15.87 mm ($\frac{5}{8}$ inch)
spring tension	7.8 N (28 ozf)

Wiper motor:

Type	Lucas 12.AUW—twin speed
Drive to wheel boxes	Rack and pinion
Armature end float	.203 to .304 mm (.008 to .012 in)
Running current	1.5 amp normal speed—2 amp high speed
Resistance, armature windings	.23 ohms to 35 ohms at 16°C (60°F)
field windings	Permag

WHEELS AND TYRES

Wheels:

Type	Pressed steel
Size	13 x 4.5J Safety rim (alloy wheels 13 x 5.5 optional)
Stud P.C.D.	107.95 mm (4¼ in)

Tyres:

Crossply (Alternative to radial ply):	Y78L, 13 Tubeless low profile
Tyre pressures, average load, front	152 KPa (22 lbf/in²)
rear	152 KPa (22 lbf/in²)
Tyre pressures, full load, front	165 KPa (24 lbf/in²)
rear	179 KPa (26 lbf/in²)
Radial ply (alternative to crossply):	XR70H, 13 tubeless, radial ply
Tyre pressures, average load, front	165 KPa (24 lbf/in²)
rear	165 KPa (24 lbf/in²)
Tyre pressures, full load, front	179 KPa (26 lbf/in²)
rear	193 KPa (28 lbf/in²)

CAPACITIES

Engine oil capacity including filter	3.40 litre (6.00 pt)
Filter capacity	0.56 litre (1.00 pt)
Transmission oil capacity, manual	1.12 litre (1.95 pt)
automatic	5.40 litre (9.50 pt)
Rear axle	1.00 litre (1.75 pt)
Cooling system including heater	6.00 litre (10.50 pt)
Fuel tank	54.60 litre 12 gal.

Dimensions:	1500 models Two door model	1750 models Four door model	TC model
Track: Front ..	1333.5 mm (52.5 in)	1333 mm (52.5 in)	1333.5 mm (52.5 in)
Rear ..	1331 mm (52.4 in)	1331 mm (52.4 in)	1331 mm (52.4 in)
Turning circle between kerbs ..	9.4 m (31.5 ft)	9.4 m (31.5 ft)	9.4 m (31.5 ft)
Wheel base ..	2438 mm (96 in)	2438 mm (96 in)	2438 mm (96 in)
Overall: height ..	1397 mm (55 in)	1397 mm (55 in)	1397 mm (55 in)
width ..	1633.5 mm (64.31 in)	1633.5 mm (64.31 in)	1633.5 mm (64.31 in)
length ..	4143 mm (163.1 in)	4222 mm (166.1 in)	4143 mm (163.1 in)
Ground clearance	165 mm (6.5 in)	165 mm (6.5 in)	165 mm (6.5 in)
Weights:			
Registration weight	Saloon Manual 887 kg (1955 lb) Coupe Manual 857 kg (1889 lb)	Saloon Manual 890 kg (1963 lb) Coupe 880 kg (1897 lb) Saloon Auto 925 kg (2037 lb) Coupe Auto 894 kg (1971 lb)	Manual 862 kg (1902 lb) Automatic 896 kg (1976 lb)
Maximum towing weights	900 kg (2000 lb)	900 kg (2000 lb)	900 kg (2000 lb)

TORQUE WRENCH SETTINGS

Engine:	Nm	lbf ft
Oil filter adaptor bolt	47.4	35
Cylinder head bolts	81.3	60
Cam carrier to cylinder head	27.0	20
Camshaft sprocket	47.0	35
Camshaft cover	8.13	6
Thermo housing to cylinder head water outlet elbow	10.8 to 13.55	8 to 10
Manifolds to cylinder head (bolts and nuts)	24.4 to 27.0	18 to 20
Carburetter studs	8.13 to 10.8	6 to 8
Water pump set screws	24.4 to 27.0	18 to 20
Pulley	24.4	18
Front cover bolts	27.0	20
Petrol pump bolts	20.3 to 27.4	15 to 18
Crankshaft pulley bolt	81.3 to 95.0	60 to 70
Timing chain guide strips	24.4 to 27.0	18 to 20
Timing cover	24.4 to 27.0	18 to 20
Pivot pin	24.4 to 27.0	18 to 20
Big end nuts	42.0 to 47.4	31 to 35
Main bearing bolts	95.0	70
Flywheel bolts	81.3	60
Oil pump mounting bolt	24.4 to 27.0	18 to 20
Sump to block $\frac{5}{16}$ in bolts	27.0 to 33.8	20 to 25
$\frac{3}{8}$ in bolts	40.6	30
Transmission manual:		
Drain plug	27.1 to 32.5	20 to 24
Transmission case top cover to case bolts $\frac{7}{16}$ in	10.18 to 14.8	8 to 11
Transmission reverse plate to rear $\frac{3}{8}$ in	10.18 to 14.8	8 to 11
Transmission rear ext. to trans case $\frac{5}{16}$	24.4 to 29.6	18 to 22
Flywheel housing securing bolts	38 to 46.2	28 to 34
Third motion shaft nut	122 to 135.5	90 to 100
Automatic transmission:		
Drive flange nut	74.5 to 81	55 to 60
Drive plate to crankshaft	67.5	50
Converter to drive plate bolts	34 to 40.6	25 to 30
Transmission case to converter housing bolts	10.8 to 17.6	8 to 13
Rear extension to transmission case bolts	40.6 to 74.5	30 to 55
Oil pan to gear box bolts	12.2 to 16.3	9 to 12
Front servo bolts	10.8 to 17.6	8 to 13
Rear servo bolts	17.6 to 36.6	13 to 27
Pump adaptor to housing screw	2.7 to 4	2 to 3
Pump adaptor to housing bolts	23 to 44.5	17 to 32
Pump adaptor to transmission case bolts	10.8 to 24.4	8 to 18
Manual shaft locknut	9.5 to 12.2	7 to 9
Pressure adaptor plug	5.4 to 6.8	4 to 5
Drain plug	10.8 to 13.5	8 to 10
Upper valve body to lower valve body screws	27.1 to 40.6	20 to 30
Lower valve body to upper valve body screws	27.1 to 40.6	20 to 30
Oil tube and end plate to valve body screws	27.1 to 40.6	20 to 30
Valve bodies to transmission case bolts	6.1 to 12.2	4.5 to 9
Cam bracket screws	27.1 to 54.2	20 to 40
Governor to counterweight screws	5.4 to 6.8	4 to 5
Governor to cover plate screws	27.1 to 65	20 to 48
Front servo adjusting screw locknut	20.3 to 27.1	15 to 20
Rear servo adjusting screw locknut	40.6 to 54.2	30 to 40
Centre support bolts	13.5 to 24.2	10 to 18
Downshift cable adaptor	10.8 to 12.2	8 to 9

Propeller and drive shaft:

	Nm	lbf ft
Centre bearing mounting screws	29.8	22
Flange retaining bolt nuts	38	28

Rear axle:

	Nm	lbf ft
Crown wheel bolts	54.2 to 68	40 to 50
Bearing cap bolts	47.4 to 61	35 to 45
Rear cover bolts	23 to 29.8	17 to 22
Pinion nut	324.2 to 378.4	240 to 280
Wheel nuts	81	60

Rear suspension:

	Nm	lbf ft
Upper shackle pin nuts $\frac{3}{8}$ in	38 to 40.6	28 to 30
Spring eye bolts nuts $\frac{7}{16}$ in	54.2 to 61	40 to 45
Spring 'U' bolt nuts $\frac{3}{8}$ in	40.6 to 47.5	30 to 35
Shock absorber to spring bracket $\frac{3}{8}$ in	38 to 40.6	28 to 30
Shock absorber to body bracket $\frac{1}{2}$ in	38 to 40.6	28 to 30

Front suspension:

	Nm	lbf ft
Ball pin retainer locknut	95 to 108	70 to 80
Eyebolt nut	67.7	50
Shock absorber retaining nuts	40.6 to 47.5	30 to 35
Tie rod fork nut	54.2 to 61	40 to 45
Tie rod to fork	40.6 to 47.5	30 to 35
Upper swivel pin nuts	47.5 to 54.2	35 to 40
Lower swivel pin nuts	34 to 40.6	25 to 30

Steering:

	Nm	lbf ft
Rack clamp bracket nuts $\frac{5}{16}$ in	24.4 to 27.1	18 to 20
Tie rod ball pin nuts $\frac{3}{8}$ in	27.1 to 32.5	20 to 24
Flexible joint pinch bolt nut	8.1 to 10.8	6 to 8
Pinion end cover retaining bolts	20.4 to 24.4	15 to 18
Pinion pre-load	1.36 to 1.58	12 to 14 lbf in
Rack yoke cover bolts	20.4 to 24.4	15 to 18
Tie rod hpusing lock nut	44.6 to 50	33 to 37
Tie rod ball spheres pre-load	3.62 to 4.18	32 to 52 lbf in
Steering column mounting bolts $\frac{5}{16}$ in	19 to 24.4	14 to 18
Flexible joint coupling bolts $\frac{5}{16}$ in	24.4 to 27.1	18 to 20
Steering column lock shear screw	14.1	19
Steering wheel nut	43.5 to 50	32 to 37
Tie rod lock nuts $\frac{1}{2}$ in	54.2 to 61	40 to 45

Brakes:

	Nm	lbf ft
Bleed screw	5.4 to 8.1	4 to 6
Master cylinder retaining nuts	20.3 to 25.8	15 to 19
Caliper retaining bolts	54.2 to 61	40 to 45
Wheel cylinder retaining bolts	5.4 to 6.8	4 to 5
Disc retaining bolts	54.2 to 61	40 to 45

Electrical:

	Nm	lbf ft
Distributor flange retaining screws	10.8 to 13.5	8 to 10
Alternator pulley retaining nut	27.1 to 40.6	20 to 30

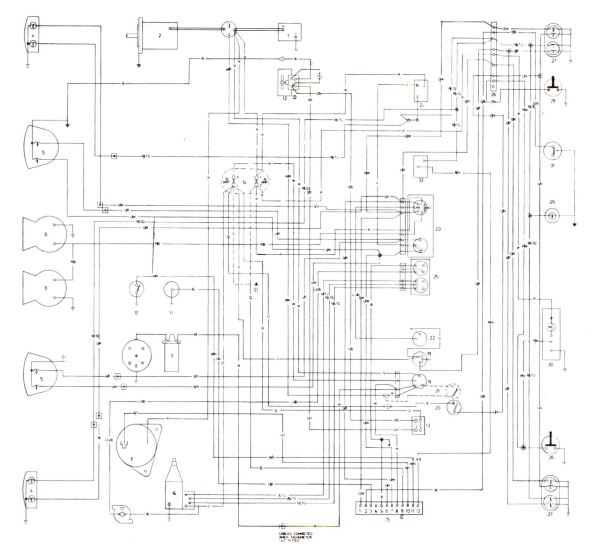

FIG 14:1 General wiring diagram

CABLES CONNECTED
WHEN TACHOMETER
NOT FITTED

Key to Fig 14:1 1 Battery 2 Starter motor 3 Starter solenoid 4 Side flasher lamp 5 Headlight 6 Horn 7 Alternator 8 Distributor 9 Coil 10 Oil switch 11 Temp. switch 12 Heater motor 13 Heater motor switch 14 Fuse box 15 Printed circuit plug 16 Wiper motor 17 Washer motor 18 Ignition switch 19 Stoplight switch 20 Reverse light switch 21 Inhibitor switch 22 Flasher unit 23 Flasher/dip switch 24 Light switch 25 Washer wiper switch 26 Body junction plug 27 Rear light 28 Door switch 29 Number plate lamp 30 Interior lamp 31 Tank unit 32 Panel light switch

Key to cable colour codes **B** Black **U** Blue **N** Brown **G** Green **LTG** Light green **O** Orange **K** Pink **P** Purple **R** Red **S** Slate **W** White **Y** Yellow

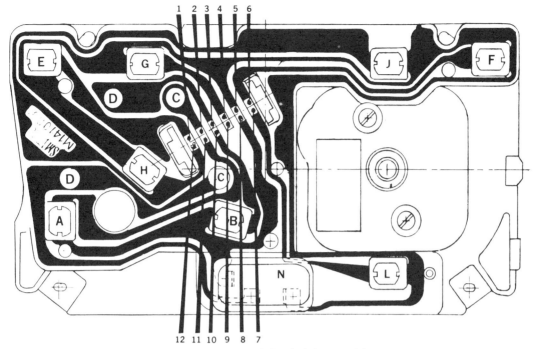

FIG 14:2   Printed circuit de luxe models

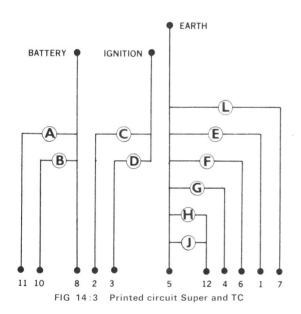

FIG 14:3   Printed circuit Super and TC

Key to Fig 14:2   **A** Oil pressure warning lamp   **B** Ignition warning lamp   **C** Fuel gauge   **D** Temperature gauge   **E** Direction indicator right hand   **F** Direction indicator left hand

Key to Fig 14:3   **G** Stop lamp warning lamp   **H** Instrument illumination lamp   **J** Instrument illumination lamp   **K** Instrument illumination lamp   **L** High beam warning lamp   **M** Time piece or tachometer feed   **N** Voltage stabilizer

Inches		Decimals	Milli-metres	Inches to Millimetres		Millimetres to Inches	
				Inches	mm	mm	Inches
	1/64	.015625	.3969	.001	.0254	.01	.00039
1/32		.03125	.7937	.002	.0508	.02	.00079
	3/64	.046875	1.1906	.003	.0762	.03	.00118
1/16		.0625	1.5875	.004	.1016	.04	.00157
	5/64	.078125	1.9844	.005	.1270	.05	.00197
3/32		.09375	2.3812	.006	.1524	.06	.00236
	7/64	.109375	2.7781	.007	.1778	.07	.00276
1/8		.125	3.1750	.008	.2032	.08	.00315
	9/64	.140625	3.5719	.009	.2286	.09	.00354
5/32		.15625	3.9687	.01	.254	.1	.00394
	11/64	.171875	4.3656	.02	.508	.2	.00787
3/16		.1875	4.7625	.03	.762	.3	.01181
	13/64	.203125	5·1594	.04	1.016	.4	.01575
7/32		.21875	5.5562	.05	1.270	.5	.01969
	15/64	.234375	5.9531	.06	1.524	.6	.02362
1/4		.25	6.3500	.07	1.778	.7	.02756
	17/64	.265625	6.7469	.08	2.032	.8	.03150
9/32		.28125	7.1437	.09	2.286	.9	.03543
	19/64	.296875	7.5406	.1	2.54	1	.03937
5/16		.3125	7.9375	.2	5.08	2	.07874
	21/64	.328125	8.3344	.3	7.62	3	.11811
11/32		.34375	8.7312	.4	10.16	4	.15748
	23/64	.359375	9.1281	.5	12.70	5	.19685
3/8		.375	9.5250	.6	15.24	6	.23622
	25/64	.390625	9.9219	.7	17.78	7	.27559
13/32		.40625	10.3187	.8	20.32	8	.31496
	27/64	.421875	10.7156	.9	22.86	9	.35433
7/16		.4375	11.1125	1	25.4	10	.39370
	29/64	.453125	11.5094	2	50.8	11	.43307
15/32		.46875	11.9062	3	76.2	12	.47244
	31/64	.484375	12.3031	4	101.6	13	.51181
1/2		.5	12.7000	5	127.0	14	.55118
	33/64	.515625	13.0969	6	152.4	15	.59055
17/32		.53125	13.4937	7	177.8	16	.62992
	35/64	.546875	13.8906	8	203.2	17	.66929
9/16		.5625	14.2875	9	228.6	18	.70866
	37/64	.578125	14.6844	10	254.0	19	.74803
19/32		.59375	15.0812	11	279.4	20	.78740
	39/64	.609375	15.4781	12	304.8	21	.82677
5/8		.625	15.8750	13	330.2	22	.86614
	41/64	.640625	16.2719	14	355.6	23	.90551
21/32		.65625	16.6687	15	381.0	24	.94488
	43/64	.671875	17.0656	16	406.4	25	.98425
11/16		.6875	17.4625	17	431.8	26	1.02362
	45/64	.703125	17.8594	18	457.2	27	1.06299
23/32		.71875	18.2562	19	482.6	28	1.10236
	47/64	.734375	18.6531	20	508.0	29	1.14173
3/4		.75	19.0500	21	533.4	30	1.18110
	49/64	.765625	19.4469	22	558.8	31	1.22047
25/32		.78125	19.8437	23	584.2	32	1.25984
	51/64	.796875	20.2406	24	609.6	33	1.29921
13/16		.8125	20.6375	25	635.0	34	1.33858
	53/64	.828125	21.0344	26	660.4	35	1.37795
27/32		.84375	21.4312	27	685.8	36	1.41732
	55/64	.859375	21.8281	28	711.2	37	1.4567
7/8		.875	22.2250	29	736.6	38	1.4961
	57/64	.890625	22.6219	30	762.0	39	1.5354
29/32		.90625	23.0187	31	787.4	40	1.5748
	59/64	.921875	23.4156	32	812.8	41	1.6142
15/16		.9375	23.8125	33	838.2	42	1.6535
	61/64	.953125	24.2094	34	863.6	43	1.6929
31/32		.96875	24.6062	35	889.0	44	1.7323
	63/64	.984375	25.0031	36	914.4	45	1.7717

UNITS	Pints to Litres	Gallons to Litres	Litres to Pints	Litres to Gallons	Miles to Kilometres	Kilometres to Miles	Lbs. per sq. In. to Kg. per sq. Cm.	Kg. per sq. Cm. to Lbs. per sq. In.
1	.57	4.55	1.76	.22	1.61	.62	.07	14.22
2	1.14	9.09	3.52	.44	3.22	1.24	.14	28.50
3	1.70	13.64	5.28	.66	4.83	1.86	.21	42.67
4	2.27	18.18	7.04	.88	6.44	2.49	.28	56.89
5	2.84	22.73	8.80	1.10	8.05	3.11	.35	71.12
6	3.41	27.28	10.56	1.32	9.66	3.73	.42	85.34
7	3.98	31.82	12.32	1.54	11.27	4.35	.49	99.56
8	4.55	36.37	14.08	1.76	12.88	4.97	.56	113.79
9		40.91	15.84	1.98	14.48	5.59	.63	128.00
10		45.46	17.60	2.20	16.09	6.21	.70	142.23
20				4.40	32.19	12.43	1.41	284.47
30				6.60	48.28	18.64	2.11	426.70
40				8.80	64.37	24.85		
50					80.47	31.07		
60					96.56	37.28		
70					112.65	43.50		
80					128.75	49.71		
90					144.84	55.92		
100					160.93	62.14		

UNITS	Lb ft to kgm	Kgm to lb ft	UNITS	Lb ft to kgm	Kgm to lb ft
1	.138	7.233	7	.967	50.631
2	.276	14.466	8	1.106	57.864
3	.414	21.699	9	1.244	65.097
4	.553	28.932	10	1.382	72.330
5	.691	36.165	20	2.765	144.660
6	.829	43.398	30	4.147	216.990

HINTS ON MAINTENANCE AND OVERHAUL

There are few things more rewarding than the restoration of a vehicle's original peak of efficiency and smooth performance.

The following notes are intended to help the owner to reach that state of perfection. Providing that he possesses the basic manual skills he should have no difficulty in performing most of the operations detailed in this manual. It must be stressed, however, that where recommended in the manual, highly-skilled operations ought to be entrusted to experts, who have the necessary equipment, to carry out the work satisfactorily.

Quality of workmanship:

The hazardous driving conditions on the roads to-day demand that vehicles should be as nearly perfect, mechanically, as possible. It is therefore most important that amateur work be carried out with care, bearing in mind the often inadequate working conditions, and also the inferior tools which may have to be used. It is easy to counsel perfection in all things, and we recognize that it may be setting an impossibly high standard. We do, however, suggest that every care should be taken to ensure that a vehicle is as safe to take on the road as it is humanly possible to make it.

Safe working conditions:

Even though a vehicle may be stationary, it is still potentially dangerous if certain sensible precautions are not taken when working on it while it is supported on jacks or blocks. It is indeed preferable not to use jacks alone, but to supplement them with carefully placed blocks, so that there will be plenty of support if the car rolls off the jacks during a strenuous manoeuvre. Axle stands are an excellent way of providing a rigid base which is not readily disturbed. Piles of bricks are a dangerous substitute. Be careful not to get under heavy loads on lifting tackle, the load could fall. It is preferable not to work alone when lifting an engine, or when working underneath a vehicle which is supported well off the ground. To be trapped, particularly under the vehicle, may have unpleasant results if help is not quickly forthcoming. Make some provision, however humble, to deal with fires. Always disconnect a battery if there is a likelihood of electrical shorts. These may start a fire if there is leaking fuel about. This applies particularly to leads which can carry a heavy current, like those in the starter circuit. While on the subject of electricity, we must also stress the danger of using equipment which is run off the mains and which has no earth or has faulty wiring or connections. So many workshops have damp floors, and electrical shocks are of such a nature that it is sometimes impossible to let go of a live lead or piece of equipment due to the muscular spasms which take place.

Work demanding special care:

This involves the servicing of braking, steering and suspension systems. On the road, failure of the braking system may be disastrous. Make quite sure that there can be no possibility of failure through the bursting of rusty brake pipes or rotten hoses, nor to a sudden loss of pressure due to defective seals or valves.

Problems:

The chief problems which may face an operator are:
1 External dirt.
2 Difficulty in undoing tight fixings
3 Dismantling unfamiliar mechanisms.
4 Deciding in what respect parts are defective.
5 Confusion about the correct order for reassembly.
6 Adjusting running clearances.
7 Road testing.
8 Final tuning.

Practical suggestion to solve the problems:

1 Preliminary cleaning of large parts—engines, transmissions, steering, suspensions, etc.,—should be carried out before removal from the car. Where road dirt and mud alone are present, wash clean with a high-pressure water jet, brushing to remove stubborn adhesions, and allow to drain and dry. Where oil or grease is also present, wash down with a proprietary compound (Gunk, Teepol etc.,) applying with a stiff brush—an old paint brush is suitable—into all crevices. Cover the distributor and ignition coils with a polythene bag and then apply a strong water jet to clear the loosened deposits. Allow to drain and dry. The assemblies will then be sufficiently clean to remove and transfer to the bench for the next stage.

   On the bench, further cleaning can be carried out, first wiping the parts as free as possible from grease with old newspaper. Avoid using rag or cotton waste which can leave clogging fibres behind. Any remaining grease can be removed with a brush dipped in paraffin. If necessary, traces of paraffin can be removed by carbon tetrachloride. Avoid using paraffin or petrol in large quantities for cleaning in enclosed areas, such as garages, on account of the high fire risk.

   When all exteriors have been cleaned, and not before, dismantling can be commenced. This ensures that dirt will not enter into interiors and orifices revealed by dismantling. In the next phases, where components have to be cleaned, use carbon tetrachloride in preference to petrol and keep the containers covered except when in use. After the components have been cleaned, plug small holes with tapered hard wood plugs cut to size and blank off larger orifices with greaseproof paper and masking tape. Do not use soft wood plugs or matchsticks as they may break.

2 It is not advisable to hammer on the end of a screw thread, but if it must be done, first screw on a nut to protect the thread, and use a lead hammer. This applies particularly to the removal of tapered cotters. Nuts and bolts seem to 'grow' together, especially in exhaust systems. If penetrating oil does not work, try the judicious application of heat, but be careful of starting a fire. Asbestos sheet or cloth is useful to isolate heat.

   Tight bushes or pieces of tail-pipe rusted into a silencer can be removed by splitting them with an open-ended hacksaw. Tight screws can sometimes be started by a tap from a hammer on the end of a suitable screwdriver. Many tight fittings will yield to the judicious use of a hammer, but it must be a soft-faced hammer if damage is to be avoided, use a heavy block on the opposite side to absorb shock. Any parts of the steering system which have been damaged should be renewed, as attempts to repair them may lead to cracking and subsequent failure, and steering ball joints should be disconnected using a recommended tool to prevent damage.

3 If often happens that an owner is baffled when trying to dismantle an unfamiliar piece of equipment. So many modern devices are pressed together or assembled by spinning-over flanges, that they must be sawn apart. The intention is that the whole assembly must be renewed. However, parts which appear to be in one piece to the naked eye, may reveal close-fitting joint lines when inspected with a magnifying glass, and, this may provide the necessary clue to dismantling. Left-handed screw threads are used where rotational forces would tend to unscrew a right-handed screw thread.

Be very careful when dismantling mechanisms which may come apart suddenly. Work in an enclosed space where the parts will be contained, and drape a piece of cloth over the device if springs are likely to fly in all directions. Mark everything which might be reassembled in the wrong position, scratched symbols may be used on unstressed parts, or a sequence of tiny dots from a centre punch can be useful. Stressed parts should never be scratched or centre-popped as this may lead to cracking under working conditions. Store parts which look alike in the correct order for reassembly. Never rely upon memory to assist in the assembly of complicated mechanisms, especially when they will be dismantled for a long time, but make notes, and drawings to supplement the diagrams in the manual, and put labels on detached wires. Rust stains may indicate unlubricated wear. This can sometimes be seen round the outside edge of a bearing cup in a universal joint. Look for bright rubbing marks on parts which normally should not make heavy contact. These might prove that something is bent or running out of truth. For example, there might be bright marks on one side of a piston, at the top near the ring grooves, and others at the bottom of the skirt on the other side. This could well be the clue to a bent connecting rod. Suspected cracks can be proved by heating the component in a light oil to approximately 100°C, removing, drying off, and dusting with french chalk, if a crack is present the oil retained in the crack will stain the french chalk.

4 In determining wear, and the degree, against the permissible limits set in the manual, accurate measurement can only be achieved by the use of a micrometer. In many cases, the wear is given to the fourth place of decimals; that is in ten-thousandths of an inch. This can be read by the vernier scale on the barrel of a good micrometer. Bore diameters are more difficult to determine. If, however, the matching shaft is accurately measured, the degree of play in the bore can be felt as a guide to its suitability. In other cases, the shank of a twist drill of known diameter is a handy check.

Many methods have been devised for determining the clearance between bearing surfaces. To-day the best and simplest is by the use of Plastigage, obtainable from most garages. A thin plastic thread is laid between the two surfaces and the bearing is tightened, flattening the thread. On removal, the width of the thread is compared with a scale supplied with the thread and the clearance is read off directly. Sometimes joint faces leak persistently, even after gasket renewal. The fault will then be traceable to distortion, dirt or burrs. Studs which are screwed into soft metal frequently raise burrs at the point of entry. A quick cure for this is to chamfer the edge of the hole in the part which fits over the stud.

5 **Always check a replacement part with the original one before it is fitted.**

If parts are not marked, and the order for reassembly is not known, a little detective work will help. Look for marks which are due to wear to see if they can be mated. Joint faces may not be identical due to manufacturing errors, and parts which overlap may be stained, giving a clue to the correct position. Most fixings leave identifying marks especially if they were painted over on assembly. It is then easier to decide whether a nut, for instance, has a plain, a spring, or a shakeproof washer under it. All running surfaces become 'bedded' together after long spells of work and tiny imperfections on one part will be found to have left corresponding marks on the other. This is particularly true of shafts and bearings and even a score on a cylinder wall will show on the piston.

6 Checking end float or rocker clearances by feeler gauge may not always give accurate results because of wear. For instance, the rocker tip which bears on a valve stem may be deeply pitted, in which case the feeler will simply be bridging a depression. Thrust washers may also wear depressions in opposing faces to make accurate measurement difficult. End float is then easier to check by using a dial gauge. It is common practice to adjust end play in bearing assemblies, like front hubs with taper rollers, by doing up the axle nut until the hub becomes stiff to turn and then backing it off a little. Do not use this method with ballbearing hubs as the assembly is often preloaded by tightening the axle nut to its fullest extent. If the splitpin hole will not line up, file the base of the nut a little.

Steering assemblies often wear in the straight-ahead position. If any part is adjusted, make sure that it remains free when moved from lock to lock. Do not be surprised if an assembly like a steering gearbox, which is known to be carefully adjusted outside the car, becomes stiff when it is bolted in place. This will be due to distortion of the case by the pull of the mounting bolts, particularly if the mounting points are not all touching together. This problem may be met in other equipment and is cured by careful attention to the alignment of mounting points.

When a spanner is stamped with a size and A/F it means that the dimension is the width between the jaws and has no connection with ANF, which is the designation for the American National Fine thread. Coarse threads like Whitworth are rarely used on cars to-day except for studs which screw into soft aluminium or cast iron. For this reason it might be found that the top end of a cylinder head stud has a fine thread and the lower end a coarse thread to screw into the cylinder block. If the car has mainly UNF threads then it is likely that any coarse threads will be UNC, which are not the same as Whitworth. Small sizes have the same number of threads in Whitworth and UNC, but in the $\frac{1}{2}$ inch size for example, there are twelve threads to the inch in the former and thirteen in the latter.

7 After a major overhaul, particularly if a great deal of work has been done on the braking, steering and suspension systems, it is advisable to approach the problem of testing with care. If the braking system has been overhauled, apply heavy pressure to the brake pedal and get a second operator to check every possible source of leakage. The brakes may work extremely well, but a leak could cause complete failure after a few miles.

Do not fit the hub caps until every wheel nut has been checked for tightness, and make sure the tyre pressures are correct. Check the levels of coolant, lubricants and hydraulic fluids. Being satisfied that all is well, take the car on the road and test the brakes at once. Check the steering and the action of the handbrake. Do all this at moderate speeds on quiet roads, and make sure there is no other vehicle behind you when you try a rapid stop.

Finally, remember that many parts settle down after a time, so check for tightness of all fixings after the car has been on the road for a hundred miles or so.

8 It is useless to tune an engine which has not reached its normal running temperature. In the same way, the tune of an engine which is stiff after a rebore will be different when the engine is again running free. Remember too, that rocker clearances on pushrod operated valve gear will change when the cylinder head nuts are tightened after an initial period of running with a new head gasket.

Trouble may not always be due to what seems the obvious cause. Ignition, carburation and mechanical condition are interdependent and spitting back through the carburetter, which might be attributed to a weak mixture, can be caused by a sticking inlet valve.

For one final hint on tuning, never adjust more than one thing at a time or it will be impossible to tell which adjustment produced the desired result.

NOTES

GLOSSARY OF TERMS

Allen key — Cranked wrench of hexagonal section for use with socket head screws.

Alternator — Electrical generator producing alternating current. Rectified to direct current for battery charging.

Ambient temperature — Surrounding atmospheric temperature.

Annulus — Used in engineering to indicate the outer ring gear of an epicyclic gear train.

Armature — The shaft carrying the windings, which rotates in the magnetic field of a generator or starter motor. That part of a solenoid or relay which is activated by the magnetic field.

Axial — In line with, or pertaining to, an axis.

Backlash — Play in meshing gears.

Balance lever — A bar where force applied at the centre is equally divided between connections at the ends.

Banjo axle — Axle casing with large diameter housing for the crownwheel and differential.

Bendix pinion — A self-engaging and self-disengaging drive on a starter motor shaft.

Bevel pinion — A conical shaped gearwheel, designed to mesh with a similar gear with an axis usually at 90 deg. to its own.

bhp — Brake horse power, measured on a dynamometer.

bmep — Brake mean effective pressure. Average pressure on a piston during the working stroke.

Brake cylinder — Cylinder with hydraulically operated piston(s) acting on brake shoes or pad(s).

Brake regulator — Control valve fitted in hydraulic braking system which limits brake pressure to rear brakes during heavy braking to prevent rear wheel locking.

Camber — Angle at which a wheel is tilted from the vertical.

Capacitor — Modern term for an electrical condenser. Part of distributor assembly, connected across contact breaker points, acts as an interference suppressor.

Castellated — Top face of a nut, slotted across the flats, to take a locking splitpin.

Castor — Angle at which the kingpin or swivel pin is tilted when viewed from the side.

cc — Cubic centimetres. Engine capacity is arrived at by multiplying the area of the bore in sq cm by the stroke in cm by the number of cylinders.

Clevis — U-shaped forked connector used with a clevis pin, usually at handbrake connections.

Collet — A type of collar, usually split and located in a groove in a shaft, and held in place by a retainer. The arrangement used to retain the spring(s) on a valve stem in most cases.

Commutator — Rotating segmented current distributor between armature windings and brushes in generator or motor.

Compression — The ratio, or quantitative relation, of the total volume (piston at bottom of stroke) to the unswept volume (piston at top of stroke) in an engine cylinder.

Condenser — See capacitor.

Core plug — Plug for blanking off a manufacturing hole in a casting.

Crownwheel — Large bevel gear in rear axle, driven by a bevel pinion attached to the propeller shaft. Sometimes called a 'ring gear'.

'C'-spanner — Like a 'C' with a handle. For use on screwed collars without flats, but with slots or holes.

Damper — Modern term for shock-absorber, used in vehicle suspension systems to damp out spring oscillations.

Depression — The lowering of atmospheric pressure as in the inlet manifold and carburetter.

Dowel — Close tolerance pin, peg, tube, or bolt, which accurately locates mating parts.

Drag link — Rod connecting steering box drop arm (pitman arm) to nearest front wheel steering arm in certain types of steering systems.

Dry liner — Thinwall tube pressed into cylinder bore

Dry sump — Lubrication system where all oil is scavenged from the sump, and returned to a separate tank.

Dynamo — See Generator.

Electrode — Terminal, part of an electrical component, such as the points or 'Electrodes' of a sparking plug.

Electrolyte — In lead-acid car batteries a solution of sulphuric acid and distilled water.

End float — The axial movement between associated parts, end play.

EP — Extreme pressure. In lubricants, special grades for heavily loaded bearing surfaces, such as gear teeth in a gearbox, or crownwheel and pinion in a rear axle.

Fade	Of brakes. Reduced efficiency due to overheating.
Field coils	Windings on the polepieces of motors and generators.
Fillets	Narrow finishing strips usually applied to interior bodywork.
First motion shaft	Input shaft from clutch to gear-box.
Fullflow filter	Filters in which all the oil is pumped to the engine. If the element becomes clogged, a bypass valve operates to pass unfiltered oil to the engine.
FWD	Front wheel drive.
Gear pump	Two meshing gears in a close fitting casing. Oil is carried from the inlet round the outside of both gears in the spaces between the gear teeth and casing to the outlet, the meshing gear teeth prevent oil passing back to the inlet, and the oil is forced through the outlet port.
Generator	Modern term for 'Dynamo'. When rotated produces electrical current.
Grommet	A ring of protective or sealing material. Can be used to protect pipes or leads passing through bulkheads.
Grubscrew	Fully threaded headless screw with screwdriver slot. Used for locking, or alignment purposes.
Gudgeon pin	Shaft which connects a piston to its connecting rod. Sometimes called 'wrist pin', or 'piston pin'.
Halfshaft	One of a pair transmitting drive from the differential.
Helical	In spiral form. The teeth of helical gears are cut at a spiral angle to the side faces of the gearwheel.
Hot spot	Hot area that assists vapourisation of fuel on its way to cylinders. Often provided by close contact between inlet and exhaust manifolds.
HT	High Tension. Applied to electrical current produced by the ignition coil for the sparking plugs.
Hydrometer	A device for checking specific gravity of liquids. Used to check specific gravity of electrolyte.
Hypoid bevel gears	A form of bevel gear used in the rear axle drive gears. The bevel pinion meshes below the centre line of the crownwheel, giving a lower propeller shaft line.
Idler	A device for passing on movement. A free running gear between driving and driven gears. A lever transmitting track rod movement to a side rod in steering gear.
Impeller	A centrifugal pumping element. Used in water pumps to stimulate flow.
Journals	Those parts of a shaft that are in contact with the bearings.
Kingpin	The main vertical pin which carries the front wheel spindle, and permits steering movement. May be called 'steering pin' or 'swivel pin'.
Layshaft	The shaft which carries the laygear in the gearbox. The laygear is driven by the first motion shaft and drives the third motion shaft according to the gear selected. Sometimes called the 'countershaft' or 'second motion shaft.'
lb ft	A measure of twist or torque. A pull of 10 lb at a radius of 1 ft is a torque of 10 lb ft.
lb/sq in	Pounds per square inch.
Little-end	The small, or piston end of a connecting rod. Sometimes called the 'small-end'.
LT	Low Tension. The current output from the battery.
Mandrel	Accurately manufactured bar or rod used for test or centring purposes.
Manifold	A pipe, duct, or chamber, with several branches.
Needle rollers	Bearing rollers with a length many times their diameter.
Oil bath	Reservoir which lubricates parts by immersion. In air filters, a separate oil supply for wetting a wire mesh element to hold the dust.
Oil wetted	In air filters, a wire mesh element lightly oiled to trap and hold airborne dust.
Overlap	Period during which inlet and exhaust valves are open together.
Panhard rod	Bar connected between fixed point on chassis and another on axle to control sideways movement.
Pawl	Pivoted catch which engages in the teeth of a ratchet to permit movement in one direction only.
Peg spanner	Tool with pegs, or pins, to engage in holes or slots in the part to be turned.
Pendant pedals	Pedals with levers that are pivoted at the top end.
Phillips screwdriver	A cross-point screwdriver for use with the cross-slotted heads of Phillips screws.
Pinion	A small gear, usually in relation to another gear.
Piston-type damper	Shock absorber in which damping is controlled by a piston working in a closed oil-filled cylinder.
Preloading	Preset static pressure on ball or roller bearings not due to working loads.
Radial	Radiating from a centre, like the spokes of a wheel.

Radius rod	Pivoted arm confining movement of a part to an arc of fixed radius.
Ratchet	Toothed wheel or rack which can move in one direction only, movement in the other being prevented by a pawl.
Ring gear	A gear tooth ring attached to outer periphery of flywheel. Starter pinion engages with it during starting.
Runout	Amount by which rotating part is out of true.
Semi-floating axle	Outer end of rear axle halfshaft is carried on bearing inside axle casing. Wheel hub is secured to end of shaft.
Servo	A hydraulic or pneumatic system for assisting, or, augmenting a physical effort. See 'Vacuum Servo'.
Setscrew	One which is threaded for the full length of the shank.
Shackle	A coupling link, used in the form of two parallel pins connected by side plates to secure the end of the master suspension spring and absorb the effects of deflection.
Shell bearing	Thinwalled steel shell lined with anti-friction metal. Usually semi-circular and used in pairs for main and big-end bearings.
Shock absorber	See 'Damper'.
Silentbloc	Rubber bush bonded to inner and outer metal sleeves.
Socket-head screw	Screw with hexagonal socket for an Allen key.
Solenoid	A coil of wire creating a magnetic field when electric current passes through it. Used with a soft iron core to operate contacts or a mechanical device.
Spur gear	A gear with teeth cut axially across the periphery.
Stub axle	Short axle fixed at one end only.
Tachometer	An instrument for accurate measurement of rotating speed. Usually indicates in revolutions per minute.

TDC	Top Dead Centre. The highest point reached by a piston in a cylinder, with the crank and connecting rod in line.
Thermostat	Automatic device for regulating temperature. Used in vehicle coolant systems to open a valve which restricts circulation at low temperature.
Third motion shaft	Output shaft of gearbox.
Threequarter floating axle	Outer end of rear axle halfshaft flanged and bolted to wheel hub, which runs on bearing mounted on outside of axle casing. Vehicle weight is not carried by the axle shaft.
Thrust bearing or washer	Used to reduce friction in rotating parts subject to axial loads.
Torque	Turning or twisting effort. See 'lb ft'.
Track rod	The bar(s) across the vehicle which connect the steering arms and maintain the front wheels in their correct alignment.
UJ	Universal joint. A coupling between shafts which permits angular movement.
UNF	Unified National Fine screw thread.
Vacuum servo	Device used in brake system, using difference between atmospheric pressure and inlet manifold depression to operate a piston which acts to augment brake pressure as required. See 'Servo'.
Venturi	A restriction or 'choke' in a tube, as in a carburetter, used to increase velocity to obtain a reduction in pressure.
Vernier	A sliding scale for obtaining fractional readings of the graduations of an adjacent scale.
Welch plug	A domed thin metal disc which is partially flattened to lock in a recess. Used to plug core holes in castings.
Wet liner	Removable cylinder barrel, sealed against coolant leakage, where the coolant is in direct contact with the outer surface.
Wet sump	A reservoir attached to the crankcase to hold the lubricating oil.

NOTES

INDEX

NOTES

Alfa Romeo Giulia 1600,
1750 1962 on
Aston Martin 1921-58
Auto Union Audi 70, 80,
Super 90, 1966 on
Audi 100 1969 on
Austin, Morris etc.
1100 Mk. 1 1962-67
Austin, Morris etc. 1100
Mk. 2, 3, 1300 Mk. 1, 2, 3
America 1968 on
Austin A30, A35, A40
Farina
Austin A55 Mk. 2, A60
1958-69
Austin A99, A110 1959-68
Austin J4 1960 on
Austin Maxi 1969 on
Austin, Morris 1800
1964 on
Austin, Morris 2200 1972 on
Austin, Morris Australian
1300, 1500 Nomad
1969 on
BMC 3 (Austin A50, A55
Mk. 1, Morris Oxford
2, 3 1954-59)
Austin Healey 100/6,
3000 1956-68
Austin Healey, MG
Sprite, Midget 1958 on
BMW 1600 1966 on
BMW 1800 1964 on
BMW 2000, 2002 1966 on
Chevrolet Corvair 1960-69
Chevrolet Corvette V8
1957-65
Chevrolet Corvette V8
1965 on
Chevrolette Vega 2300
1970 on
Chrysler Valiant V8
1965 on
Chrysler Valiant Straight
Six 1966-70
Citroen DS 19, ID 19
1955-66
Citroen ID 19, DS 19, 20,
21 1966 on
Datsun 1200 1970 on
Datsun 1300, 1400, 1600
1968-72
Datsun 240C 1971 on
Datsun 240Z Sport 1970 on
De Dion Bouton
1899-1907
Fiat 124 1966 on
Fiat 124 Sport 1966 on
Fiat 125 1967 on
Fiat 128 1969 on
Fiat 500 1957 on
Fiat 600, 600D 1955-69
Fiat 850 1964 on
Fiat 1100 1957-69
Fiat 1300, 1500 1961-67
Ford Anglia Prefect 100E
1953-62
Ford Anglia 105E, Prefect
107E 1959-67

Ford Capri 1300, 1600
1968 on
Ford Capri 2000, 3000
1969 on
Ford Classic, Capri
1961-64
Ford Consul, Zephyr,
Zodiac, 1, 2 1950-62
Ford Corsair Straight
Four 1963-65
Ford Corsair V4 1965-68
Ford Corsair V4 2000
1969-70
Ford Cortina 1962-66
Ford Cortina 1967-68
Ford Cortina 1969-70
Ford Cortina Mk. 3
1970 on
Ford Escort 1967 on
Ford Falcon 6 1964-70
Ford Falcon XK, XL
1960-63
Ford Falcon V8 (U.S.A.)
1965-71
Ford Falcon V8 (Aust.)
1966 on
Ford Pinto 1970 on
Ford Maverick 1969 on
Ford Mustang V8 1965-71
Ford Thames 10, 12,
15 cwt 1957-65
Ford Transit 1965 on
Ford Zephyr Zodiac Mk. 3
1962-66
Ford Zephyr Zodiac V4,
V6, Mk. 4 1966-72
Ford Consul, Granada 1972
Hillman Avenger 1970 on
Hillman Hunter 1966 on
Hillman Imp 1963-68
Hillman Imp 1969 on
Hillman Minx 1 to 5
1956-65
Hillman Minx 1965-67
Hillman Minx 1966-70
Hillman Super Minx
1961-65
Holden V8 1968 on
Holden Straight Six
1948-66
Holden Straight Six
1966 on
Holden Torana 4 Series
HB 1967-69
Jaguar XK120, 140, 150,
Mk. 7, 8, 9 1948-61
Jaguar 2.4, 3.4, 3.8 Mk.
1, 2 1955-69
Jaguar 'E' Type 1961 on
Jaguar 'S' Type 420
1963-68
Jaguar XJ6 1968 on
Jowett Javelin Jupiter
1947-53
Landrover 1, 2 1948-61
Landrover 2, 2a, 3 1959 on
Mazda 616 1970 on
Mercedes-Benz 190b,
190c, 200 1959-68

Mercedes-Benz 220
1959-65
Mercedes-Benz 220/8
1968 on
Mercedes-Benz 230
1963-68
Mercedes-Benz 250
1965-67
Mercedes-Benz 250
1968 on
Mercedes-Benz 280
1968 on
MG TA to TF 1936-55
MGA MGB 1955-68
MGB 1969 on
Mini 1959 on
Mini Cooper 1961 on
Morgan 1936-69
Morris Marina 1971 on
Morris Australian Marina
1972 on
Morris Minor 2, 1000
1952-71
Morris Oxford 5, 6 1959-71
NSU 1000 1963 on
NSU Prinz 1 to 4 1957 on
Opel Ascona, Manta
1970 on
Opel GT 1900 1968 on
Opel Kadett, Olympia 993cc
1078cc 1962 on
Opel Kadett, Olympia 1492,
1698, 1897cc 1967 on
Opel Rekord C 1966 on
Peugeot 204 1965 on
Peugeot 404 1960 on
Peugeot 504 1968-70
Porsche 356A, B, C 1957-65
Porsche 911 1964-69
Porsche 912 1965-69
Porsche 914 S 1969 on
Reliant Regal 1952 on
Renault R4, R4L, 4 1961 on
Renault 6 1968 on
Renault 8, 10, 1100 1962 on
Renault 12, 1969 on
Renault R16 1965 on
Renault Dauphine
Floride 1957-67
Renault Caravelle 1962-68
Rover 60 to 110 1953-64
Rover 2000 1963 on
Rover 3 Litre 1958-67
Rover 3500, 3500S 1968 on
Saab 95, 96, Sport
1960-68
Saab 99 1969 on
Saab V4 1966 on
Simca 1000 1961 on
Simca 1100 1967 on
Simca 1300, 1301, 1500,
1501 1963 on
Skoda One (440, 445, 450)
1955-70
Sunbeam Rapier Alpine
1955-65
Toyota Corolla 1100 1967 on
Toyota Corona 1500 Mk. 1
1965-70

Toyota Corona 1900 Mk. 2
1969 on
Triumph TR2, TR3, TR3A
1952-62
Triumph TR4, TR4A
1961-67
Triumph TR5, TR250,
TR6 1967 on
Triumph 1300, 1500
1965 on
Triumph 2000 Mk. 1, 2.5 PI
Mk. 1 1963-69
Triumph 2000 Mk. 2, 2.5 PI
Mk. 2 1969 on
Triumph Herald 1959-68
Triumph Herald 1969-71
Triumph Spitfire, Vitesse
1962-68
Triumph Spitfire Mk. 3, 4
1969 on
Triumph GT6, Vitesse
2 Litre 1969 on
Triumph Toledo 1970 on
Vauxhall Velox, Cresta
1957-72
Vauxhall Victor 1, 2, FB
1957-64
Vauxhall Victor 101
1964-67
Vauxhall Victor FD 1600,
2000 1967 on
Vauxhall Victor 3300,
Ventora 1968 on
Vauxhall Victor FE
Ventora 1972 on
Vauxhall Viva HA 1963-66
Vauxhall Viva HB 1966-70
Vauxhall Viva, HC Firenza
1971 on
Volkswagen Beetle 1954-67
Volkswagen Beetle 1968 on
Volkswagen 1500 1961-66
Volkswagen 1600 Fastback
1965 on
Volkswagen Transporter
1954-67
Volkswagen Transporter
1968 on
Volkswagen 411 1968 on
Volvo 120 1961-70
Volvo 140 1966 on
Volvo 160 series 1968 on
Volvo 1800 1960 on

NOTES

NOTES

NOTES